Praise for *Crystal Magic*

"Sandra's book is balanced with spiritual, scientific, and historical information. It is easy to understand and makes learning crystals and minerals fun and inspiring. I highly recommend this for anyone looking to explore the magical world of crystals."

—Heather Nichols, owner of Stones and Stuff

Crystal
Magic

© Jessica Weiser

About the Author

Sandra Kynes is an explorer of history, myth, and magic. Although she is a member of the Order of Bards, Ovates and Druids, she travels a solitary Goddess-centered path through the Druidic woods. She likes to develop creative ways to explore the world and integrate them with her spiritual path, which serves as the basis for her books. Sandra has lived in New York City, Europe, and England. She now lives in coastal New England in a Victorian-era house with her family, cats, and a couple of ghosts. In addition to writing, she is a yoga instructor and Reiki practitioner. Sandra enjoys connecting with nature through gardening, hiking, bird watching, and ocean kayaking. Visit her website at www.kynes.net.

Crystal Magic

Mineral Wisdom for Pagans & Wiccans

SANDRA KYNES

Llewellyn Publications
Woodbury, Minnesota

First Edition
First Printing, 2017

Book design by Donna Burch-Brown
Cover design by Cassie Kanzenbach

Alexandrite on page 44 © Joe Budd Photography, courtesy of The Arkenstone, iRocks.com; Goshenite on page 73, Chrysoberyl on page 90, Chrysocolla Quartz on page 93, Chalcotrichite on page 101, Onyx on page 169 and Red Zircon on page 243 © The Arkenstone, iRocks.com; Cat's-eye on page 84 © Lyle Koehnlein; Rainbow Obsidian on page 167 photo taken by Jordan Loveless, courtesy of Earth, Wind, Fire & Ice, Chadds Ford, PA, http://www.etsy.com/shop/EarthWindFireandIce1; all other art from Shutterstock.com and iStockphoto.com.

Llewellyn Publications is a registered trademark of Llewellyn Worldwide Ltd.

Library of Congress Cataloging-in-Publication Data
Names: Kynes, Sandra, author.
  Title: Crystal magic : mineral wisdom for pagans & wiccans / Sandra Kynes.
  Description: First American Edition. | Woodbury : Llewellyn Worldwide, Ltd.,
    2017. | Includes bibliographical references and index.
  Identifiers: LCCN 2017029255 (print) | LCCN 2017035164 (ebook) | ISBN
    9780738754161 (ebook) | ISBN 9780738753416 (alk. paper)
  Subjects: LCSH: Crystals--Miscellanea. | Precious stones--Miscellanea. |
    Magic. | Wiccans. | Neopagans.
  Classification: LCC BF1442.C78 (ebook) | LCC BF1442.C78 K96 2017 (print) |
    DDC 133/.2548—dc23
  LC record available at https://lccn.loc.gov/2017029255

Llewellyn Worldwide Ltd. does not participate in, endorse, or have any authority or responsibility concerning private business transactions between our authors and the public.
  All mail addressed to the author is forwarded, but the publisher cannot, unless specifically instructed by the author, give out an address or phone number.
  Any Internet references contained in this work are current at publication time, but the publisher cannot guarantee that a specific location will continue to be maintained. Please refer to the publisher's website for links to authors' websites and other sources.

Llewellyn Publications
A Division of Llewellyn Worldwide Ltd.
2143 Wooddale Drive
Woodbury, MN 55125-2989
www.llewellyn.com

Printed in the United States of America

Other Books by Sandra Kynes

Plant Magic

Bird Magic

Herb Gardener's Essential Guide

Star Magic

Mixing Essential Oils for Magic

Llewellyn's Complete Book of Correspondences

Change at Hand

Plant Magic

Sea Magic

Your Altar

Whispers from the Woods

A Year of Ritual

Gemstone Feng Shui

Forthcoming Books by Sandra Kynes

365 Day of Crystal Magic

Llewellyn's Complete Book of Essential Oils

Contents

INTRODUCTION

Crystals are popular with Pagans and Wiccans because they provide a simple and effective way to add power to magic and ritual. The fascination and use of crystals dates to ancient times when they served as bling and much more. Through the ages, crystals have functioned as symbols of power, wealth, beauty, and prestige and as tokens of love.

While some gemstones attract attention with their rich colors, others seem to play with the light or shine from within. Many cultures considered certain stones to have metaphysical qualities because their mysterious beauty seemed to echo the forces of nature. Although specific attributes of particular gemstones varied among the ancient cultures, there was a universal belief in their protective power. The Mesopotamians recorded fifty-four important stones that they used as magical amulets.[1] Drawing on some of the oldest texts of India, Vedic astrologers associated crystals with the celestial power of the sun, the moon, and the planets. Later in medieval times, gemstones became associated with the constellations of the Western zodiac. Today's widespread use of birthstones is a remnant of these practices.

1. Michael C. Howard, *Transnationalism in Ancient and Medieval Societies: The Role of Cross-Border Trade and Travel* (Jefferson, NC: McFarland & Company, 2012), 114.

Similar to other areas of the natural world, such as herbs and other plants, gemstones enhance ritual and magic. While it is easy to work with crystals on a superficial level, with a little more knowledge we are able to tap into the deeper power and wisdom of the mineral kingdom. When we take time to explore and learn as much as we can about the natural world, we follow in the footsteps of the wise women and men of the past who developed a working knowledge of the world around them and lived in magic.

It does not take a degree in mineralogy to understand the basic properties and characteristics of crystals. In turn, mineralogy helps us discover the many subtle tools crystals have to offer. Formed by dynamic processes—the powerful creative and destructive forces of the ever-changing earth—crystals enhance ritual and magic work. While the inner structure of crystals can amplify energy, their optical properties and other characteristics provide nuances that enhance magic work and enrich our daily lives.

With *Crystal Magic,* I have come full circle back to writing about crystals and gemstones. My first book, *Gemstone Feng Shui,* had the very specific focus of using crystals in place of the traditional accoutrements for the ancient Chinese practice of feng shui. Since then, it has been my ambition to pull together the information from years of research into another book about crystals, but this book would focus on their use for Pagans and Wiccans.

Crystal Magic is divided into two parts beginning with "History, Science, and Working with Stones." The first chapter provides a historical perspective on the use of gemstones since ancient times, including astrology, divination, and medicinal applications. While the second chapter may seem a little scientific and nerdy, learning about the various characteristics and how crystals are created adds to our knowledge base and supports the more effective use of gemstones. Also included is information on simulated and synthetic stones as well as red flags for spotting fakes. The third chapter is devoted to buying and preparing stones; the fourth provides an overview of their magical uses. The fourth chapter also includes a new form of crystal grid based on the inner structure of crystals.

The second part of the book is entitled "A Compendium of Stones." It contains entries for more than one hundred varieties of minerals, which include identification details and historical information. Also provided is the pronunciation of mineral names. Of course, each entry contains magical information. This part of the book provides a foundation for understanding the rich cultural background of crystals to aid you in developing your own unique methods for using them.

The appendices provide two quick-reference guides to magical attributes and correspondences (appendix A) and associated deities (appendix B). A glossary of mineralogical terms provides a reference for words that most of us do not encounter in our everyday lives.

Not all crystals or gemstones are minerals from the earth. These non-mineral or organic gemstones include substances such as amber, pearl, and jet. Regarded as a gemstone, coral is not included in this book because so many of the world's reefs are endangered and I do not want to encourage people to support this destruction by purchasing coral. If you already have some, please use it to focus your willpower and send healing energy to the reefs and oceans.

Throughout this book, I have used the words *gemstone, mineral, stone,* and *crystal* interchangeably, even though there are differences. As already mentioned, some gemstones are non-mineral but most are minerals. Of the several thousand types of minerals, only about seventy or eighty are gem quality. Three major factors qualify a mineral as a true gemstone: the stone's beauty, durability, and scarcity. Finally, although it is a fuzzy area of semantics, it is generally accepted that a "stone" has been handled and/or shaped by human hands whereas a "rock" is regarded as raw material.

Working with crystals strengthens our connection with the dynamic natural world. Although we can simply use these stones to boost spells or represent the elements in ritual, learning more about them provides a foundation upon which we can continue to build knowledge throughout our lives. Following a path of learning adds fullness to our lives as we develop our unique skills and creative expression in the craft. Now, let's step into the enchanting and powerful kingdom of minerals.

Part One

History, Science, and Working with Stones

This part of the book provides a historical perspective on how gemstones have been used since ancient times, including astrology, divination, and medicinal applications. We will learn about the earth's dynamic processes that create crystals and how crystals are categorized by their inner structures. Also included are details on optical characteristics, special phenomena, and information on simulated and synthetic stones. From the scientific details, we move to magic and learn about buying, preparing, and using crystals.

Chapter 1

FROM BLING TO MAGIC:
A HISTORY OF CRYSTALS

The use of crystals most likely began when people noticed pretty colored stones that may have reflected light in an unusual way. According to geoarchaeologist George Rapp (1930–), the earliest gemstones that caught people's attention were probably found along riverbanks.[2] Worn smooth by being tumbled against rocks, shiny colorful stones must have looked otherworldly. In addition, their appearance in water or among ordinary rocks must have made them seem mysterious.

According to Japanese folklore, quartz was created from the breath of a white dragon. Similarly, the folklore of India explained red gemstones as drops of blood from a slain celestial dragon. That fabled dragon's blood may have been carnelian, which the Sumerians and Mesopotamians imported from the Indus Valley. In addition to India, a vast area stretching from Turkey to Afghanistan was a rich source, where many types of minerals were collected from riversides or rocky areas. Exported from Afghanistan as early as 4000 BCE, lapis lazuli was used to decorate temples in Egypt and Mesopotamia.[3] The Sumerians were also fond of this stone and used

---

2. George R. Rapp, *Archaeomineralogy* (New York: Springer-Verlag, 2002), 87.

3. Howard, *Transnationalism in Ancient and Medieval Societies*, 115.

it for a wide range of objects. The Phoenicians traded Baltic amber throughout the Mediterranean as early as 2000 BCE.[4] This early gemstone trade expanded under the auspices of the Roman Empire.

Although it takes a great deal of skill to carve certain types of stones—because of their hardness—engraved and carved crystals have been found throughout the ancient world. These crystals were used for sacred and secular objects and jewelry. Carved, cylindrical seals were commonly used by the Babylonians to apply wax to objects for identification purposes. These seals were often worn as personal ornamentation. Instead of cylinders, the Romans made flat seals and often wore them as signet rings. According to legend, one of the most famous seal rings belonged to the Israelite King Solomon, who used its power for his magic work.

Becoming a major supplier for trade, the Egyptians were the first to mine gemstones rather than simply collect them from scattered surface rocks or riverbeds. For their own use, Egyptians decorated the tombs of pharaohs and other important people with gemstones. Crystals also functioned as votive offerings to the dead and deities. Symbolizing rebirth, carnelian was frequently used for funerary objects. According to myth, Isis used a carnelian amulet to protect the dead. For the living, Egyptians not only wore gems as jewelry but also crushed some minerals such as malachite into a powder for cosmetic use.

In Asia and Mesoamerica, jade was the most dominantly used and valued stone. Around 3000 BCE, the Chinese began carving objects from jade.[5] Because of its durability, this stone was a symbol of immortality and was frequently placed in tombs to aid the deceased in the afterlife. In the New World, the Olmec mined jade as early as 1000 BCE.[6]

Early Written Records

The Ebers papyrus from Egypt (c. 1500 BCE) and the *Sushruta Samhita* from India (c. 700 BCE) not only detailed the medicinal uses of plants but also preparations made with powdered minerals.[7] In later centuries, Greek physician Pedanius Dioscorides (c. 40–90 CE) also wrote about the use of minerals for medical treatments; a practice that continued well into the Middle Ages and beyond.

4. Anna S. Sofianides and George E. Harlow, *Gems & Crystals from the American Museum of Natural History* (New York: Simon and Schuster, 1990), 20.

5. Dale Anderson, *Ancient China* (Chicago: Raintree, 2005), 7.

6. Ibid.

7. K. Mangathayaru, *Pharmacognosy: An Indian Perspective* (New Delhi, India: Pearson, 2013), 2.

Many other people also explored the world of minerals. The writings of Theophrastus (c. 372–287 BCE), a Greek philosopher, naturalist, and devoted pupil of Aristotle, are regarded as some of the earliest texts on mineralogy. Also, five of the thirty-seven books on natural history written by Roman scholar Pliny the Elder (c. 23–79 CE) were about minerals.

The Bible also contains descriptions of gemstones. Functioning as symbols and sources of power, the stones in the breastplates of the high priests of Israel were part of an oracular device to interpret God's will. Elsewhere in the ancient world, the Mesopotamians used pairs of oracular stones to answer yes/no questions. Also, the Byzantine scholar and writer Photius of Constantinople (c. 820–891 CE) wrote about oracular stones being cast like dice.

Occasionally, the names of stones in ancient texts cause confusion. For example, some scholars believe the term *carbuncle* was a specific reference to almandine garnet, while others consider it to have been a catchall name for red stones. Likewise, the name *emerald* comes from the Greek word *smaragdos*, which was used for many types of green stones.[8] In addition, lapis lazuli was often called *sapphirus,* making it difficult to determine whether an ancient reference meant lapis lazuli or sapphire.

Medieval Europe

As mentioned, Vedic astrologers associated crystals with celestial bodies. The Chinese also linked certain gems with their zodiac. Not surprisingly, during the Middle Ages in Europe gemstones became associated with the planets and constellations in Western astrology. In addition to the zodiac, Heinrich Cornelius Agrippa (1486–1535), author of *Three Books of Occult Philosophy,* regarded fifteen stars as particularly powerful for magic. He associated certain gemstones with each of these stars. Although stones contained concentrated power on their own, drawing down celestial energy into them was a way to boost one's own power and purpose.

The magical properties and spiritual values of crystals were often enhanced by the fact that they came from mysterious, faraway lands. As if that was not enough, symbols were engraved onto gemstones to focus and direct their power. European nobility cited King Solomon as the leading example for wearing jewelry inscribed with magical formulas for protection.

....
8. Walter Schumann, *Gemstones of the World*, 5th ed. (New York: Sterling Publishing, 2006), 106.

While there was a brisk trade in crystals during the Middle Ages, it furnished jewelry and items for the nobility and wealthy classes. Ordinary people could not afford such luxuries. For them there were herbs. Although herbs were regarded as magically and medicinally potent, gemstones were believed to have greater power.

Minerals in Healing and Magic

Just as the classic herbals—books about herbs—were popular in the Middle Ages, so too were lapidaries—books about minerals. French theologian Bishop Marbode (1035–1133) was the author of one well-known lapidary. Written as a long poem, his *Book of Stones* described the properties of sixty minerals. German theologian, scientist, and philosopher Albertus Magnus (c. 1200–1280) wrote *The Book of Secrets of the Virtues of Herbs, Stones and Certain Beasts*. The section on gemstones became a standalone treatise called *The Book of Minerals*. It included the descriptions and powers of ninety-nine gemstones along with their use in alchemy, astrology, and magic. While we may consider it unusual for a Christian church official such as Marbode to write about the magical properties of gemstones, in his time crystals were regarded as mystical and important because their powers overlapped with those of saints' relics.

Swiss physician and alchemist Theophrastus von Hohenheim (1493–1541)—who called himself Paracelsus—noted that one quest of alchemy was to make medicinal elixirs.[9] In addition, he was influential in promoting the use of minerals for healing purposes. This is a common practice that continues today and not just among alternative healers. For example, the mineral *bismuth subsalicylate* is the active ingredient in Pepto-Bismol.®

In addition to the use of minerals in medicinal preparations, wearing them also provided healing energy. Medieval physicians used complicated astronomical calculations to determine which stones were appropriate for a patient's ailment. While the color of a stone revealed a person's state of health, a change in the stone's color was believed to predict impending death or bad behavior on the part of the wearer.

Crystals were regarded as a bridge between the visible and invisible—between matter and spirit. From the Middle Ages through the Renaissance, crystallomancy (crystal gazing) was a popular form of divination. Credited with making it all the rage, John Dee (1527–1608) was a mathematician, astrologer, occult philosopher, and adviser to Queen Elizabeth I. Dee is most famous for his scrying work with Edward Kelley using a crystal ball that he

---

9. Glenn Sonnendecker, *Kremers and Urdang's History of Pharmacy*, 4th ed. (Philadelphia: J. B. Lippincott Company, 1986), 40.

referred to as a show stone and angelic stone.[10] Their work resulted in the Enochian alphabet and system of magic.

Although a crystal ball, glass bowl, or mirror was usually used for scrying, holding a crystal in the right hand after it was properly prepared was also believed to produce visions. Some stones were believed to actually speak or to enable a person to shape shift. In addition, it was common practice to use a stone as a muse for stoking creativity.

Fashioning Stones

The ancient methods for fashioning gemstones consisted of smoothing away jagged edges and polishing them to bring out their colors. In ancient times, India was the center of this work, and it was where many methods were perfected. However, it was not until the Middle Ages that cutting or faceting gemstones came into general practice. Faceting a stone gives it a number of flat surfaces (facets) that enhance the way light is reflected or absorbed.

Faceting requires a good understanding of the optical properties, hardness, and cleavage of a stone. Mineral cleavage is the predictable manner in which a stone can be smoothly broken. Although it was gaining in popularity, the art of faceting had limited practice in the Near East, where it was believed that too much cutting would reduce a stone's mystical powers.

It was not until the fifteenth century in Italy that diamonds became the "king" of gemstones. This was when skilled artisans were able to cut this hardest of stones. More importantly, they developed special faceting techniques that brought out the diamond's sparkling beauty.[11] From Italy, gemstone faceting spread to other parts of Europe, and over the centuries, many other types of cuts have been developed. Some cuts are unique to a particular type of stone—such as diamond or emerald—to bring out their specific qualities. Some styles of faceting become a fashion rage and then fade, while others remain classic.

Now that we have a brief cultural overview of gemstones and their uses, let's look into the science of crystals.

....

10. Eric G. Wilson, *The Spiritual History of Ice: Romanticism, Science, and the Imagination* (New York: Palgrave MacMillan, 2003), 13.

11. Rapp, *Archaeomineralogy*, 89.

Chapter 2

THE SCIENCE
OF CRYSTALS

The ancient Greeks believed crystals to be a form of non-melting ice. In fact, the word *crystal* comes from the Greek word *krystallos*, which in turn came from the word *kryos* meaning "ice cold." [12] This theory regarding ice is not completely farfetched if you consider how a crystal usually feels cool to the touch. In addition, clear crystals often look like ice. Luckily, there is a great deal more information available today that continues to reveal more about the importance of minerals. According to David Vaughan, professor of mineralogy at the University of Manchester, England, and other scientists, minerals played an important role in the origin and evolution of life on Earth. Minerals provided organic molecules with basic raw material for metabolic processes and a surface upon which they could grow into more complex molecules and eventually higher organisms. Essential to the production of vitamins, enzymes, bones, energy, and much more, minerals continue their important role of supporting life.

Why should scientific information matter to Pagans and Wiccans? Knowing how crystals are formed helps us understand why their energy is so dynamic and powerful. Being familiar

....
12. Ian F. Mercer, *Crystals* (Cambridge, MA: Harvard University Press, 1990), 58.

with crystal characteristics provides for more effective and personalized use. In addition, we may find that certain crystal structures work especially well for our individual energy and magic. This information also aids in selecting the stones with which we may want to work.

Each type of mineral is defined by its chemical composition and crystal structure. However, while two minerals can have the same chemical composition, the conditions under which they are created can produce very different crystal structures. For example, the carbon composition of diamond and graphite is almost identical, but the conditions through which they are formed produce drastically different results. Pencil lead is not nearly as exciting as a diamond ring.

As mentioned, crystals are perfect for magic work because they are formed by dynamic processes—the powerful creative and destructive forces of the natural world. The earth itself is dynamic and constantly changing. Because of this, minerals are continually formed, broken down, and re-formed. Their formation comes from four processes called crystallization from molten rock, precipitation from an aqueous solution, chemical alteration, and recrystallization. Some crystals are formed through a combination of these processes.

In the first process, crystallization from molten rock, elements are combined under high temperatures and pressure. As the elements cool, minerals are formed. Examples of gemstones from this process include diamond, beryl, peridot, topaz, and zircon.

As the name of the second process suggests, precipitation from an aqueous solution, water is involved in forming minerals. In this process, water dissolves and moves chemical elements from one place to another. During transport or at their new location, the chemical elements interact with others. Opal and calcite are examples of minerals that result from this process. In addition, opal actually contains 3 to 10 percent water.

Composed of chemical elements, minerals are only stable under certain conditions and change as conditions change. This is the basis of the third process, chemical alteration. Oxidation is an example of this process. The gemstones azurite and malachite are formed through the oxidation of chalcopyrite and contain a little more than 50 percent copper.

In the fourth process, recrystallization, the atoms of minerals are re-formed under heat and pressure. When a mineral that was formed by the first process, crystallization, is subjected to intense heat and pressure again, a chemical reaction causes their atomic structures to change. Gemstones that are formed in this way include diopside, emerald, and kyanite.

These four processes determine a mineral's shape, color, and internal structure. As mentioned, even though minerals may have the same chemical composition, the processes under which they are created can produce very different results.

Crystal Structures

The molecules of nearly all minerals have a regular internal pattern called a crystal structure or crystal system. In the late eighteenth century, French mineralogist René-Just Haüy (1743–1822) discovered these internal structures.[13] Although a crystal's inner structure has a specific and simple geometric shape, its outer form is usually very different and often more complex.

The exterior of a crystal has surfaces called faces or planes. In order for crystals to develop these faces, they need room to grow. The giant selenite crystals in the Cueva de los Cristales (Cave of Crystals) in northern Mexico is an extreme example of how some crystals can grow when unimpeded. While there are many potential exterior shapes, crystals are classified into seven systems according to the symmetry of their inner geometric structures. An eighth system called amorphous is used to denote a lack of specific inner structure.

The first system called cubic or isometric, is the most symmetrical. The others decrease in symmetry. Knowing a stone's inner structure provides a simple but powerful way to use a unique crystal grid, which is introduced in chapter 4.

Table 1. Crystal Systems and Attributes

Category	Attributes	Examples
Cubic or Isometric	Square inner structure; exterior shapes include cube, octahedron, rhombic dodecahedron; no double refraction; no pleochroism	Diamond, fluorite, garnet, spinel
Tetragonal	Rectangular inner structure; exterior shapes include four- and eight-sided pyramids and prisms; potential double refraction; potential pleochroism is usually dichroic	Apophyllite, zircon

13. Marc Rothenberg, ed., *The History of Science in the United States: An Encyclopedia* (New York: Garland Publishing, 2001), 145.

Table 1. Crystal Systems and Attributes (cont.)

Category	Attributes	Examples
Hexagonal	Hexagon inner structure; exterior shapes include six-sided prisms and pyramids, twelve-sided pyramids, double pyramids; potential double refraction; potential pleochroism is usually dichroic	Aquamarine, beryl, emerald, heliodor, morganite
Trigonal, a subsystem of Hexagonal	Triangular inner structure; exterior shapes include three-sided prism and pyramids, rhombohedron; potential double refraction; potential pleochroism is usually dichroic	Amethyst, citrine, quartz, ruby, sapphire, tourmaline
Orthorhombic	Diamond-shaped inner structure; exterior shapes include single and double pyramids, rhombic prisms; potential double refraction; potential pleochroism is usually trichroic	Andalusite, celestite, chrysoberyl, peridot, topaz
Monoclinic	Parallelogram inner structure; exterior shapes include prisms with inclined end faces; potential double refraction; potential pleochroism is usually trichroic	Azurite, diopside, kunzite, moonstone, staurolite
Triclinic	Trapezium inner structure; exterior shapes usually have paired faces; potential double refraction; potential pleochroism is usually trichroic	Labradorite, kyanite, rhodonite, turquoise
Amorphous	Lacks specific internal structure; no double refraction; no pleochroism	Amber, jet, moldavite, obsidian, opal

As mentioned in the introduction, several non-mineral gemstones from organic sources are included in this book. Amber is fossilized sap from ancient pine trees. Pearls, beginning as irritants inside oysters and a few other mollusks, come from the watery depths of the ocean. Jet is woody material that was buried in sediment and compacted into a form of coal. Although petrified wood came from an organic source, minerals seeped into the wood and preserved it over time. Petrified wood has become popular as a tumbled stone.

The Optical Properties of Crystals

Light does not always pass straight through a stone; instead, it can be deflected or refracted (bent) at various angles according to its crystal structure. As light passes through some stones, it is split and each ray is refracted at different angles. This is called double refraction, and it can make a stone appear extra sparkly.

Double refraction is also responsible for pleochroism, an effect whereby a stone appears to be a different color or hue when viewed from different directions. A stone that is dichroic exhibits two different colors or hues. Topaz and apatite are examples of stones that may exhibit two colors. A stone that is trichroic, such as staurolite and iolite, shows three colors or hues. Tourmaline may be dichroic or trichroic. Opaque stones are not usually pleochroic.

Some gemstones exhibit what is called a color change phenomenon. These stones appear different colors depending on the light in which they are viewed—natural or artificial. For example, alexandrite is green when viewed in daylight but red under incandescent light.

Crystals that exhibit unusual special effects are referred to as phenomenal stones. One example is the cat's-eye, which displays one of the most dramatic effects. Parallel fibers, needles, or channels within a stone create the cat's-eye. This effect is also called *chatoyancy* from the French *chat*, "cat," and *oeil*, "eye." [14]

Another phenomenon called an asterism is more commonly known as a star. This pattern is formed by tiny needlelike inclusions that radiate at various angles from the center of the stone. Most famously known to occur in sapphires, stars can also occur in rubies, garnet, iolite, and other types of crystals.

Other Special Characteristics

Inclusions, which are imperfections within a stone, provide crystals with additional characteristics and personality. Inclusions can be in a solid, liquid, or gas form. For example, microscopic air bubbles cause the cloudiness in some amber. Inclusions can consist of other minerals, such as rutile that is frequently found in garnet, quartz, and spinel.

14. Schumann, *Gemstones of the World*, 53.

The terms *brilliance, fire,* and *luster* are often used when describing stones. Brilliance applies only to transparent gemstones and refers to light that is reflected from the interior of the stone. Brilliance can be enhanced or increased by cutting a stone in a particular fashion. For example, the diamond cut was developed to bring out the brilliance of a diamond. This cut also works well for other types of stones. Other highly brilliant stones include sphene, ruby, sapphire, and zircon.

Similar to brilliance, fire describes how light is refracted from within a stone. Instead of light being reflected, it is split into multiple rays that display a spectrum of colors. This differs from double refraction, which splits light into only two rays. Diamond, sphene, garnet, and zircon are examples of stones that exhibit fire.

Unlike brilliance or fire, luster describes the effect of light reflected from the surface of a stone. Luster has categories that describe everything from metallic and sparkling to dull.

Table 2. Surface Lusters

Name	Appearance	Examples
Metallic	A sheen similar to polished metal	Hematite, pyrite
Adamantine or Diamond	Sparkling like a diamond or lead crystal glass	Cerussite, diamond, garnet, sphene
Vitreous or Glassy	Like a freshly washed glass; one of the most common lusters	Aquamarine, chrysoberyl, sapphire, spinel
Greasy	Shiny like an ink or a grease spot on paper	Serpentine, garnet, jadeite, peridot
Resinous	Less shiny than greasy; like the appearance of resin	Amber, staurolite
Pearly	Like a pearl or mother-of-pearl on the interior of some seashells	Charoite, opal
Silky	Exhibits a ray of light like a piece of silk	Malachite, tiger's-eye
Waxy	A dull shine as though it has a coating of wax	Carnelian, jasper, turquoise
Dull or Matt	Color appears flat; many stones appear dull before polishing or tumbling	Rhodonite

Another characteristic called transparency describes the amount of light that passes through a crystal. Transparency has three categories of transparent, translucent, and opaque. Light can pass through a transparent crystal whereas only some light passes through a translucent stone. An opaque stone will block any light from passing through it.

Synthetic and Simulated Gems and the Art of Deception

Stones classified as gemstones can be very expensive, which has led to the creation of human-made substitutes. Substitutes are not necessarily bad; they allow us to have certain types of jewelry that we might not otherwise be able to afford. While we know a substitute stone is not the real thing, it can look like the natural one and we like it. Unfortunately, imitation stones are sometimes passed off as the real thing.

Stones that are human made fall into two categories called synthetic and simulated. A synthetic gem is very close to the real thing and often takes an expert to tell the difference. This type of stone is created in a lab and has the same chemical composition and structure found in nature. A simulated stone does not have the chemical composition and structure of the real crystal, but simply fools the eye. For example, glass is often used to imitate a diamond. Unlike synthetic gems, simulated stones can often be spotted as fakes even by laypeople.

In addition to synthetic and simulated stones, there is a type of tinkering referred to as augmentation. Augmenting is the practice of altering one type of stone with heat, irradiation, staining, or oiling so it looks like a more expensive gemstone. Another way of altering a stone is called luster enhancement, which involves the use of wax to make it shinier and increase its appeal.

Tinkering with the appearance of gemstones is not new. In fact, altering stones dates back to the ancient Romans who discovered that heating light-colored stones such as chalcedony would produce the darker colors they preferred. The Romans also made imitation stones from glass and paste.

Marketing also causes a problem by creating names that sound similar to or allude to stones that are more expensive. Sapphirine and emeraldine are examples of names that are used to associate common minerals with more expensive gems. By no means an exhaustive list, table 3 provides examples of misleading names that you may encounter.

Table 3. Misleading Marketing Names of Crystals

Marketing Name	Actual Stone	Marketing Name	Actual Stone
Alexandrine	Synthetic alexandrite	Evening emerald	Peridot
American ruby	Garnet	German lapis	Blue jasper or azurite
Balas ruby	Red spinel	Indian jade	Aventurine
Blue moonstone	Tinted chalcedony	Japanese opal	Plastic
Brazilian sapphire	Blue tourmaline	Mountain jet	Obsidian
California moonstone	Quartz	Rainbow moonstone	Labradorite
Cape May diamond	Quartz	Rose zircon	Synthetic pink spinel
Cape ruby	Pyrope garnet	Spanish topaz	Citrine
Ceylon opal	Moonstone	Smoky topaz	Smoky quartz
Colorado topaz	Citrine	Turquenite	Howlite dyed blue
Emeraldite	Green tourmaline	Water sapphire	Iolite

This overview of crystal structures and optical properties provides us with a fundamental understanding of various characteristics that make crystals so fascinating. Next, we'll explore where to purchase them and how to prepare them for magical use.

Chapter 3

SELECTING AND PREPARING STONES

There is no right or wrong way to buy crystals. However, if you are planning an excursion specifically to buy them for magic, take time before leaving home to think about the purpose for the stones you seek. Sometimes you may want to put together a shopping list before stepping out the door. If you are like me, you will find it easy to be sidetracked like a kid in a candy store. At other times, you may want to be serendipitous and see which stones attract you.

When buying gemstone jewelry, most of us prefer stones with few or no imperfections. For magic work, the opposite is often the case. Inclusions, frost, or minor flaws that might detract from gemstone jewelry actually reveal more of a particular stone's character and can be more interesting for magic work.

Over time, you may want to assemble different sets of stones for specific uses. Like other magic or ritual tools, stones accumulate energy and intent, which increases their potency. Stones used specifically for working with the elements can be selected by color or origin. For example, stones to represent the element fire can be chosen for their red, orange, or yellow colors. Alternatively, you could choose peridot or obsidian, as these are born of volcanic action.

As you begin to assemble various sets of gemstones, you may want to match the size of the stones within each set as closely as possible to maintain balance. When this is not possible, for example peridot is usually available only in small pieces, use several small stones with an aggregate size that is equal to others you plan to use with them. Follow your intuition. If two pieces of peridot look and feel equal to others in a set, use two. If the energy of three pieces feels appropriate, then that is what you should use.

Sources for Acquiring Crystals

There are many sources for crystals, including the Internet. However, I usually recommend buying a stone in person so you can hold it in your hands to interact with its energy and determine if it is right for you. Making purchases in person also allows you to assess the size and shape of the stone, which you cannot do easily on the web. However, if you do not have a local source for crystals and gemstones or if you cannot find a particular stone in your area, try the Internet. Since many websites also offer buying over the phone, you may be able to speak with someone to describe the size and shape you want. Also, check the vendor's return policy in case you do not get what you had expected.

While many types of stores offer crystals, use caution, as proper labeling is sometimes an issue. Earth science stores and museum gift shops are usually dependable. And, of course, rock and fossil shops are great sources. Plus, you can count on them to identify the less well-known types of stones correctly. If you are lucky, your local metaphysical shop owner may also be a rockhound, giving you the best of both worlds.

In addition to stores, look for mineral fairs, shows, or swaps. These are excellent venues for finding an incredible range of crystals as well as learning more about them. Often at these venues, stones are sold with a provenance. Not only will you know where and when it was mined or found, you will find out who owned it over the years. I purchased a piece of celestine not only for its beauty and energy, but also for the fact that it was taken from the earth the year I was born. This has become a very special stone for me.

Once you have found a crystal that you want to buy, take a few moments to hold it between your palms to sense its energy as you think of how you are planning to use it. Don't expect a thunderbolt or choir of angels to let you know you have found the right one. Clues tend to be subtle or you just might "know" it is the right stone for you.

Also, listen to your intuition, especially if something doesn't feel right. You may not be able to pinpoint what makes you feel a certain way with a particular stone but if this happens, it is just not the right one with which you should work. Do not take it personally;

just listen to your heart of hearts. In addition, sometimes stones choose us. While one stone may not want to go home with you, you may find that another almost jumps into your hand.

Stones that you trade or receive from friends can be very special and the ones that you find yourself are gifts from Mother Earth. If you are not sure about the identification of a stone that you find or receive from a friend, take it to a rock shop or mineral show and ask for advice. Don't be shy; most rockhounds are happy to share their knowledge. One nice thing about exchanging crystals with friends is that you will know more of a stone's history, which can make it particularly special for you.

Rough vs. Tumbled

The debate ebbs and flows as to which is better: rough (in a natural state) or tumbled stones. This is a personal decision because our energy and the energy of a stone are unique. Rough stones show more of their basic characteristics, while tumbled or faceted ones often reveal more of their beauty. It comes down to how you feel when you hold the stone.

Labradorite is one of my favorites. It has its own special flash of iridescent colors called labradorescence. This flash is prevalent when labradorite is tumbled and very subtle when the stone is rough. I like working with both. With the rough labradorite, I like to think of the labradorescent flashes as a secret message between the stone and me.

Preparing Crystals for Use

Whichever way a stone comes into your life, it should be cleaned and prepared—even one that comes from your best friend. This is especially important when you purchase crystals. Cleaning a stone will remove unwanted or negative energy that it may have picked up through previous handling. Cleaning will enable a clear, pure flow of energy and help you get the most power from the stone. In addition, it will allow the stone to function more richly and fully with your energy and for your purpose. Gemstones should be cleaned separately to keep their power focused on their own energy.

Over time, you may feel that a stone has lost its potency, which is an indication that it needs to be cleaned and recharged. (See the section on charging a stone in the next chapter.) A stone that has been used to remove negativity should be cleaned immediately or set aside and not reused until it is cleaned.

Salt is especially effective for cleaning crystals. Sea salt is traditionally recommended; however, this should be a case-by-case decision. Because it comes from the ocean, sea salt is imbued with the power of the waves and the cleansing intention of water. Salt that comes from the body of Mother Earth will enhance the grounding power of a crystal. Be sure to use pure salt because some types contain aluminum or chemicals. Another decision with salt cleansing is whether to do it wet or dry.

Saltwater can be collected from the ocean, a bay, or an inlet. If you do not live near the coast, you can create it by dissolving a large pinch of sea salt in a small jar or bowl of spring water. Avoid using tap water, as it contains fluoride and other chemicals that are not appropriate for energetic cleansing. The downside to a saltwater cleaning is that it may leave a slight film on the stone's surface, which may alter the stone's luster. For a dry cleaning, you will need enough salt to bury the gemstone. Whichever method you use for salt cleansing, close your eyes and visualize the salt draining away old energy. Leave the stone in place overnight in the dry salt or saltwater.

Another popular way to clean a crystal is by moonlight. This takes a little longer than using salt, but if you want to draw on the power of Luna, it is worth the wait. Find a windowsill in your home that gets at least several hours of moonlight during the full moon. Place the gemstone on that windowsill for three nights beginning with the night before the full moon.

A crystal that has been used to remove negativity should be cleaned before it is used again. An effective method for cleaning such a stone is to place it in dry salt or saltwater and then put in the light of a waning moon for several nights. Luna will take the negativity with her as she goes away. A stone placed outside or on a windowsill on the night of a new moon will be open to receive energy. The light of a waxing moon will help boost the power of a stone.

A gentle method for cleaning a crystal is to bury it in a bowl of dried herbs or flower petals for a week. When cleaning this way, you can coordinate the type of herb with your intended use for the stone. For example, use thyme with a piece of moss agate that you plan to use to attract abundance. If you want a stone to be powerfully grounded, bury it outside in the earth or inside in a cup of soil for three days.

Another method for cleaning a stone's energy is through smudging. Use a cauldron or fireproof bowl to burn a little sage, cedar, or mugwort, and then pass the gemstone through the smoke. You don't need to generate a thick pall of smoke, just enough for a gentle wafting will do nicely. As with the herbal cleansing, you can coordinate the herbs for smudging with your intended use for the stone.

A very personal method for cleansing a stone is to use your own energy. Hold the crystal in both hands in front of your heart. Close your eyes and visualize universal energy running through your body from head to toe. Bring your awareness to the energy above your head. It may help to visualize it as soft white, pink, or lavender light. Feel it gently touch the crown of your head, then move down, activating your third-eye chakra, which is between and slightly above the eyebrows. As this energy descends to the throat and chest, it activates the heart chakra.

From here, visualize the energy moving along your arms to your hands and into the stone. Visualize the light pulsing and glowing around the stone. Now imagine it moving back up your arms, then down your spine, legs, and into your feet. Become aware of the bottoms of your feet—you may feel a tingling sensation. Visualize the energy moving from your feet into the floor and eventually into the ground, taking away old energy and any negativity with it.

After cleaning a new crystal by whatever method you choose, take time to sit with it. Cradle it in your hands and welcome it into your life. Be receptive to the energy of the stone and establish a connection with it by visualizing the movement of energy from your heart to the stone. Also, be receptive to energy coming back to you.

Chapter 4

CRYSTALS AND MAGIC

Crystals provide an easy, effective, and discreet way to engage in magical practices. After cleaning a stone, there is one more step to prepare it for magical use. This is called charging a crystal.

Charging a Crystal

When we work with magical energy, we shape it with our intention and willpower through visualization and then send it out with our own energy. Charging a crystal is simply focusing our intent and willpower into the stone to enable its energy to work more effectively with ours. If you have cleaned a crystal with your energy as outlined in the previous chapter, it is already becoming attuned to you.

Place a clean crystal on your altar. Rub your palms together, and then put your left palm on your stomach and your right palm over your heart. The left hand is over the solar plexus chakra, which is the seat of courage and power. This will activate the energy of this chakra and move it up to the heart chakra, which is being activated with the right hand. The heart chakra is the seat of love and compassion. It serves to moderate the energy of the solar plexus, which can be overpowering. When channeled together, these chakras produce a flow of powerful energy.

With your hands in these positions, visualize the energy of both chakras expanding and merging. When you feel the energy expand, pick up the crystal and hold it between your hands. Bring your attention down to your feet, and then draw earth energy up through your body. By drawing earth energy, you are tapping into a continuous flow that will enhance but not deplete your own energy. This will also keep you grounded.

Hold your hands in front of your heart as you cradle the crystal. Think of your particular purpose for the stone. Visualize your energy moving from your heart center, down your arms, and into the crystal to give it your intention and to pattern it with your willpower. Continue to hold the stone for another moment or two, and then wrap it in a soft cloth and place it on your altar until you are ready to work with it.

For general-purpose stones, simply think of sharing their energy in your home and magic work. Chanting or singing as you do this initial work with a stone helps to raise energy and strengthen your bond with it.

Magical Practices

As mentioned in the previous chapter, gemstones can be chosen by color or origin when used to represent the elements. For the element fire, select stones with fiery colors or choose peridot or obsidian, as these are born of volcanic action. For the element water, soothing blue stones work well as do pearls and opal. Pearls, of course, come from the sea, and opals actually contain water molecules. Transparent or translucent yellow, white, or blue stones work well to represent air, or choose a delicate crystal cluster. Coming from the earth, most gemstones can represent this element; however, some such as andalusite and moss agate may feel more effective. While details on associated elements are included with each stone in part 2 of this book, ultimately listen to the guidance of your intuition.

Like candles, crystals can be used for spells according to color. For example, pink for romance, red for passion, blue for harmony, green for prosperity, and so forth. Table 4 provides a few details for a range of basic colors.

Table 4. Magical Associations of Basic Colors

Black	Authority, banish, bind, break hexes, defense, determination, grounding, power, protection, release, reversal, security, wisdom
Blue	Astral realm, blessings, communication, forgiveness, harmony, healing, inspiration, intuition, relationships, truth, visions

Brown	Balance, concentration, family, grounding, home, justice, protection, renewal, stability, travel
Green	Abundance, acceptance, adaptability, balance, fertility, growth, independence, prosperity, strength, trust, well-being
Orange	Ambition, attraction, changes, creativity, goals, intelligence, luck, pleasure, reconciliation, success, support
Pink	Affection, balance, compassion, friendship, generosity, love, marriage, romance, sensuality, warmth
Purple	Awareness, dedication, enlightenment, freedom, justice, luck, protection, psychic abilities, spirits, spirituality, transformation, wisdom
Red	Action, ambition, courage, desire, fertility, love, loyalty, lust, motivation, passion, rebirth, sexuality, willpower
White	Clarity, compassion, consciousness, harmony, healing, love, peace, purification, truth, unity
Yellow	Communication, confidence, faith, happiness, imagination, inspiration, knowledge, skills, wisdom, wishes

Whether or not you plan to use a crystal in a spell, place one among the items you prepare for magic work to give them an energy boost. For example, place a piece of malachite on your altar overnight with the things you are going to use for a spell to attract money. You may also want to store a crystal with your ritual tools to empower your gear. Because stones such as clear quartz or blue topaz are associated with purification and consecration, they can keep the energy around your tools sacred.

Crystals are commonly placed around the home to neutralize negativity and foster protection. Placing stones on your desk at work can be an effective and discreet way to engender harmony or to provide a shield against negative energy. Crystals can be placed in the garden to enhance growth or to connect with fairies, devas, and other nature spirits. They also make nice offerings for these magical beings. Staurolite is particularly attractive to fairies.

Stones associated with certain deities can be used to represent them on your altar, or they can serve as offerings to your favorite goddess or god. During my pilgrimage to Ireland, I left crystals in special places as offerings. Information on associated deities is provided with each stone in part 2 and in the appendix B quick reference guide.

Just as certain herbs aid dreamwork, so too do particular crystals. Place a piece of amethyst, moonstone, or smoky quartz in a sachet and hang it on your bedpost or set it on your bedside table. In addition, garnet and other stones are helpful for remembering dreams.

Many types of crystals are especially helpful for healing. They can be held in the hands for meditation, placed on the body for energy work, or worn as jewelry. Also, arrange stones on the altar of a healing circle to aid in sending energy to someone in need.

Crystal Grids

Using multiple crystals is a powerful way to boost energy. A crystal grid is created by laying out stones in a geometric pattern, then working with the energy to direct it for your purpose. While there are many grid patterns to choose from, I like to work with the shape of a crystal's inner structure. As previously mentioned, despite a crystal's outer shape its inner structure may be quite different because it is based on the mineral's crystal system. For example, rose quartz is in the trigonal crystal system, which means its inner structure is a triangle. Refer to table 5 for a guide to crystal system shapes.

Decide on a location for your crystal grid where it can remain in place for as long as you feel it is appropriate. Choose stones that are associated with your purpose. Staying with rose quartz as an example, let's say you want to draw love into your life. You can use three pieces of rose quartz to represent the corners of a triangle or you can use more stones to create the three sides of a triangle. You can also fill in the entire shape of the triangle with as many stones as you feel are appropriate. In addition, you do not need to use all the same type of stone. Choose others that align to your purpose and have the same inner structure. In our example, we could also choose pink calcite and amethyst because they are associated with love and have trigonal inner structures.

Spend a few minutes in meditation or just sit quietly before setting up your grid. A grid can be small to fit on your altar or lay it out on the floor and make it large enough to sit within it. Once it is set up, close your eyes, hold your hands over it, and think about your purpose. Visualize your energy moving into the crystals and the energy of the crystals moving through the grid. Remove your hands and take a few minutes to sit with the grid as you visualize your purpose. Write a few thoughts on a piece of paper and place it, along with pictures or other small objects, within the grid to add energy and support for your purpose. As time goes by, you may want to recharge the grid with another visualization.

Table 5. Crystal Structures as Grid Shapes

Crystal System	Shape of Inner Structure	
Cubic/Isometric	Square	
Tetragonal	Rectangle	
Hexagonal	Hexagon	
Trigonal	Triangle	
Orthorhombic	Diamond	
Monoclinic	Parallelogram	
Triclinic	Trapezium	
Amorphous	Represent the lack of inner structure with a circle	

The Special Power of Certain Stones

The shapes of some crystals make them perfect for specialized use. Crystals that are naturally pointed help to focus and send energy. In fact, a long, thin crystal can be used in place of a wand. It just needs to be large enough to hold comfortably. A smaller crystal point can be affixed to the end of a wand.

Some stones grow in pairs. These twinned crystals are effective in doubling the power of spells. Calcite, fluorite, and many others often form in pairs. In addition to twins, many types of stones grow in groups or clusters. This occurs when multiple crystals form from a common base. When used magically, clusters of crystals provide an amazing boost to energy. Clusters can be instrumental for almost any use.

Occasionally, a crystal may stop growing and then start again. In translucent crystals, these growth patterns can be seen as faint outlines, like ghostly crystals held within. Known as phantom crystals, these stones are a symbol of the soul as well as transformation. Meditate or sit quietly with a phantom crystal to enhance and deepen your spirituality. It may also help guide you on your chosen path.

Crystals and Divination

You don't always need a crystal ball for crystal gazing. A phantom or twined stone or a crystal that has inclusions—internal frost or imperfections—works well for crystal gazing. Sit in a darkened room with only one candle lit. Hold the crystal in front of the candle flame and with a soft gaze look through the stone. While this method of scrying takes patience and practice, it is a rewarding form of divination. Do not expect to see images in the crystal. Its effectiveness is in opening the mind to receive information.

As previously mentioned, in ancient times a simple yes/no divination was performed with two stones of equal size and shape. A bright colored stone represented the affirmative answer and a dark one, the negative. Both were placed in a pouch and after posing a question, one stone was drawn. The process was repeated two more times for confirmation. For your own practice, decide which stone means yes and which means no. Keep them in a pouch from which they can be drawn without seeing them. After meditating on a question, draw a stone from the pouch. Put it back and repeat the process two more times for confirmation.

Birthstones, Stars, Planets, and Constellations

Wearing birthstone jewelry is a simple way to connect with the constellations of the zodiac. However, there are so many more stars in the sky and we can tap into their energy, too. Since ancient times, gemstones have been used as talismans and amulets empowered by drawing down the energy of stars. We can also tap into the power of meteor showers.

Decide which star, planet, or constellation you want to work with and follow the same procedure as charging a crystal. After drawing up earth energy and bringing the crystal in front of your heart center, visualize drawing down the energy of the star, planet, or constellation. Feel the energy move through the crown chakra on top of your head. Pull the energy down through your body, and then visualize the energy expanding. When you feel that you cannot hold the energy any longer, release it down your arms into the crystal. Hold the stone for another moment or two, and then wrap it in a cloth and place it on your altar until you are ready to work with it.

In addition to working with star or planetary magic, crystals charged in this way add energy to enhance astrology work. You may also want to consider charging birthstone jewelry for loved ones in this way. Also, charge and attach a special crystal to a pet's collar.

Another way to work with stars that combines the idea of a crystal grid is a method I explained in my book *Star Magic*. Instead of a geometric grid, lay out stones in the pattern of the constellation with which you want to work.

Stones, Herbs, and Oils

Although herbs are often considered less powerful than crystals, the synergy between herbs and crystals can boost and enhance magical energy. For example, for a love spell you might combine the use of pink calcite with dill, marjoram, and/or roses. For a spell of luck, use malachite with rosemary, peppermint, and violets.

Oils are often used to consecrate crystals, too. The synergy will boost the vibrational energy of both the stone and the oil. A tiny dab of oil is all that is needed. Avoid bathing the stone in oil as this may subdue its luster or other optical phenomena.

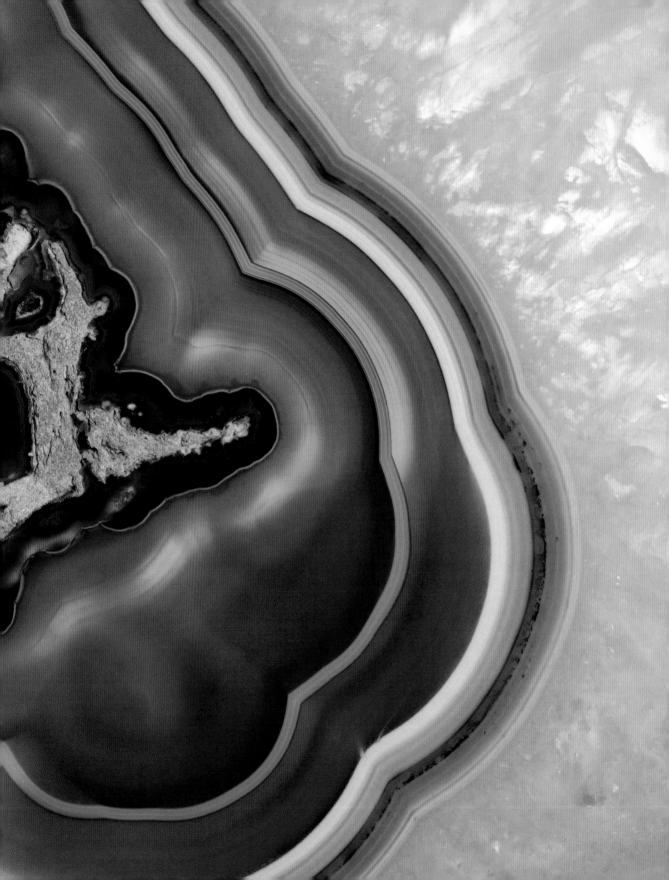

Part Two

A Compendium of Stones

This section is an easy-to-use, go-to reference. It contains entries for more than one hundred types of crystals, including identification details and historical information. This is intended to help you recognize crystals and to provide a foundation for understanding the rich background of their cultural use. Details on how to pronounce mineral names are also included. Of course, each entry contains suggestions for magical applications. This section is intended to inform and inspire you to develop your own methods for using crystals as magical tools.

Agate

Pronunciation: AG-it

Agates are known for their wide range of colors and patterns. Found along the River Achates in Sicily, Greek naturalist Theophrastus named this stone *achate*.[15] The Sumerians and Mesopotamians used agate for beads, seals, and ceremonial ax heads. For Egyptians, agates served as amulets. The Minoans of Crete and Mycenaeans of mainland Greece used these stones for jewelry, as did the Romans, who were especially fond of agate for signet rings. Agate was valued during the Middle Ages and often used as talismans for luck. Adorning the scabbards of swords and daggers in the Middle East, agate was believed to staunch the bleeding of wounds. It was also employed medicinally for this purpose.

Agate colors include black, blue, brown, gray, green, orange, pink, purple, red, white, and yellow. Most agates have multiple colors that are structured into wavy bands, flowing patterns, or concentric designs. Usually, they are named according to their pattern or predominant color. Agates have a trigonal inner structure, their luster is greasy or vitreous, and they range from translucent to opaque.

In general, agate fosters abundance, wealth, and love. It strengthens our connection with the natural world and is instrumental for grounding energy. As an all-purpose stone of protection, agate is especially effective for psychic protection. Use it for weather working and to

....

15. Patti Polk, *Collecting Agates and Jaspers of North America* (Iola, WI: Krause Publications, 2013), 9.

weather the storms of life. Agate helps to deal with everyday problems and stress. It is also instrumental to release what we no longer need in our lives. As a stone of high energy, it aids in personal growth, self-confidence, and maintaining inner strength. Agate also attracts luck.

Most types of agate are associated with the element earth. In general, their astrological influence comes from the moon, the fixed star Procyon, and the zodiac constellations of Cancer, Capricorn, Libra, and Virgo. Agate is also associated with the god Asclepius.

Black Agate

This variety of agate can be completely black or it may have a little white banding. It is a supportive stone that fosters courage and success. Black agate also fosters peaceful energy and healing. Use it to boost the power of spells and to spark creativity. This stone is associated with the element fire.

Black with White Veining

As its name suggests, this variety of agate is predominantly black with white, spidery veining. During medieval times, it was used as a talisman to guard against danger. This is a stone of beauty and strength. It fosters receptive energy and piques intuition to warn of potential danger or problems.

Blue Lace Agate

See separate entry.

Brown Agate

Also known as tawny agate

This stone is predominantly dark brown with wavy bands of lighter browns, tans, or white. While this agate boosts courage and provides support during conflict, it is also helpful in setting goals and achieving successful outcomes. It is instrumental in spells to attract money. Associated with the home and healing, use brown agate to give thanks for your blessings. This stone is associated with the element fire.

Fire Agate

This variety of agate has rich, rusty colors and an iridescence that gives off flashes of orange. It is opaque with a vitreous or waxy luster. Fire agate aids in dealing with problems, especially those related to sexuality. It is also helpful to add spark to your sex life. In addition, this stone fosters a sense of security. As expected, it is associated with the element fire. Its astrological influence comes from Mercury and the zodiac constellation of Aries.

Green Agate

Predominantly dark green, this stone has varying patterns of lighter colors. Fertility, love, and healing are the hallmarks of this agate. It fosters personal growth and strengthens family ties. This stone is helpful to gain insight in unusual situations. Green agate also boosts energy for spells. Its astrological influence comes from Mercury.

Moss Agate
Also known as mocha stone

This variety of agate is usually colorless with green, brown, or red mosslike inclusions, which are the source of its name. Like tree agate, it is sometimes called *mocha stone*. Moss agate brings strength while balancing energy and emotions. It is also a stone of abundance and hope. This agate engenders harmony and optimism in the home. It fosters creativity and can be used to aid garden growth. Moss agate's astrological influence comes from Mercury and the zodiac constellations of Aquarius, Gemini, Taurus, and Virgo.

Red Agate
Also known as blood agate

Predominantly red, this stone has swirling patterns or bands of brown, yellow, lighter red, and/or white. While red agate is a stone of love, action, and protection, it is also helpful for generating healing energy. It bolsters determination and aids in overcoming obstacles. This stone is particularly effective for protection spells. Red agate is associated with the element fire and the goddess the Morrigan. Its astrological influence comes from Mercury and the zodiac constellation of Aquarius.

Snakeskin Agate

With a scalelike pattern that resembles the skin of a snake, this stone is instrumental in working with animals and raising energy for animal magic. It also aids in dealing with sexual issues. Snakeskin agate is associated with the element fire. Its astrological influence comes from Mercury and the zodiac constellation of Scorpio.

Tree Agate
Also known as dendritic agate and mocha stone

Looking like a design on a frosty window, this variety of agate can be colorless, gray, or white with dark patterns that often resemble a branching tree. Associated with agriculture and personal well-being, this is a stone of abundance. Use it for introspection and growth when seeking wisdom. Tree agate is associated with the element air. Its astrological influence comes from Mercury and the zodiac constellations of Gemini and Taurus.

Alexandrite

Pronunciation: al-ex-ZAN-drite

Alexandrite is a rare type of chrysoberyl known for its stunning phenomenon of changing color from green to red depending on the type of light in which it is viewed. This feature prompted it to be described as "an emerald by day and ruby by night." Discovered on the birthday of Russian Czar Alexander II in 1834, it was named in honor of him by Finnish mineralogist Nils Nordenskjold (1792–1866).[16] In addition to the name, this stone was fashionable with the Russian aristocracy because it exhibited the imperial colors. Alexandrite was especially popular from the late nineteenth into the early twentieth century throughout Europe.

Alexandrite is green to blue green in daylight and red to reddish purple in artificial light. A cross-shaped twinning of crystals is common in this stone. Although rare, it can exhibit a cat's-eye effect. Alexandrite is transparent with an orthorhombic inner structure. It has a vitreous or greasy luster.

Alexandrite enhances the power of other stones with which it is used. On its own, this stone strengthens personal power and spirituality. It is instrumental for opening the psyche to one's higher self. Alexandrite supports and can hasten success and transformation. Wear it to aid adaptability. Alexandrite is a stone of love, faith, and self-respect that also fosters joy. Use it to stimulate psychic abilities and dreams or to aid in astral travel. This stone also attracts good fortune and prosperity.

Alexandrite is associated with the elements earth and water. Its astrological influence comes from Venus and the zodiac constellations of Gemini, Pisces, and Scorpio.

16. Cally Oldershaw, *Firefly Guide to Gems* (Toronto, Canada: Firefly Books, 2003), 59.

Amazonite

Pronunciation: AM-uh-zuh-nite

Also known as Amazon stone and green feldspar

Although this variety of feldspar was named for the Amazon River, it is not found in the immediate vicinity of the river. In addition, while it is mined in Brazil, it is found in several other locations around the world. Amazonite was used for jewelry in Egypt as early as 4000 BCE and in Mesopotamia and India around 2000 BCE.[17] Held in high esteem, the Sumerians used it ornamentally in the tombs of important people. Carved amazonite was used as talismans by the Egyptians and placed in the tombs of kings, including Tutankhamen. For the living, this stone was carved into figurines of deities, vases, and kohl makeup pots. It was frequently used in combination with turquoise and lapis lazuli. The Aztec and Maya included amazonite in mosaics to represent the ongoing cycle of renewal and the growth of vegetation.

Amazonite can be blue-green, colorless, green, white, or yellow. The most popular stones have irregular patterns of green or blue-green colors. This stone has a triclinic inner structure and a vitreous luster. It ranges from translucent to opaque. Amazonite fluoresces a weak olive-green color.

Amazonite is useful to clear and focus the mind, sharpen intuition, and open psychic channels to receive inspiration. Its grounding energy is emotionally soothing, aids communication, and fosters unity. Amazonite brings stability and helps build relationships that are based on trust. A stone of hope and growth, it is effective in charms to aid fertility or

17. Rapp, *Archaeomineralogy*, 100.

manifest desires and goals. In the right hands, it fosters strength, leadership, and success. This stone brings honor when it is deserved. Use amazonite to dispel negativity and invite harmony into your life and home. Also, use it to attract luck. Place amazonite on your Samhain altar to wish loved ones a good journey in the afterlife.

Amazonite is associated with the elements earth and water. Its astrological influence comes from Uranus and the zodiac constellation of Virgo.

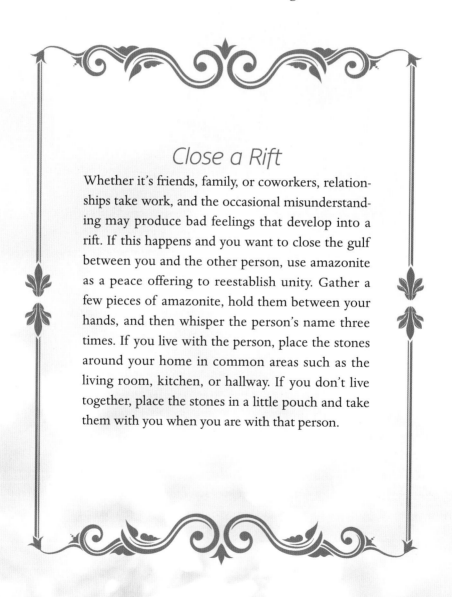

Close a Rift

Whether it's friends, family, or coworkers, relationships take work, and the occasional misunderstanding may produce bad feelings that develop into a rift. If this happens and you want to close the gulf between you and the other person, use amazonite as a peace offering to reestablish unity. Gather a few pieces of amazonite, hold them between your hands, and then whisper the person's name three times. If you live with the person, place the stones around your home in common areas such as the living room, kitchen, or hallway. If you don't live together, place the stones in a little pouch and take them with you when you are with that person.

Amber

Pronunciation: **AM-bur**

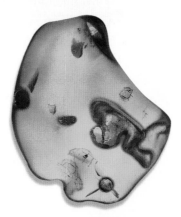

Highlighted in the film *Jurassic Park*, amber is the fossilized resin of ancient pine trees (*Pinus succinifera*). The fascination with and use of amber dates to the Stone Age. A cave in the French Pyrenees yielded stores of amber dating to approximately 13,000 BCE.[18] Used throughout the ancient world, Baltic amber was considered the best type and came to be regarded as "the gold of the north." In the past, it was variously named sea stone, strand amber, and succinate.

The Etruscans carved amber into ornaments—most often animal shapes—to use as talismans. According to Greek myth, amber was formed from the tears of the Heliades, the daughters of sun god Helios, when they mourned the death of their brother Phaëthon. Amber carvings were dedicated to divinities, and amulets were placed in graves to ensure a smooth transition into the otherworld. Because of its pleasing odor when burned, amber was used as temple incense throughout Asia. In medieval Europe, an amber bead necklace placed on a baby was believed to protect it from witchcraft and sorcery. Worn by older children, amber beads were believed to protect against bronchial problems and numerous other ailments.

Amber ranges from pale yellow to brown and reddish brown and from transparent to opaque. It has a vitreous luster and is classified as amorphous, for its lack of an inner

18. Lance Grande and Allison Augustyn, *Gems and Gemstones: Timeless Natural Beauty of the Mineral World* (Chicago: University of Chicago Press, 2009), 280.

structure. Like topaz and tourmaline, amber can become electrically charged, attracting dust and other small particles. Radial cracks called sun spangles are artificially created by heating a piece of amber.

Because of its age, amber is instrumental for connecting with ancestors and seeking ancient wisdom. It brings mental clarity and illumination that supports creativity. This stone helps to manifest change through gentle motivation. Burn a small piece before ritual or magic work to clear your space. Amber's power of purification boosts the energy of spells, especially for protection and success. This stone helps to foster honesty and stability in a relationship. Its calming energy aids in healing, especially from grief. Leave a piece of amber as an offering for tree spirits or for the fairies. Because it is so full of light, amber is perfect for the Yule altar.

Amber is associated with the elements earth and fire. Its astrological influence comes from Mercury, the sun, and the zodiac constellations of Aquarius, Cancer, Leo, and Sagittarius. Amber is associated with the deities Apollo, Danu, Freya, Helios, and Njord.

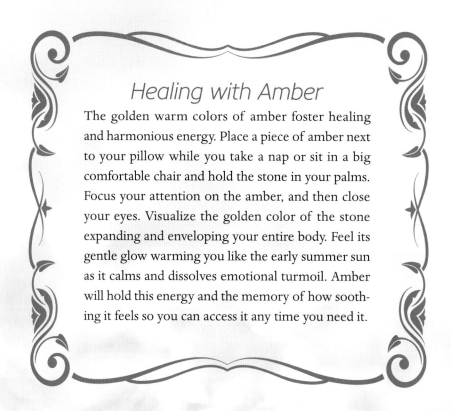

Healing with Amber

The golden warm colors of amber foster healing and harmonious energy. Place a piece of amber next to your pillow while you take a nap or sit in a big comfortable chair and hold the stone in your palms. Focus your attention on the amber, and then close your eyes. Visualize the golden color of the stone expanding and enveloping your entire body. Feel its gentle glow warming you like the early summer sun as it calms and dissolves emotional turmoil. Amber will hold this energy and the memory of how soothing it feels so you can access it any time you need it.

Amethyst

Pronunciation: AM-uh-thist

As the most highly valued quartz, amethyst has enjoyed a long history of popularity that has rarely waned. From the pharaohs of Egypt to British monarchs, this gemstone has been used in countless royal jewelry. Mined in Egypt during the First Dynasty (2920–2770 BCE), amethyst was used for beads, bracelets, amulets, and funeral scarabs.[19] The Romans and the high priests of Israel also used amethyst. On Crete, the Minoans used it for cylinder seals. According to ancient legend, this stone was thought to cause the wearer to have unusual and bewildering dreams.

During the Middle Ages, amethyst was believed to be an antidote against poison. In northern Europe, it was used as a charm against witchcraft. According to Leonardo de Vinci, it increased intelligence and dispelled evil thoughts.[20] By the mid-seventeenth century, amethyst was as precious as diamonds.[21] The name of this stone was derived from the Greek *amethustos* meaning "sober" in reference to the belief that it kept the wearer from becoming intoxicated.[22]

---

19. Rapp, *Archaeomineralogy*, 91.

20. Grande and Augustyn, *Gems and Gemstones*, 87.

21. Henry G. Smith, *Gems and Precious Stones: With Descriptions of Their Distinctive Properties* (Sydney, Australia: Charles Potter, 1896), 59.

22. Oldershaw, *Firefly Guide to Gems*, 154.

The color of amethyst encompasses many shades of purple and violet, even reddish violet. It ranges from transparent to translucent with a vitreous to greasy luster. It has a trigonal inner structure. Very pale-colored amethyst stones are called rose de France.

A gemstone of awareness and wisdom, amethyst is a great healer and spiritual guide. It is good for calming and focusing the mind and tapping into one's intuition. This stone is a great tool for divination and dreamwork and for fine-tuning psychic abilities. It is instrumental for grounding energy before and after ritual or magic work. Its energy can purify altars and tools. Carry it for protection or when seeking justice. Use amethyst in spells to achieve goals or help manifest love. Use it to foster harmony, growth, and peace. It is a stone of change and transformation that also offers stability and strength. Amethyst opens the channels for communication on all levels, including contacting spirits. Keep it in your workspace to stimulate inspiration and creative expression.

Amethyst is associated with the element water. Its astrological influence comes from Jupiter, Neptune, Pluto, the fixed star Antares, and the zodiac constellations of Aquarius, Capricorn, Pisces, Sagittarius, and Virgo. This stone is also associated with the deities Bacchus, Diana, Dionysus, Justitia, and Venus.

Amethyst Quartz
Also known as amethystine quartz

Although mostly amethyst, this stone also contains white quartz. Ranging from translucent to opaque, it is pale lilac to violet with whitish striping or swirls. The Phoenicians used amethyst quartz for cylinder seals; the Assyrians used it for seals, amulets, and jewelry. Although in today's gem trade it is considered of lesser quality, energetically the white quartz adds extra power to the amethyst.

Ametrine

Pronunciation: AM-uh-trine *or* AM-uh-treen

Also known as bolivianite and trystin

Just as this stone's name is a combination of amethyst and citrine, so too is its mineral composition. It has distinct zones or bands of purple amethyst and brownish-yellow citrine. Ametrine is transparent with a vitreous to greasy luster and has a trigonal inner structure.

Although the two colors of this stone are on opposite sides of the color wheel, this pairing of complementary opposites creates a balance of energies. With harmony and strength, this stone brings the physical and spiritual aspects of life into equilibrium. Ametrine provides a calm atmosphere that encourages reflection and introspection. Often, along with this comes clarity and a new level of spiritual awareness and growth. The soothing energy of ametrine helps to deal with loss and negative emotions and any type of negative energy or people. Ametrine is effective for cleansing the aura and ritual space. Fostering healing energy, this stone ushers in renewal and stability. Ametrine is both a guardian and a guide when working with spirits. It also aids in contacting spirit guides. Use it to focus energy for decision-making and spellwork.

Ametrine is associated with the elements air, fire, and water. Its astrological influence comes from Jupiter, the sun, and the zodiac constellation of Libra.

Andalusite

Pronunciation: **an-duh-LOO-site**

This stone was named for Andalusia, the province in Spain where it was discovered. The transparent variety of andalusite was nicknamed poor man's alexandrite. While it does not change color, transparent andalusite is strongly pleochroic, presenting two colors similar to alexandrite when viewed from different angles.

Andalusite can be brown, greenish brown, orange brown, reddish brown, yellowish brown, gray, pink, white, yellow, or yellow green. It ranges from transparent to opaque and has an orthorhombic inner structure. Its luster ranges from vitreous to dull. Transparent green andalusite is regarded as a top-quality gem.

Andalusite is a stone of manifestation that can keep your energy grounded during times of change. Use it to bolster determination to achieve success, especially when you are in a leadership role. This stone is effective for dispelling negative energy and works well for pre-ritual preparations. It also enhances memory and aids in past-life work or dreamwork. Wear or carry andalusite to attract luck or to provide protective energy. Associated with spirituality, it is an ideal altar stone for ritual and a focus stone for meditation.

Andalusite is associated with the element earth. Its astrological influence comes from the zodiac constellation of Virgo.

Chiastolite

Pronunciation: kye-AS-tuh-lite

Also known as cross stone and luck stone

This opaque andalusite is the most common variety. It is popular for the pronounced X or cross pattern that is revealed when a crystal is cut horizontally. This stone's name was derived from the Greek *khiastos* meaning "marked with an X" in reference to the Greek letter *khi/chi*.[23] Chiastolite found near Santiago de Compostella in Spain, an important Christian pilgrimage site, gave rise to its name cross stone. Also known as the luck stone, it was worn in medieval times as a charm for good luck as well as an amulet for protection. Fairies are particularly fond of this stone.

23. Michael R. Collings, *Gemlore: An Introduction to Precious and Semi-Precious Stones,* 2nd ed. (Rockville, MD: The Borgo Press, 2009), 39.

Angelite

Pronunciation: AYN-juhl-ite

Also known as blue anhydrite

Although alabaster was a favored material for carvings in ancient Egypt, second on their list was white or pale blue anhydrite. It was commonly used to make small vases, cosmetic jars, and flasks in the shape of animals. Erroneously called blue marble, blue anhydrite was used for statuettes, which were found in tombs dating to the Middle Kingdom (c. 1938–1650 BCE).[24] Ground into a powder, this stone was used as a pigment on the walls of Amenhotep III's tomb. It continued to be used for wall paintings in Europe through the Middle Ages. This stone earned the common name angelite because its particular shade of blue was regarded as a heavenly color for centuries. The mineral name was derived from the Greek *anhydros,* meaning "waterless."[25] This is in reference to the fact that anhydrite forms from dehydrated gypsum.

Angelite ranges from bluish to violet and transparent to translucent. It has a vitreous luster and an orthorhombic inner structure.

....

24. Paul T. Nicholson and Ian Shaw, eds., *Ancient Egyptian Materials and Technology* (New York: Cambridge University Press, 2006), 23.

25. Nicholas Eastaugh, et al., *Pigment Compendium: A Dictionary and Optical Microscopy of Historical Pigments* (Burlington, MA: Butterworth-Heinemann, 2008), 19.

As its name implies, this stone is perfect for communicating with the angelic realm. It is instrumental for interpreting messages and calling on angels for support in magic work. Angelite is especially helpful to foster compassion, generosity, and forgiveness. Although its energy is gentle, this stone functions as a guardian and protector, especially when seeking to transform your life. It is effective for dreamwork, developing psychic skills, and expanding awareness. Angelite is helpful in quieting anxiety and stress. Use it to foster self-acceptance.

Angelite is associated with the elements air and water. Its astrological influence comes from the moon, Neptune, and the zodiac constellation of Aquarius.

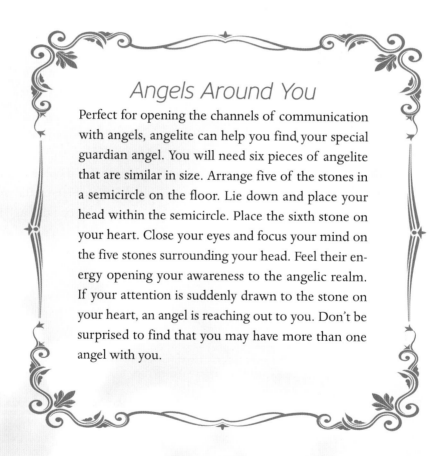

Angels Around You

Perfect for opening the channels of communication with angels, angelite can help you find your special guardian angel. You will need six pieces of angelite that are similar in size. Arrange five of the stones in a semicircle on the floor. Lie down and place your head within the semicircle. Place the sixth stone on your heart. Close your eyes and focus your mind on the five stones surrounding your head. Feel their energy opening your awareness to the angelic realm. If your attention is suddenly drawn to the stone on your heart, an angel is reaching out to you. Don't be surprised to find that you may have more than one angel with you.

Apatite

Pronunciation: **AP-uh-tite**

Although this mineral is a common source of phosphorus, apatite can also produce gem-quality stones. Its name is derived from the Greek *apatao,* meaning "to cheat" or "to deceive," due to the ease in which it can be mistaken—or intentionally substituted—for more expensive stones such as beryl and tourmaline.[26] In ancient Egypt, apatite was used for beads and as a cosmetic pigment. In the Near East, this stone was used for cylinder seals.

Apatite can be blue, colorless, green, pink, violet, or yellow. It ranges from transparent to translucent and has a vitreous or greasy luster. Apatite has a hexagonal inner structure. It may exhibit a cat's-eye effect when cut en cabochon, which is a smooth dome shape.

Apatite is especially powerful for self-work. Whether there is a need to improve your self-image or overcome shyness, this stone helps to find love and harmony within. It also aids in accepting the foibles of other people and situations that you cannot change. In addition, apatite enhances communication on all levels. It supports psychic abilities and is especially helpful for developing clairaudience and clairvoyance skills. Use it around your home and in spells to attract abundance and love. This stone is also instrumental for healing and dealing with grief. Place it on your desk or in your work area for focus and inspiration to stoke the fires of creativity. Hold a piece of apatite during meditation to deepen spirituality.

Apatite is associated with the elements air, earth, and fire. Its astrological influence comes from the zodiac constellation of Virgo.

....

26. Oldershaw, *Firefly Guide to Gems,* 89.

Asparagus Stone

Pronunciation: **uh-SPAR-uh-gus** *or* **uh-SPARE-uh-gus**

This variety of green apatite was so named because its color resembles the vegetable's particular shade of green. Asparagus stone is an aid when seeking any form of knowledge. Its healing energy is especially helpful in fostering harmony.

Moroxite

Pronunciation: **muh-ROCKS-ite**

This variety of apatite is blue to greenish blue and often strongly dichroic, appearing blue or yellow from different angles. Its name was derived from a type of phosphate used by the Greeks for bleaching linen. This is a stone of beauty that is helpful to release unwanted things from your life. It is instrumental in finding the appropriate way to extend a peace offering to reconcile a relationship. This stone also fosters healing energy. Use it before divination or other practices to activate the psyche.

Apophyllite

Pronunciation: **uh-POF-uh-lite** *or* ap-uh-FIL-ite

While this stone's name is applied to a small group of common minerals, most collectors rarely make the distinction. The name comes from the Greek *apo,* meaning "to be off," and *phyllos,* "leaf." [27] Like a tree losing its leaves, this mineral flakes apart when heated due to the loss of water in its structure. In the past, this mineral was called ichthyophthalmite or "fisheye stone" because it can sometimes have a pearly luster like a fish's eye. [28]

Too soft to use for jewelry, the popularity of apophyllite is due to its beautiful crystals that can take the form of cubes or rectangular prisms that terminate in four-sided pyramids. Collectors also like it for its clusters of upright crystals that form a spray or fan-shaped array.

Most commonly colorless, apophyllite can also be green, gray, pink, reddish, or white. It has a tetragonal inner structure and ranges from transparent to translucent. Its luster can be vitreous or pearly. This stone fluoresces yellow or orange.

Apophyllite is a spiritual stone that brings balance, clarity, and wisdom. It is instrumental when seeking self-knowledge. It stimulates intuition and aids in learning how to trust inner wisdom. It also aids in establishing connection with the astral realm. Use apophyllite to purify your ritual area or to lighten the energy anywhere in your home. To remove stress and invite happiness into your life, hold a piece of apophyllite as you sit quietly and let its energy wash over you.

....

27. Arthur Thomas, *Gemstones: Properties, Identification and Use* (London: New Holland Publishers (UK), 2008), 71.

28. Klaus K. E. Neuendorf, James P. Mehl, Jr., and Julia A. Jackson, eds., *Glossary of Geology,* 5th ed. (Alexandria, VA: American Geological Institute, 2005), 31.

Apophyllite is associated with the element earth. Its astrological influence comes from the zodiac constellation of Taurus.

Green Apophyllite

This variety of apophyllite ranges from pale green to bluish green. It is weakly dichroic appearing blue green or pale, yellowish green from different angles. This stone aids in personal growth and transformation. Use green apophyllite to open your energy field when you need to be receptive.

Aquamarine

Pronunciation: auk-wah-muh-REEN

This popular variety of beryl takes its name from the Latin *aqua marina* meaning "water of the sea" because it is reminiscent of the soothing colors of the Mediterranean.[29] Used in Greece as early as 500 to 300 BCE, legends tell of it being favored by mermaids.[30] Particularly valued by sailors or anyone who went to sea, aquamarine was used as a talisman for good luck and protection. The Romans, who used it for jewelry, believed it could quell seasickness. By the Middle Ages, aquamarine was believed to counteract the effects of poison and was used for various medicinal purposes. During this time, aquamarine was also considered an oracle stone. In China, it was used for figurines and seals, and in Turkey, large stones were fashioned into dagger hilts.

Aquamarine ranges from light to deep blue but is most famous for its blue-green or sea-green hues. Ranging from transparent to translucent, it has a vitreous luster and hexagonal inner structure. Aquamarine is dichroic, appearing colorless to light blue or blue from different angles. Although very rare, it can exhibit a cat's-eye effect or a six-rayed star. This stone is often heat-treated to create bluer stones for use in the gem trade.

Most famously used for protection, aquamarine is a good stone to take along when traveling. It is a stone of purification that functions well in banishing spells and to initiate renewal. Aquamarine enhances communication and supports healthy relationships, especially in marriage. Promoting tranquility, it aids in dealing with loss and grief. Aquamarine also fosters feelings of love and happiness. Use it to stir energy for inspiration and creativity

29. Jen Altman, *Gem and Stone: Jewels of Earth, Sea, and Sky* (San Francisco: Chronicle Books, 2012), 26.

30. Robert Simmons and Naisha Ahsian, *The Book of Stones: Who They Are and What They Teach* (East Montpelier, VT: Heaven & Earth Publishing, 2007), 49.

and for guidance when seeking wisdom. It also stimulates psychic abilities. This stone supports mental clarity and promotes healing. In addition, aquamarine fosters independence on all levels.

As expected, aquamarine is associated with the element water. Its astrological influence comes from the moon, Neptune, and the zodiac constellations of Aquarius, Aries, Gemini, Libra, Pisces, Scorpio, and Virgo.

Call on the Power of the Sea

Place a sea green candle on your altar along with seashells, a string of pearls, driftwood, starfish, beach pebbles, or sand. Prepare several pieces of aquamarine by sprinkling a pinch of sea salt over them. If you have a recording of ocean waves, play it or simply imagine the sound. Light the candle, and then stand in front of your altar holding the aquamarine crystals. Visualize waves breaking on the beach, and then raise the crystals as you say:

Spirit of the Sea, Mother Ocean,
bless these crystals with your motion.
With your wisdom as my guide;
may their energy rise like the tide.

Blow out the candle and wrap the crystals in a blue cloth until you need them for a spell or ritual.

Aragonite

Pronunciation: **uh-RAH-guh-nite** *or* **A-ruh-guh-nite**

In 1796, German geologist Abraham Gottlob Werner (1750–1817) named this stone for the city of Molina de Aragon in Spain where it was first discovered.[31] Frequently found in caves forming stalactites and stalagmites, aragonite has the same chemical composition as calcite but differs in its crystal structure. This mineral is a component of organic substances and is responsible for the iridescent surfaces of pearls and the mother-of-pearl interior of mollusk shells.

Aragonite generally forms long, thin crystals that are frequently twinned. Multiple crystals often form structures called sixlings, which can have a starlike shape. The aragonite formation called *flos-ferri*, meaning "flowers of iron," is reminiscent of intricate branching coral.[32] Although this name alludes to great strength, these crystals are actually quite fragile.

Aragonite can be blue, brown, colorless, gray, pink, reddish, white, or yellowish green. Ranging from transparent to opaque, its luster can be vitreous, resinous, or dull. Aragonite has an orthorhombic inner structure. This stone fluoresces a weak green, pink, or yellow color.

....

31. Ernest H. Nickel and Monte C. Nichols, *Mineral Reference Manual* (New York: Springer Science + Business Media, 1991), 9.

32. Cheryl Angelina Koehler, *Touring the Sierra Nevada* (Reno, NV: University of Nevada Press, 2007), 262.

A stone of balanced calm energy, aragonite is instrumental for relieving stress. Use it before magic work or after ritual to heighten your senses and to ground and center your energy. Holding a small crystal cluster aids in building confidence and provides guidance when seeking truth. It also fosters acceptance of people and/or situations. Keep it with your divination tools to cleanse any unwanted energy they may have picked up during use. Also, use this stone for healing circles to support and send energy to those in need.

Aragonite is associated with the elements air and water.

Blue Aragonite

This variety of aragonite ranges from pale blue to robin's egg blue. The color is often mottled or has faint veining. This stone of compassion and growth aids in self-healing. It also helps to fine-tune intuition and to develop psychic abilities.

Aventurine

Pronunciation: uh-VEN-chuh-reen *or* uh-VEN-chuh-rin

Also known as aventurine quartz

Aventurine is a type of quartz in which tiny inclusions produce a sheen of glittering reflections called aventurescence. This mineral takes its name from the famous aventurine glass of Italy, which was accidentally created when copper filings were spilled into molten glass. This stone is called aventurine quartz to distinguish it from aventurine feldspar, which is an old mineral name for sunstone.

The consensus among mineralogists is that aventurine is the mineral Pliny referred to as *sandastros*, a stone he described as having stars shining from within. In ancient times, aventurine had a wide range of uses from ax heads and seal stones to decorative jewelry.

With green as its most prevalent color, aventurine also occurs in various shades of blue, golden brown, or reddish brown. Its aventurescent sheen is caused by inclusions of mica, hematite, or goethite flecks that often give it a speckled appearance. This stone has a trigonal inner structure, ranges from translucent to opaque, and has a vitreous or waxy luster.

This is a stone of confidence and courage that can lift emotions and boost energy. Use it when seeking clarity for making decisions or for initiating change. It is an aid for attracting prosperity and finding opportunities. Use it in spells when seeking justice or when removing something that is unwanted from your life. This stone also provides protection and fosters a sense of well-being. Aventurine sparks the imagination for creative work and for finding solutions to problems. It is an aid for building friendships and community bonds.

Aventurine is associated with the elements air and earth. Its astrological influence comes from Mercury, Uranus, Venus, and the zodiac constellations of Aquarius, Aries, and Virgo.

Green Aventurine

This variety of aventurine has often been used as an alternative to the more expensive jade. Green aventurine is helpful in attracting money, luck, and success. It is also calming and supports healing, especially from heartbreak. This stone fosters compassion and friendship. It also bolsters inner strength. Meditate with it to gain insight for personal happiness and to help find independence.

Azurite

Pronunciation: AZ-uh-rite *or* AZ-uhr-ite

Also known as chessylite

T his stone's greatest use has been as a pigment dating back to approximately 6000 BCE when it was used on the walls of the shrines at Çatalhüyük in Anatolia, Turkey.[33] Azurite was a component in the famous pigment called Egyptian blue that had widespread use in the Mediterranean region throughout the Greek and Roman periods. On opposite sides of the world, the ancient Chinese and Maya also used it for pigment. In addition, azurite was the source for the most important blue in European paintings from the Middle Ages and Renaissance into the seventeenth century.[34] This pigment was also used for medieval manuscripts.

In Babylon, azurite was used for cylinder seals, and in the American Southwest, it found use as small axes and spear points. The word azure was derived from the medieval Latin name for the stone, *lazurium*, which in turn, had come from the Persian *lajward*, meaning "blue."[35] The name *chessylite* honors the area of Chessy in France, which is a location where azurite is found.

---

33. David A. Scott, *Copper and Bronze in Art: Corrosion, Colorants, Conservation* (Los Angeles: Getty Publications, 2002), 108.

34. Elisa Bergslien, *An Introduction to Forensic Geoscience* (Hoboken, NJ: Wiley-Blackwell, 2012), 299.

35. Oldershaw, *Firefly Guide to Gems*, 80.

This stone can be various shades of deep blue. It has a greasy or vitreous luster and ranges from translucent to opaque. Azurite has a monoclinic inner structure. It is pleochroic, appearing different hues from different angles.

Azurite is a stone of awareness supporting clairvoyance and all forms of psychic skills. Use it to sharpen intuition and to provide insight for divination and dreamwork. This stone is helpful for dispelling negativity, removing obstacles, and dealing with challenges. It also aids in making decisions. Azurite's calming energy subdues anxiety and empowers the emotions by fostering stability. Wear or carry a piece of azurite to aid in any form of communication or self-expression. As a spiritual stone, it provides growth and transformation. It supports contact with spirit guides.

Azurite is associated with the element water and the deities Brigid, Epona, Manannan, and Ogma. Its astrological influence comes from Saturn, Venus, and the zodiac constellations of Capricorn and Sagittarius.

Azurmalachite

Pronunciation: AZ-er-MAL-uh-kite
Also known as azure-malachite and azurite malachite
This stone is a blue and green mix of azurite and malachite. It brings the power of malachite to the calming energy and insight of azurite.

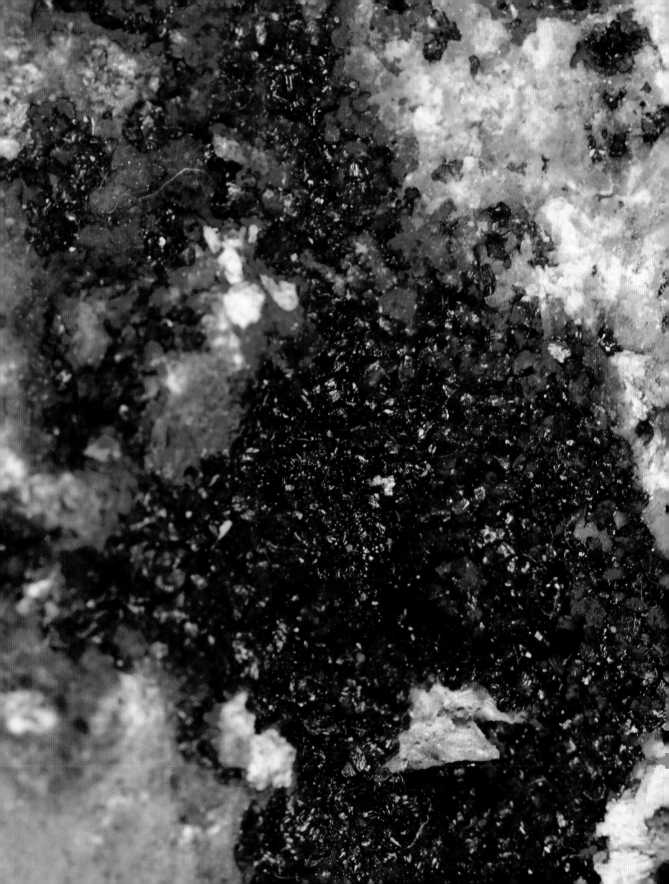

Barite

Pronunciation: BAIR-ite *or* BAR-ite

Also known as baryte, bologna stone, and heavy spar

The name of this mineral comes from the Greek *baryos,* meaning "heavy" or "dense," due to its unusually heavy weight.[36] Because there is scientific disagreement as to the spelling of the name, both barite and baryte are regarded as acceptable. In 1603, shoemaker and amateur alchemist Vincenzo Casciarolo of Bologna, Italy, thought he had discovered the long sought after philosopher's stone when the barite he had collected was found to be luminescent.[37] This is an effect where a stone becomes bright under a light source and then retains some of its brightness for a time in the dark. This property earned barite a flurry of nicknames such as lapis solaris, luciferin stone, shining stone, and sun stone.[38]

Barite is popular with collectors because of its bladed crystals that can form a desert rose or a cockscomb (rooster's crest). As the most common barium mineral, it is used predominantly by industry. Its applications range from paper, paint, glass, and insulation manufacturing to barium "milk shakes" for medical radiography.

Barite is colorless or white and tinged blue, brown, green, red, or yellow. It is often multicolored with colors forming in bands. With a vitreous or pearly luster, barite ranges from

36. Eastaugh, et al., *Pigment Compendium,* 46.

37. Marco Piccolino and Nicholas J. Wade, *Galileo's Visions: Piercing the Spheres of the Heavens by Eye and Mind* (New York: Oxford University Press, 2014), 57.

38. Ibid.

transparent to opaque and has an orthorhombic inner structure. It fluoresces a blue-green, gray, or white color.

The spiritual energy of this stone makes it especially effective for working with spirit guides and angels. It enhances the flow of psychic energy and is an aid for remembering and interpreting dreams. Barite also supports astral work. This stone provides guidance for decisions that require overcoming obstacles or solving problems. Barite also supports relationships and fosters loyalty.

Barite is associated with the element air. Its astrological influence comes from Uranus and the zodiac constellation of Aquarius.

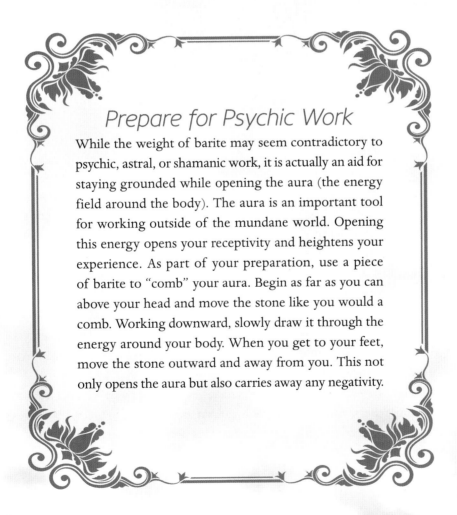

Prepare for Psychic Work

While the weight of barite may seem contradictory to psychic, astral, or shamanic work, it is actually an aid for staying grounded while opening the aura (the energy field around the body). The aura is an important tool for working outside of the mundane world. Opening this energy opens your receptivity and heightens your experience. As part of your preparation, use a piece of barite to "comb" your aura. Begin as far as you can above your head and move the stone like you would a comb. Working downward, slowly draw it through the energy around your body. When you get to your feet, move the stone outward and away from you. This not only opens the aura but also carries away any negativity.

Beryl

Pronunciation: BER-uhl

Beryl is actually a group of minerals. The most famous are the deep green beryls called emerald and the blue or greenish blue ones called aquamarine, which are covered in separate entries. While beryls of gemstone quality are called precious beryls, others are known as common beryls because they are often cloudy and opaque. The name *beryl* comes from the ancient Greek *beryllos*, which was originally applied to many green or bluish-green gemstones but later used only for beryl.[39]

Quarried by Egyptians along the Red Sea as early as 1650 BCE, beryls were exceptionally popular for jewelry from ancient times through the nineteenth century.[40] In India, beryls were made into beads and crystal balls. In fact, during the Middle Ages a crystal ball was referred to as a beryl or sphera, and Paracelsus referred to a type of divination using a crystal as ars beryllistica.[41]

Known for its perfect and often large crystals, beryl can grow up to three feet long and sometimes more. Beryl can be blue, green, golden, pink, white, or yellow. It ranges from transparent to opaque and has a vitreous luster. This stone has a hexagonal inner structure.

39. Gavin Linsell, *Gems TV: Guide to Gems & Jewelry* (Doncaster, England: Insignia Books, 2009), 25.

40. Frederick Brewster Loomis, *Field Book of Common Rocks and Minerals* (New York: G. P. Putnam's Sons, 1948), 126.

41. György E. Szönyi, *John Dee's Occultism: Magical Exaltation through Powerful Signs* (Albany, NY: State University of New York Press, 2004), 200.

Beryl stimulates communication and aids in living up to one's potential. It supports relationships, especially marriage, and clears the way for acceptance and reconciliation when needed. This stone fosters optimism and a sense of well-being. Use it to banish anything unwanted from your life or to help you meet challenges. Carry a piece of beryl for smooth travel or to bolster courage. This stone supports magic work by aiding concentration and raising energy levels. Beryl also boosts healing and spiritual growth.

Most beryls are associated with the element water. Their astrological influence comes from Mars, the moon, Neptune, the fixed star Sirius, and the zodiac constellations of Cancer, Capricorn, Libra, and Scorpio. They are associated with the deities Neptune, Poseidon, and Tiamat.

Goshenite

Pronunciation: **GOH-shun-ite**
Also known as lucid beryl and white beryl

This clear, transparent beryl is often used as an imitation diamond. Although it was named for Goshen, Massachusetts, where it was found in modern times, it was known and used by the ancient Greeks. Early eyeglass lenses were made from this stone. Goshenite is especially effective in bringing clarity to situations and relationships.

Heliodor

Pronunciation: **HEE-lee-uh-dawr**

Though discovered in 1910, the name of this beryl comes from the Greek *helios* and *doron,* meaning "gift from the sun." [42] It ranges from golden to greenish yellow and transparent to translucent. The more lemony colored stones have been called golden beryl. Associated with the mind, this beryl aids learning and study. Use it for support when developing psychic skills. This stone also boosts willpower. Heliodor is associated with the element fire and the god Helios. Its astrological influence comes from the sun and the zodiac constellation of Leo.

....
42. Schumann, *Gemstones of the World,* 112.

Morganite

***Pronunciation:* MOR-gun-ite *or* MAWR-gun-ite**

Named for the nineteenth-century banker J. P. Morgan (1837–1913), who was an avid gem collector, this stone ranges from soft pink and lilac pink to salmon pink. It is dichroic, appearing pink or colorless from different angles. This is the beryl to call on for support from angels in your magic work. It is also effective for guidance in everyday matters and aids in attracting love. Place morganite on your altar for aid when seeking wisdom through meditation. In addition, this stone's calming energy relieves stress and fosters emotional healing, especially from heartbreak.

Red Beryl

Also known as red emerald

Formerly named bixbite for mineralogist Maynard Bixby (1853–1935), who discovered it in 1904, this type of beryl is more rare than emerald.[43] Because of the confusion with another mineral discovered by Bixby that was named bixbyite, the straightforward name of red beryl came into use. Ranging from translucent to opaque, this stone's color covers reddish shades from strawberry to raspberry. Red beryl is dichroic, appearing purplish red or orange red from different angles. This stone aids in matters of the heart and supports loving relationships.

43. Oldershaw, *Firefly Guide to Gems*, 129.

Bloodstone

Also known as blood jasper and heliotrope

The use of bloodstone dates to the prehistoric people of western Scotland, who used this hard stone as a knapping tool to shape flint into arrowheads, scrapers, and blades. The name *heliotrope* comes from the Greek *helios* and *tropos,* meaning "sun turner," which stems from the belief that it could turn the sun's rays red.[44]

The Greeks and Romans used bloodstone for seal stones, cameos, and a range of decorative objects. Their athletes wore it in the belief that it would provide endurance. The Egyptians used this stone as a general talisman. From ancient times through the Middle Ages, bloodstone was regarded as a powerful healing stone. In medieval Europe, it was believed to give the wearer the gift of prophecy. In addition, it was called the martyr's stone because of the legend that green jasper at the foot of the cross was stained with drops of blood from Jesus, which resulted in this stone. Due to the popularity of this story, bloodstone was believed to possess special powers and was favored by Christians for religious carvings. It was also regarded as a stone of prophecy.

Bloodstone is multicolored dark green or bluish green with flecks of red. It ranges from translucent to opaque and vitreous to waxy. It has a trigonal inner structure.

A crystal of honesty, integrity, and justice, bloodstone is effective for attracting luck, success, and money. Use it to bolster strength and buffer aggression. Bloodstone shows us how to be adaptable when dealing with obstacles and when making decisions, especially in business. Use it to add energy in all forms of divination. Bloodstone boosts the power of spells in general and is an aid when banishing spirits. This stone boosts confidence, especially when

44. Schumann, *Gemstones of the World*, 144.

developing new skills. As a spiritual stone, it enhances faith and healing and is instrumental when seeking renewal.

Bloodstone is associated with the element fire and the goddesses Badb and the Morrigan. Its astrological influence comes from Mars and the zodiac constellations of Aries, Capricorn, Libra, Pisces, and Scorpio.

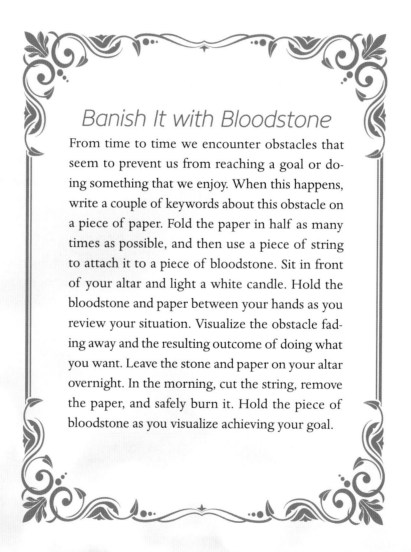

Banish It with Bloodstone

From time to time we encounter obstacles that seem to prevent us from reaching a goal or doing something that we enjoy. When this happens, write a couple of keywords about this obstacle on a piece of paper. Fold the paper in half as many times as possible, and then use a piece of string to attach it to a piece of bloodstone. Sit in front of your altar and light a white candle. Hold the bloodstone and paper between your hands as you review your situation. Visualize the obstacle fading away and the resulting outcome of doing what you want. Leave the stone and paper on your altar overnight. In the morning, cut the string, remove the paper, and safely burn it. Hold the piece of bloodstone as you visualize achieving your goal.

Blue Lace Agate

Possibly the most popular of all agates, this stone was discovered in Namibia in the 1960s.[45] It is widely used for jewelry and small carvings. What this stone lacks in history, it makes up for with powerful energy.

Aptly named, blue lace agate has lacy bands or wavy patterns of powder blue and white colors. It has a trigonal inner structure, a vitreous luster, and ranges from translucent to opaque.

Popular for calming and grounding energy, this agate is a major healer. Wear it to aid your own healing or use it to send energy to others. Keep a piece in your pocket during stressful times to promote patience and to subdue anger. This stone fosters hope, peace, and trust, and engenders true friendship. Use it to dispel fear and build confidence. For the home, it aids in attracting happiness and harmony. Blue lace agate is instrumental in angel magic and is supportive for spiritual development. Meditate with it when seeking wisdom and transformation. As an aid to manifest your desires, blue lace agate is influential for removing obstacles that may inhibit the changes you want to make in your life. This stone invites inspiration for self-expression and clarity for all forms of communication.

Blue lace agate is associated with the elements air and water. Its astrological influence comes from Mercury and the zodiac constellation of Pisces.

....
45. Staff Writer, *Fodor's South Africa,* 6th ed. (New York: Fodor's Travel Publications, 2015), 241.

Calcite

Pronunciation: KAL-site

Also known as calcspar and lime spar

Along with quartz, calcite is one of the most common minerals on Earth. Known for its well-formed crystals, it is one of the most widely collected. This mineral's name comes from the Latin *calx* meaning "lime." [46] Calcite is a component of chalk, limestone, and many types of marble. Present in ocean water, this mineral is a building block for the shells and bones of sea animals. As for humans, the Egyptians and Phoenicians carved large pieces of calcite into storage jars. The Mesopotamians used this stone for jars and vessels, which were often placed in graves.

Calcite can be black, blue, brown, colorless, gray, green, orange, pink, red, white, or yellow. It ranges from transparent to nearly opaque, and its luster is vitreous or dull. Calcite has a trigonal inner structure. Its crystals are frequently twinned.

Enhancing awareness and consciousness, calcite supports and aids work in the astral realm. It provides protection wherever you are. Use it to develop and support divination and psychic skills. Calcite is a motivator for finding opportunities and achieving goals. This stone is instrumental for sparking creativity. In addition, it fosters stability and comfort.

Calcite is associated with the element water. Its astrological influence comes from Venus and the zodiac constellation of Cancer.

....

46. Rapp, *Archaeomineralogy*, 106.

Blue Calcite

This variety of calcite can be varying shades of blue, occasionally with white veining. It is instrumental for purifying energy in ritual space and any area where magic work is performed. It is an aid for healing the emotions, especially after the breakup of a relationship. Blue calcite supports the development of psychic skills and provides protection.

Clear Calcite

Also known as Iceland spar

This is a colorless, transparent variety of calcite that has been used to make prisms for optical equipment. It is the "sunstone" of the Vikings, who used it to polarize light, which allowed them to find the sun for navigation on overcast days. Providing insight and clarity, this spiritual stone is the perfect tool for introspection and guidance. It also brings inspiration. Clear calcite aids communication and is instrumental in manifesting what you seek. Use it in esbat rituals to focus energy or during psychic work. Its astrological influence comes from the moon.

Green Calcite

This variety of calcite can be pale to emerald green. It reduces fear and brings emotional balance. Use green calcite in spells to attract money and prosperity to your household. This stone boosts the power of intuition and stokes the imagination. It is also a stone of protection. Green calcite is associated with the element earth.

Orange Calcite

The color of this stone ranges from pale to bright orange. It helps to expand awareness and energize creativity. It boosts confidence and courage and helps to overcome shyness. Orange calcite is associated with the element fire. Its astrological influence comes from the sun.

Pink Calcite

This stone can be an opaque creamy pink or a transparent pale pink to salmon pink. The grounding energy of pink calcite fosters healing and well-being. It also encourages growth and aids in attracting love.

Red Calcite

The color of this stone encompasses a wide variety of reds, including pinkish red and orange red. Aiding spiritual growth, this is the calcite to use for renewal. Use it in divination and dreamwork, especially for guidance to interpret messages. This stone also stimulates inspiration. Red calcite is associated with the element fire. Its astrological influence comes from the sun.

White Calcite

Also known as alabaster

This variety of calcite is the famous alabaster of ancient Egypt, which was used for exquisitely carved objects. The Egyptians associated this gleaming stone with the sun. The Assyrians used white calcite for amulets, seals, and vases. In medieval times, white calcite mortar was used to cover walls as a base for murals. This stone is instrumental for cleansing the aura and purifying ritual space and tools. It stimulates creativity and boosts the energy of other stones.

Carnelian

Pronunciation: car-NEEL-yuhn

Also known as cornelian

There are two theories about this stone's name. One is that it was derived from the Latin *carneus* meaning "fleshy." [47] The other is that it was named for the cornel or cornelian cherry (*Cornus mas*), which is actually a type of dogwood tree and not a true cherry. [48] During the Middle Ages, gem merchants called it carneolus.[49]

As abundant as pebbles in many riverbeds in India, the earliest artifacts made with carnelian date to approximately 7000 or 6000 BCE.[50] Carnelian was also abundant in the Egyptian desert. This stone was used throughout the ancient world for amulets, seal stones, jewelry, and inlay in furniture and coffins. The royal tombs of Ur in Sumer (present-day southern Iraq) contained carnelian beads. The Egyptians and Persians buried their dead with carnelian amulets "as a charm for new flesh to be put on in rebirth." [51] Carnelian was also believed to protect the dead in the afterlife. The Greeks and Romans favored it for jewelry, especially intaglios. While carnelian was believed to prevent health problems in the Far East, in the Middle East and Europe it was used to protect against the plague.

47. Rapp, *Archaeomineralogy*, 93.

48. Schumann, *Gemstones of the World*, 142.

49. Clifford Frondel, ed., *Dana's The System of Mineralogy*, vol. 3: *Silica Minerals*, 7th ed. (New York: John Wiley & Sons, 1962), 207.

50. Rapp, *Archaeomineralogy*, 93.

51. William Stewart, *Dictionary of Images and Symbols in Counseling* (London: Jessica Kingsley Publishers, 1998), 96.

The color of carnelian ranges through a wide variety of reds, including orange red. Although rare, it can be a yellowish color. When the colors are banded, it is occasionally referred to as carnelian agate. Carnelian ranges from vitreous to waxy and can be translucent or opaque. It has a trigonal inner structure.

Since ancient times, carnelian has served as a stone of protection that aids in dealing with aggression. It protects those who have passed beyond the veil and seek rebirth. It also aids those who grieve in this world. In addition, it provides psychic protection when traveling in the astral realm. Carnelian is a stone of communication that helps to vocalize your wants and needs. It also helps when making decisions. Carnelian provides a channel for inspiration whether you want to stoke creativity or find wisdom. When meeting challenges, this stone's energy boosts courage and confidence and fosters success. Carnelian is also associated with fertility. Use it to dispel negativity, reverse spells, and remove anything that is unwanted from your life.

Carnelian is associated with the element fire, the god Odin, and the goddess Isis. Its astrological influence comes from Mercury, Saturn, the sun, Venus, and the zodiac constellations of Aries, Cancer, Capricorn, Leo, Scorpio, Taurus, and Virgo.

Sard

This stone is a brownish-colored variety of carnelian. It is covered in a separate entry on page 202.

Cat's-Eye

Also known as cymophane, oriental cat's-eye, and true cat's-eye

Although a number of other stones such as quartz, ruby, tourmaline, and others can produce a cat's-eye effect, chrysoberyl exhibits it most strikingly and is the only one rightfully known simply as *cat's-eye* without reference to the type of mineral. Quartz cat's-eye also produces a strong effect, but it is not as dramatic as chrysoberyl.

As mentioned in part 1, the cat's-eye effect—also called chatoyancy—is caused by fine parallel inclusions within the stone. Resembling the slit of a cat's eye, these inclusions produce a luminous line that seems to move as the stone is rotated. This effect is most pronounced when the stone is cut en cabochon.

The name *cymophane* was derived from the Greek meaning "to appear wavelike." [52] According to legend, cat's-eye has been used as a charm against evil spirits, essentially watching out for the welfare of its wearer.

While cat's-eye usually ranges from greenish yellow to honey brown, it can also be dark brownish green, slightly bluish, or orange. Ranging from transparent to translucent, it has a vitreous or greasy luster and an orthorhombic inner structure. The quartz cat's-eye can be brown, gray, green, white, or yellow. It ranges from semitransparent to translucent, has a vitreous luster, and a trigonal inner structure.

Cat's-eye and quartz cat's-eye are perfect for working with animals, especially familiars. They are strongly protective. As a stone of insight and intuition, both types of cat's-eye

52. David Federman, *Modern Jeweler's Consumer Guide to Colored Gemstones* (New York: Van Nostrand Reinhold, 1990), 44.

stimulate awareness and creativity. Use them in spells to attract luck and wealth. They also foster generosity, happiness, and optimism. These stones strengthen willpower and aid in the quest for knowledge. In addition, they support growth and transformation.

Cat's-eye and quartz cat's-eye are associated with the element earth and the goddess Bast. Their astrological influence comes from Mercury, Venus, and the zodiac constellations of Capricorn, Gemini, and Pisces.

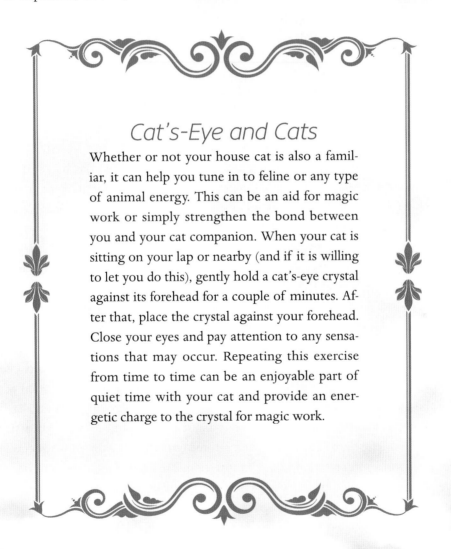

Cat's-Eye and Cats

Whether or not your house cat is also a familiar, it can help you tune in to feline or any type of animal energy. This can be an aid for magic work or simply strengthen the bond between you and your cat companion. When your cat is sitting on your lap or nearby (and if it is willing to let you do this), gently hold a cat's-eye crystal against its forehead for a couple of minutes. After that, place the crystal against your forehead. Close your eyes and pay attention to any sensations that may occur. Repeating this exercise from time to time can be an enjoyable part of quiet time with your cat and provide an energetic charge to the crystal for magic work.

Celestine

Pronunciation: si-LES-tin *or* SEL-uh-stine

Also known as celestite

The name of this stone comes from the Latin *caelestis* meaning "celestial," which is quite appropriate for its ethereal quality. [53] Because of this, it may be a surprise that celestine is widely used as an industrial mineral. It is an important ingredient in fireworks and flares because it burns bright red. It is also used in the manufacture of paint, glass, and ceramics.

The Greeks included celestine in a pigment known as *strontium white*, which artists used for many centuries. Even though its crystals can be quite beautiful, celestine is not often used for jewelry because of its brittleness.

Celestine can be bluish white, colorless, grayish white, greenish blue, pale pink, reddish, or multicolored. It ranges from transparent to translucent and has a greasy, pearly, or vitreous luster. This stone has an orthorhombic inner structure.

Celestine is instrumental in spiritual development and growth. It is especially effective for working with the angelic realm. Use celestine to raise the spiritual vibration of your home and lift the moods of family members. Its calming energy brings healing, harmony, and inner peace. It also helps to relieve anxiety and stress. Celestine fosters compassion and self-worth, bringing clarity and closure to fractured emotions. It is an aid when developing skills for magic, communication, and self-expression. Use it to heighten awareness for work in the astral realm. Celestine also boosts motivation and provides stability. It is particularly effective when working with star magic.

Celestine is associated with the element air and the goddess Athena. Its astrological influence comes from Neptune and Venus.

....

53. Oldershaw, *Firefly Guide to Gems*, 82.

Cerussite

Pronunciation: **suh-RUS-ite** *or* **SEER-uh-site**

The name of this mineral was derived from the ancient Greek word for "white lead ore," which evolved into *cerussa* in Latin.[54] In the past, it was also called white lead spar. Mining this stone along the Red Sea coast, the Egyptians used cerussite for trade with other countries. For themselves, they used it mainly for cosmetics. Cerussite was carved for ornamental objects in Babylon and Turkey, and in China, it was a component in the enamel for glazed pottery.

Today, faceted cerussite crystals are prized because, due to its brittleness, this stone is difficult to cut and only highly skilled craftspeople can manage it. Mineral collectors like it for its sparkle and its intricate twinning crystals that often form V-shaped chevrons or multiple crystals that form sixlings. Cerussite is also an industrial mineral used in cement, as a pigment for white paint, and as pottery glaze.

Cerussite is brownish, colorless, gray, grayish black, or white. Occasionally, it can have a blue or green tinge. Crystals can grow up to two feet long. This stone ranges from transparent to translucent and has an adamantine, vitreous, or greasy luster. Its inner structure is orthorhombic. Cerussite fluoresces bluish, green, pink, or yellow.

The grounding energy of this stone is especially helpful when raising awareness and seeking transformation. It also aids in keeping one's feet on the ground while journeying in the astral realm. Use this stone to foster respect but only when it is warranted. Cerussite brings clarity to all forms of communication. Employ its energy to initiate changes in your life.

Cerussite is associated with the element earth.

....

54. Rapp, *Archaeomineralogy*, 208.

Chalcedony

Pronunciation: kal-SED-nee *or* KAL-suh-doe-nee

Also known as blue chalcedony, common chalcedony, and true chalcedony

Mineralogists use the name *chalcedony* for a group of cryptocrystalline quartz such as agate, chrysoprase, bloodstone, jasper, carnelian, and onyx. They also use this name for a specific bluish white or gray variety of crystal. To avoid confusion, the name chalcedony is used in this book for the latter.

The name of this stone was derived from Chalcedon, an ancient port city near present-day Istanbul, Turkey. The Babylonians and Greeks used chalcedony for cylinder and cone-shaped seals. It was also popular for decorative carvings and for jewelry, especially cameos. Greek sailors used it as an amulet to protect them from drowning. During the Middle Ages, chalcedony was believed to have the power to ward off ghosts.

Chalcedony is bluish gray with a waxy or dull luster. It is translucent and has a trigonal inner structure. This stone fluoresces bluish white.

Chalcedony is a healing stone that subdues anger and brings peaceful balance to the emotions. When it comes to communication, chalcedony is an aid in learning how to listen. It can also help you find the right words in delicate situations. Its subtle energy is instrumental for psychic work, especially clairvoyance. Chalcedony is helpful for dreamwork and is an aid for remembering and interpreting them. Also, use it to support past-life work, especially when it is emotionally charged. This stone is an aid for learning how to accept and deal with new situations when they take you out of your comfort zone.

Chalcedony is associated with the element water. Its astrological influence comes from the moon, the fixed star Deneb Algedi, and the zodiac constellations of Cancer and Capricorn.

Charoite

Pronunciation: **CHAR-uh-ite**

Charoite is a rock-forming mineral that is relatively new to the marketplace. It was first discovered in eastern Siberia in 1949 but not confirmed as a unique mineral species until 1978.[55] Although it is often reported to have been named for the Chara River in Russia, mineralogist and professor Mikhail Evdokimov noted that this stone's name actually comes from the Russian word *chary* because of the impression it gives—*chary* means "magic charm."[56]

The colors of this stone range from pale lilac to deep purple with swirling or streaking patterns of black or white. It ranges from translucent to opaque with a vitreous luster. Charoite has a monoclinic inner structure and fluoresces a red color.

Charoite is a stone that supports community efforts for building unity and trust. With strong spiritual energy, it is ideal for dedication and purification rituals. For issues of the self, charoite fosters inner strength, helps deal with shyness, and inspires personal growth. Use this stone to activate the left brain/logical part of the mind when learning a new skill or studying for exams. This stone's swirling pattern aids in getting energy moving, which is especially effective for ritual and magic. The energy of this stone is also a boon for psychic work and divination. As the root of its name implies, it is instrumental as a magic charm, especially for protection when engaged in these activities. This stone also wards off negativity and subdues fear. On a mundane level, charoite can help you go with the flow when you need to accept what you cannot change.

Charoite is associated with the element water.

....

55. Mikhail D. Evdokimov, "Charoite: A Unique Mineral from a Unique Occurrence" *Gems and Gemology*, vol. 33, no. 1 (Spring 1997): 74.

56. Ibid.

Chrysoberyl

Pronunciation: KRIS-uh-ber-uhl

Also known as chrysolite

Known in antiquity but not properly identified, the name of this stone comes from the Greek *chrysos,* meaning "golden," and *beryllos,* "beryl." [57] Because of its hardness, chrysoberyl may have been one of the stones used as a stone-cutting tool by the ancient Egyptians. Chrysoberyl was finally identified as a distinct species in 1789 by German geologist Abraham Gottlob Werner. [58] Known as chrysolite—a name that was also used for peridot and topaz—the Brazilian name of *crisolita* for chrysoberyl adds to the confusion.

Chrysoberyl was especially popular as a gemstone during the late Victorian era. Mineral collectors find this stone attractive for its frequent heart-shaped twinning of crystals. It also forms trillings, which are starlike structures created by three intergrown crystals that radiate from a common center.

The yellow hues of chrysoberyl can be brownish yellow, golden yellow, yellow, or yellowish green. It can also be bluish green or a faint olive green. While gem-quality crystals are generally transparent, most chrysoberyl ranges from translucent to opaque. It has an orthorhombic inner structure and its luster is greasy or vitreous. While a well-cut, gem-quality chrysoberyl gemstone has a great deal of brilliance, it lacks the fire of a diamond.

This stone fosters a deep-seated sense of confidence and self-respect. It supports emotional healing and opens the heart for deep compassion and the ability to forgive. It is effective in spells to attract abundance as long as the gains are generously shared with others.

---

57. Thomas, *Gemstones,* 110.

58. Keith Proctor, "Chrysoberyl and Alexandrite from the Pegmatite Districts of Minas Gerais, Brazil," *Gems and Gemology,* vol. 24, no. 19 (Spring 1988): 74.

Use this stone to provide clarity and perspective for issues great and small. The energy of chrysoberyl brings optimism and peace of mind. In addition, it can be instrumental in sparking a sense of renewed purpose.

Two other varieties of chrysoberyl, alexandrite and cat's-eye, are covered separately. All three types of chrysoberyl are chemically the same but differ in their optical properties.

Chrysoberyl is associated with the element air. Its astrological influence comes from the sun, Venus, the zodiac constellation of Leo, and the fixed star Vega.

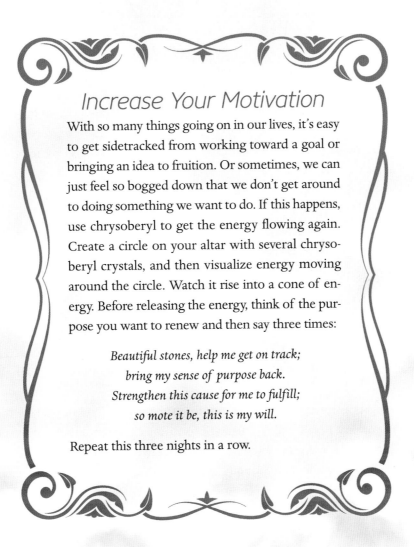

Increase Your Motivation

With so many things going on in our lives, it's easy to get sidetracked from working toward a goal or bringing an idea to fruition. Or sometimes, we can just feel so bogged down that we don't get around to doing something we want to do. If this happens, use chrysoberyl to get the energy flowing again. Create a circle on your altar with several chrysoberyl crystals, and then visualize energy moving around the circle. Watch it rise into a cone of energy. Before releasing the energy, think of the purpose you want to renew and then say three times:

Beautiful stones, help me get on track;
bring my sense of purpose back.
Strengthen this cause for me to fulfill;
so mote it be, this is my will.

Repeat this three nights in a row.

Chrysocolla

Pronunciation: **kris-uh-KOL-uh**

Chrysocolla is a bit of an enigma because it is alternately described as having a cubic, monoclinic, or orthorhombic inner structure. This is because chrysocolla frequently pseudomorphs, meaning that it chemically replaces another mineral. When this occurs, chrysocolla takes on that mineral's inner structure.

Chrysocolla's name comes from the Greek *chrysos,* meaning "gold," and *colla,* "glue," due to its resemblance to material used for soldering gold.[59] Reference to this stone first appeared in the writings of Theophrastus in 315 BCE.[60]

Although chrysocolla is soft and easily broken, when it is intergrown with quartz it can be cut for jewelry and ornamental carvings. The only ancient example of carved chrysocolla is a figurine amulet found in an Egyptian child's burial. The Egyptians occasionally used this mineral for eye makeup but valued it more as a pigment for wall paintings. Chrysocolla continued to be used as a pigment in Europe until the seventeenth century.[61]

This stone can be blue, sky blue, blue green, or bright green. It ranges from translucent to opaque and its luster is vitreous or greasy. Chrysocolla is amorphous, lacking an inner crystal structure.

Chrysocolla is a stone of peace that aids in resolving problems, especially those that arise in a relationship. Because of its enigmatic form, it can aid in transformation and shape shifting, which makes it a good choice for shamanic work. Despite its own changeability, this stone offers stability and grounding. Its powerful energy can boost spells and fan

59. Proctor, "Chrysoberyl and Alexandrite from the Pegmatite Districts of Minas Gerais, Brazil," (Spring 1988): 74.

60. Oldershaw, *Firefly Guide to Gems,* 79.

61. Eastaugh, et al., *Pigment Compendium,* 110.

the sparks of creativity. Bringing us closer to the natural world, chrysocolla helps to raise awareness, hone the senses, and facilitate the reception of wisdom from other realms. This stone can both attract love and aid in recovering from a breakup. With calming energy, chrysocolla is instrumental in opening the portals for dreamwork.

Chrysocolla is associated with the elements earth and water. Its astrological influence comes from Venus and the zodiac constellations of Gemini, Taurus, and Virgo.

Chrysocolla Quartz

This stone is a combination of quartz and chrysocolla. Even though chrysocolla has strong energy on its own, the presence of quartz boosts it even more. In addition, it is an especially grounding stone.

Eilat Stone
Pronunciation: ey-LAHT

This blue-green stone is a mixture of chrysocolla, turquoise, and malachite from the mines near Eilat in southern Israel. When working with this stone you may find varying combinations of energy and power from all three minerals.

Chrysoprase

Pronunciation: KRIS-uh-praise

Also known as chrysophrase

Although this stone's name is less than glamorous coming from the Greek *chrysos* and *prason,* meaning "golden leek" in reference to its color, chrysoprase has been prized as a gem since ancient times.[62] The ancient Greeks, Romans, and Egyptians used chrysoprase for jewelry and other ornamental objects. In Egyptian jewelry, it was often set with lapis lazuli. The popular use of chrysoprase continued through the Middle Ages. Poland was an important source for chrysoprase until the mines were worked out in the fourteenth century. The Holy Roman Emperor Charles IV (1316–1378) may have helped to hasten this depletion by covering the walls of St. Wenceslas chapel in Prague with chrysoprase. Many European monarchs favored chrysoprase for jewelry.

Most often yellowish to apple green, chrysoprase can be a darker olive or jade green, too. Stones that come from "down under" have the misleading nickname of *Australian jade.* Chrysoprase ranges from translucent to opaque with a vitreous or waxy luster. It has a trigonal inner structure.

Chrysoprase is effective in banishing spells to remove anything unwanted from your life. It also helps to ward off nightmares to allow for peaceful sleep. Use it in any type of spell to support your willpower and intention. This is a stone for the emotions fostering compassion, adaptability, and balance. It also helps to deal with envy and anger. Chrysoprase dispels loneliness by attracting healthy friendships and kindling a true sense of happi-

62. Oldershaw, *Firefly Guide to Gems,* 169.

ness. Also, use it as a good luck charm to attract abundance and success. It is instrumental when seeking wisdom and personal growth.

Chrysoprase is associated with the element earth and the goddess Vesta. Its astrological influence comes from Venus and the zodiac constellations of Libra and Taurus.

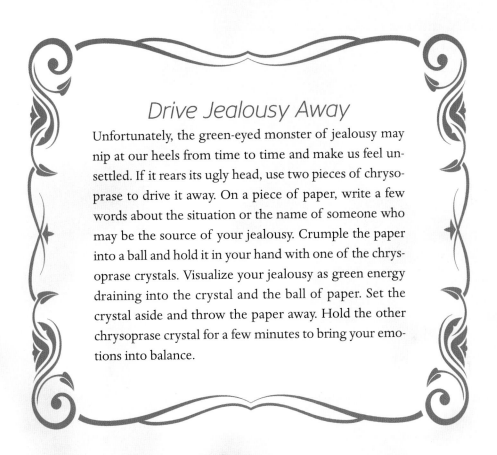

Drive Jealousy Away

Unfortunately, the green-eyed monster of jealousy may nip at our heels from time to time and make us feel unsettled. If it rears its ugly head, use two pieces of chrysoprase to drive it away. On a piece of paper, write a few words about the situation or the name of someone who may be the source of your jealousy. Crumple the paper into a ball and hold it in your hand with one of the chrysoprase crystals. Visualize your jealousy as green energy draining into the crystal and the ball of paper. Set the crystal aside and throw the paper away. Hold the other chrysoprase crystal for a few minutes to bring your emotions into balance.

Citrine

Pronunciation: SIH-treen, SIH-trin, or sih-TREEN

The rarest member of the quartz family, citrine takes its name from the Old French *citrin* meaning "lemon," which refers to its color.[63] Since ancient times, citrine was prized for jewelry and seal stones beginning with the Greeks approximately 400 BCE.[64] It was sometimes called sunstone and thought capable of holding sunlight. The Romans also used it for jewelry, especially for intaglio work. In addition to its beauty, citrine was carried for protection against snakebites. During the Middle Ages, it was worn to ward off the plague. This stone's popularity for jewelry continued through the nineteenth century. While it is sometimes passed off as the more expensive topaz, a great deal of citrine on the market is actually heat-treated amethyst or smoky quartz.

Citrine ranges from pale to dark yellow to golden brown. Darker stones are sometimes called *Madeira citrine*. Citrine ranges from transparent to translucent. It has a vitreous luster and trigonal inner structure. Citrine is weakly dichroic, appearing as various shades of yellow from different angles.

This stone is a symbol of abundance, hope, optimism, and success. Its solar aspect radiates power to manifest change and strengthen willpower. By its very nature citrine invites happiness and harmony into the home. It brings clarity for interpreting dreams and visions and supports all forms of psychic work. This stone can be used to raise energy for ritual and to boost spells. It also provides protection. Citrine fosters creativity, especially when

63. Oldershaw, *Firefly Guide to Gems*, 156.

64. Rapp, *Archaeomineralogy*, 96.

establishing goals. Use it for luck when beginning something new. Citrine aids in solving problems and bringing people together. With a high spiritual vibration, it provides guidance and growth for all aspects of life.

Citrine is associated with the element fire. Its astrological influence comes from Mars, Mercury, the sun, and the zodiac constellations of Aries, Gemini, Leo, Libra, and Scorpio.

Build Harmony in Your Home

A way to foster happiness and maintain a sense of harmony is to keep positive energy flowing throughout your home. Dab four citrine crystals with a drop of lavender essential oil, and then carry them as you walk through every room in your house. Begin at the front door and visualize how energy moves around furniture and other objects in each room. Wherever you feel energy getting stuck, move the crystals in a sweeping motion as you say:

May the energy move and flow,
as peace and harmony beings to grow.

After going through your entire home, place one of the crystals in each of the cardinal directions to act as sentinels to keep positive energy flowing.

Corundum

Pronunciation: **kuh-RUHN-duhm**

Pure corundum is a colorless, common mineral that is sometimes used as an ornamental stone, but mostly as an abrasive for industrial grinding and polishing. However, this mineral also produces two gem-quality varieties: ruby and sapphire. Both are second only to diamond in hardness. The word *corundum* comes from the Hindu name for this stone, *kurund*, which most often referred to ruby. Gem-quality corundum in any color except red is called sapphire. Ruby and sapphire are covered in separate entries.

Cuprite

Pronunciation: KOO-prite

Also known as ruby copper

Cuprite is a minor copper ore that was named from the Latin *cuprum*, meaning "copper." [65] Prior to being described and named in 1845 by German mineralogist Wilhelm von Haidinger (1795–1871), cuprite was known as red copper ore.[66] Actually, cuprite is not such a "new" mineral. According to archaeological findings, the Mesopotamians, Egyptians, and Chinese used cuprite to make red glass as early as 1600 BCE.[67] Glassmaking with cuprite was also done by the Romano-Celts of Britain. In addition to glass, this mineral was used for the production of bronze in Europe and pre-Columbian Peru.

Cuprite is popular with mineral collectors because of its cube-shaped crystals and deep red reflections. Gem-quality cuprite is rare and too soft to be used for jewelry.

Cuprite is crimson red and sometimes so dark that it almost appears black. It ranges from translucent to opaque, has an adamantine to almost metallic luster, and a cubic inner structure.

65. A. C. Bishop, A. R. Woolley, and W. R. Hamilton, *Cambridge Guide to Minerals, Rocks and Fossils,* 2nd ed. (New York: University of Cambridge Press, 2001), 40.

66. Richard V. Gaines, et al., *Dana's New Mineralogy: The System of Mineralogy of James Dwight Dana and Edward Salisbury Dana,* 8th ed. (New York: John Wiley & Sons, 1997), 204.

67. Andrew J. Shortland, Ian C. Freestone, and Thilo Rehren, eds., *From Mine to Microscope: Advances in the Study of Ancient Technology* (Havertown, PA: Oxbow Books, 2009), 201.

Cuprite is an aid when dealing with problems and letting go of relationship issues. Use this stone in banishing spells to remove whatever is unwanted from your life. Its grounding energy fosters security as it eases anxiety and fear. It is instrumental for stabilizing the emotions and for dealing with sex on a mature level. With receptive energy, this stone fosters empathy and compassion while protecting one's own emotions. Cuprite is a lightning rod for inspiration, giving creative energy a major boost. This stone also supports past-life work.

Cuprite is associated with the element earth. Its astrological influence comes from Venus and the zodiac constellation of Aquarius.

Chalcotrichite

***Pronunciation:* kal-kuh-TREEK-ite *or* kal-kuh-TRIK-ite**
This variety of cuprite forms small, sparkly, needlelike crystals. Its name comes from the Greek word meaning "hairy copper" because of its appearance.[68] Despite the size of its crystals, chalcotrichite carries all the energy and attributes of larger ones.

....
68. Oldershaw, *Firefly Guide to Gems*, 53.

Danburite

Pronunciation: **DAN-buh-rite**

This mineral was named for the town of Danbury, Connecticut, where it was first discovered and described in 1839 by mineralogist Charles Shepard (1804–1866).[69] It has since been found in other areas of the world. Although danburite is used as an alternative to diamond because of its brilliance, it lacks the fire of that more expensive stone. Well-faceted yellow danburite can be difficult to distinguish from golden-colored topaz. Danburite is popular with mineral collectors because of its prismatic clusters.

Usually colorless, danburite can also be gray, light brown, pale pink, white, or yellow. Yellow-colored stones are sometimes marketed under the name sunshine danburite. Danburite ranges from transparent to translucent and can have a vitreous, greasy, or waxy luster. Danburite's inner structure is orthorhombic. It fluoresces a sky-blue color.

Although its energy is soft, danburite is instrumental for raising awareness and bringing clarity to all forms of communication whether on the earthly or angelic plane. This stone stimulates the mind for psychic work and heightens sensitivity for channeling. It aids spiritual growth and provides the courage to question beliefs. Meditating with danburite provides guidance when seeking truth. In addition, this stone fosters peace and patience. Fairies are intrigued by danburite and enjoy it when given to them as gifts.

Danburite is associated with the element air. Its astrological influence comes from Uranus and the zodiac constellations of Aquarius and Leo.

....

69. Peter Cristofono, *Rockhounding New England: A Guide to 100 of the Region's Best Rockhounding Sites* (Guilford, CT: Morris Book Publishing, 2014), 6.

Pink Danburite

This variety of danburite ranges from pale to rosy pink. Like many pink stones, it is valuable as a love charm for attracting romance and fostering a balanced love of self. It also supports spirituality and radiates healing energy.

Desert Rose

Also known as petrified rose and sand rose

Whlie several minerals form roselike clusters, barite and gypsum are the most common and beautiful. With an embedded dusting of sand, circular clusters of these flat crystals resemble roses. The name *barite* comes from the Greek *barys,* meaning "heavy" in reference to its weight when compared with other crystals of similar size.[70] Likewise, the name *gypsum* was derived from the Greek *gypsos,* meaning "plaster," which describes one of its major applications.[71]

Gypsum was used for plaster and mortar by the Mesopotamians and the Egyptians, who used it in their pyramids dating to 3000 BCE.[72] In Europe, its use as mortar continued into medieval times. Similarly today, gypsum is used in the manufacture of plasters and wallboard. The use of barite in the process of making pigments for pottery and wall paintings began in ancient China. Today barite is mined for the automotive, petroleum, paint, and medical industries. Both types of desert roses are popular with mineral collectors and are sometimes made into jewelry.

Barite desert rose ranges from colorless to reddish to white. It has an orthorhombic inner structure. For more about barite, refer to its separate entry. Gypsum desert rose can be

70. Oldershaw, *Firefly Guide to Gems,* 83.

71. Ibid.

72. Jessica Elzea Kogel, et al., eds., *Industrial Minerals & Rocks: Commodities, Markets, and Uses,* 7th ed. (Littleton, CO: Society for Mining, Metallurgy, and Exploration, 2006), 519.

brown, colorless, gray, red, white, or yellow. It has a monoclinic inner structure. As desert roses, both minerals are opaque.

With the ability to form beautiful roses, these industrial minerals show us that we can balance the mundane, practical side of life with beauty and spirituality. With peaceful energy, desert roses are especially helpful for meditation and inward journeys. In addition, they are a boon for dreamwork and psychic work. Use desert rose to boost love spells and spark lusty romance. These roses are also an aid for past-life work and for tapping into the wisdom of the ancients.

Desert rose is associated with the element air. Its astrological influence comes from Venus and the zodiac constellation of Libra.

All You Need Is Love and a Rose

For centuries, the rose has been one of the greatest symbols of love and devotion. Whether you are in a long-term relationship or any intimate relationship, you can still experience feelings of love. Crystals are instrumental for tapping into the energy of universal love and can function like a conduit, drawing this love into our lives. Keep a desert rose in your home, at your workplace, and even in your car to surround yourself with the energy of love and to serve as reminders of love. If you have a garden, place a desert rose outside to extend this energy around your property.

Diamond

Pronunciation: DYE-mund *or* DYE-uh-mund

Diamond has been considered the king of gemstones since ancient times, and the word *diamond* comes from the Greek *adamas,* meaning "invincible" in reference to it being the hardest natural substance.[73] While it was known in India at least 2,300 years ago, no attempt was made to facet this stone because it was believed that cutting a diamond would destroy its magical power.[74] Even though Pliny mentioned diamonds, they were not regarded as particularly valuable, as the Romans could not figure out how to cut them. In Egypt and the Middle East, diamond was regarded as a stone of good fortune. In medieval Europe, it was believed to protect against evil spirits and demons.

When faceting was achieved in the Middle Ages, stonecutters sought to increase the diamond's optical effects to bring out its brilliance and fire. However, it was not until the early twentieth century that the brilliant cut, also known as the diamond cut, was brought to a high level of perfection. While all diamonds are a symbol of love, pink ones embody romance, devotion, and fidelity. In addition to aiding fertility, pink diamonds are soothing and help to reduce stress.

In addition to representing power and authority, diamonds continue to be a great symbol of love. The tradition of giving a diamond engagement ring began in 1477 with the Holy Roman Emperor Maximilian I (1459–1519) and Mary Duchess of Burgundy (1457–1482).[75]

....

73. Oldershaw, *Firefly Guide to Gems,* 46.

74. Ibid.

75. Sofianides and Harlow, *Gems & Crystals from the American Museum of Natural History,* 38.

Although we may think of diamonds as being beautiful and valuable, three quarters of all diamonds are of low-quality, industrial grade.

While the purest diamonds are colorless, this stone can range from white to black and almost all colors of the spectrum. Diamonds with rich colors are called fancy diamonds. This stone ranges from transparent to translucent. It has a cubic inner structure and an adamantine luster. Uncut diamonds may have a greasy luster.

In addition to being a symbol of power and wealth, this stone is an emblem of love, trust, and commitment. Its energy provides protection, healing, and support when seeking justice. The power of diamond amplifies energy, builds emotional strength, and unites people through reconciliation. This stone attracts abundance, luck, and prosperity. In addition, it brings clarity to psychic work, especially clairaudience and clairvoyance. Diamond also engenders confidence and courage, and aids in meeting challenges and overcoming obstacles. It also supports spirituality and faith.

Diamond is associated with the element fire. Its astrological influence comes from Mars, the sun, Venus, the fixed star Algol, and the zodiac constellations of Aries, Leo, Libra, Pisces, Taurus, and Virgo. This stone is also associated with the deities Danu and the Dagda.

Diopside

Pronunciation: die-OP-side *or* die-OP-sid

This mineral's name was derived from Greek, meaning "double appearance," which may refer to its dichroism.[76] In Mesopotamia, Egypt, and the Middle East, diopside was used for ceramic glazes. The Olmec of Central America used it for jewelry but most often for ornamental objects. They were especially fond of jade and frequently used diopside-jadeite, a stone that is a mix of the two minerals.

Diopside is black, brown, colorless, green, pink (rare), grayish white, or yellow. It has a monoclinic inner structure, vitreous luster, and ranges from transparent to opaque. It is dichroic, appearing with different hues from different angles depending on the color of the stone. Diopside crystals are short and often twinned. In addition, this stone can produce four-rayed stars. It fluoresces a green, orange, violet, or yellow color.

The grounding energy of diopside keeps us in balance with the natural world. It helps to fine-tune intuition and aids in connecting with animals and the fairy realm. Diopside also aids in working with spirit guides. This stone is instrumental to raise energy for healing or spiritual growth. Use it in love spells and in charms when seeking forgiveness. It also supports divination practices. Employ diopside in dedication rituals or use it to build community bonds.

Diopside is associated with the element earth. Its astrological influence comes from Jupiter and Saturn.

....
76. Schumann, *Gemstones of the World*, 206.

Chrome Diopside

Pronunciation: krome di-OP-side

This variety of diopside ranges from vivid to emerald green. Occasionally it can be transparent or exhibit a cat's-eye effect. While it has become popular for jewelry, this stone is somewhat soft and needs to be handled with care. Chrome diopside is especially helpful when working with spirit guides.

Violane

Pronunciation: VEE-uh-lane

From Italy, this variety of diopside ranges from violet to light blue and from translucent to opaque. It is mostly used for ornamental objects. Keep this stone on your altar to support spiritual growth.

Dioptase

Pronunciation: die-OP-taze

Dating to 6000 BCE, dioptase was used as a pigment in the Middle East to add color to pottery and to outline the eyes of statues.[77] With a color that can rival emerald, dioptase was often misidentified as such in the past. Because it was a lot less expensive, this stone was referred to as the emerald of the poor. In the past, it was also called achrite and copper emerald.[78]

Too fragile for a ring stone and usually too small to cut, dioptase crystals are mostly used for pendants and brooches. Mineral collectors value this stone for its crystals that form in masses. The name of this mineral was derived from the Greek *dia,* meaning "through," and *optomai,* "to see," which refers to the visibility of its internal lines of cleavage.[79]

This stone ranges from blue green to emerald green. It is weakly dichroic appearing dark emerald or light emerald green from different angles. Ranging from transparent to translucent, dioptase has a vitreous luster and a trigonal inner structure.

Dioptase is a stone of abundance that fosters comfort, prosperity, and well-being. It brings emotions into balance to promote healing and to engender forgiveness. It is ideal for finding personal truth and recovering self-respect. Holding this stone during meditation aids in finding the wisdom you seek. Use dioptase in spells or as a charm to attract love. It is also effective in banishing spells. In addition, it reduces stress.

This stone is associated with the element water. Its astrological influence comes from Jupiter, the moon, and Venus.

....

77. Dominique Collon, *Ancient Near Eastern Art* (Los Angeles: University of California Press, 1995), 42.

78. Oldershaw, *Firefly Guide to Gems,* 96.

79. Ibid.

Dolomite

Pronunciation: DOE-luh-mite *or* DOL-uh-mite

In addition to the mineral itself, the name *dolomite* refers to the rock that contains approximately 50 percent of the mineral along with calcite and limestone. The dolomite rock is sometimes distinguished by the name dolostone. When dolostone is transformed into a metamorphic rock—which means it is subjected to extreme heat and pressure—it is called dolomitic marble or dolomite marble. Marble generally consists of recrystallized calcite and/or dolomite. Dolomite is slightly harder than calcite.

Both dolomite stone and marble were used by the Egyptians to make bowls, pitchers, and ornamental carvings. It was also used for paving stones and blocks for buildings. Along with limestone and calcite, dolomite was used in constructing the famous pyramids at Giza.

Originally called *dolomie*, dolomite was named in honor of French mineralogist Dieudonné (Deodat) de Dolomieu (1750–1801), who first described the mineral in the 1790s.[80] The Dolomite Mountains in northern Italy were named after the mineral. Too soft for jewelry, dolomite is used as an ornamental stone. Mineral collectors like its distinctively curved crystals. Both the mineral and the rock have wide use in industry for furnace linings, metal processing, and building materials. The mineral is also used in making paper, pottery, glass, and paint.

Dolomite can be brown, colorless, pink, white, or yellow. Ranging from transparent to translucent, it has a vitreous or pearly luster and a trigonal inner structure. Its curved crystals are sometimes saddle shaped and occasionally twinned. It fluoresces a pink or orange-

----

80. Bruce Cairncross, *Field Guide to Rocks & Minerals of Southern Africa* (Cape Town, South Africa: New Struik Publishers, 2004), 93.

red color. Once used as a synonym for dolomite, the term *bitter spar* is often used for brown dolomite, which is especially good for grounding negative energy.

Dolomite (mineral, rock, or marble) is a stone of gentle, calm energy that brings stability, balance, and comfort. Fostering compassion, it provides support for emotional situations. It releases negative energy and subdues anger and fear. This stone helps to deal with sorrow as well as stress. In addition, it kindles—or rekindles—optimism and enthusiasm. Dolomite also helps to maintain a quiet spirituality that is deeply integrated with everyday life.

Dolomite is associated with the element earth. Its astrological influence comes from the zodiac constellation of Aries.

Pearl Spar

This variety of dolomite ranges from white to pinkish and has a pearly luster. It is especially effective for dealing with anger and ratcheting down emotional upsets.

Dumortierite

Pronunciation: doo-MAWR-tee-uh-rite *or* doo-MOR-tee-uh-rite

In 1881, French mineralogist Ferdinand Gonnard (1833–1923) named this mineral in honor of his former university colleague, French paleontologist Eugene Dumortier (1801–1876).[81] However, like a number of other "new" minerals, this one was known and used in ancient times. The people of Tiburón Island, located in the Gulf of California off the coast of Mexico, used powdered dumortierite for ceremonial face paint. In Peru, small carved dumortierite cylinders have been found in pre-Columbian burials.

Because of its softness, this stone has limited use as jewelry and is most often carved into beads. For ornamental objects, it is often sculpted into egg or sphere shapes. Because it can withstand high temperatures, dumortierite is used in the manufacture of porcelain, particularly for spark plugs.

The most prized color of dumortierite is an intense, deep blue violet that resembles, but is more vivid than, sodalite. Dumortierite can also be black, brown, pink, reddish brown, or white. It frequently contains white or black veining, streaking, or spots. This mineral ranges from transparent to opaque. It has a vitreous or dull luster and an orthorhombic inner structure. Dumortierite is strongly pleochroic. It has a weak fluorescence of sky blue or violet.

Dumortierite is a stone of self-discipline that helps to keep life organized and bring clarity of purpose. It aids in learning and honing mental skills and in developing psychic

---
81. Oldershaw, *Firefly Guide to Gems*, 100.

talents, especially clairvoyance and clairaudience. It bolsters memory and aids past-life work. This stone opens the channels for easy communication with spirit guides. Use it for dreamwork to aid in receiving and understanding messages. Dumortierite invites insight and stimulates creativity. Its calm energy subdues and redirects impatience.

Dumortierite is associated with the element air. Its astrological influence comes from Saturn and the zodiac constellation of Leo.

Denim Dumortierite

This variety of dumortierite is a slightly lighter blue, resembling the color of denim. While it carries all the properties of dumortierite, its energy is very gentle.

Dumortierite Quartz

This variety is intergrown with quartz crystals, giving it a pale blue color. The presence of quartz amplifies the energy of the dumortierite.

Emerald

Pronunciation: **EM-er-uhld** *or* **EM-ruhld**

Emerald is the most precious variety of beryl and the fourth hardest gemstone after diamond, sapphire, and ruby. Emeralds were mined in Egypt on the Red Sea coast east of Aswan as early as 3000 BCE, long before Cleopatra's name was associated with the site.[82] The Egyptians used this stone for jewelry, scarabs, and decorative objects. Included on sarcophagi, emerald—like the color green—was a symbol of renewal. The Romans were also fond of this stone. According to ancient Vedic texts, it was worn as a sacred talisman in India. During the Middle Ages, emeralds were used for scrying and worn as protection against evil spirits. Throughout Europe, emeralds were held in high esteem for their many medicinal and spiritual properties. In the New World, the Aztec and Inca also had a high regard for this gemstone. Spanish explorers traced the source of emeralds to Colombia at a place called Somondoco, "god of the green stones."[83]

Beginning with the Arabic *zumurrud*, which meant "green," this stone's name evolved into the Greek *smaragdos*, "green stone," then *smeraldo* in Italian, and *emeraude* in French.[84] The inclusions in emeralds are called *jardin*, French for "garden," which is appropriate for this stone's lush green color.[85] Emeralds are unusual in that their inclusions are like fingerprints, providing information on where each stone originated. Faceting known as the

82. Ibid., 122.

83. Robert Webster, *Gems: Their Sources, Descriptions and Identification*, 3rd ed. (Boston: Newnes, 1975), 85.

84. John Sinkankas and Terry Ottaway, eds., "The Legendary Green Beryl," *Emeralds of the World:* extraLapis English no. 2 (Arvada, CO: Lapis International, 2002), 4.

85. Carol Clark, *Tropical Gemstones* (Hong Kong: Periplus Editions (HK), 1998), 32.

emerald cut is intended to bring out the depth of color rather than sparkle, as does the diamond cut.

The color of this stone ranges from the famous emerald green to medium green and slightly yellowish green. Emerald ranges from transparent to translucent. It has a vitreous luster and a hexagonal inner structure. Some stones are dichroic, appearing green and blue green or yellow green from different angles.

Emerald's power of protection extends to hexes and enchantment. It is especially helpful for safe, easy travel and for security in general. As a stone of the emotions, it is effective in spells to find love or to combat jealousy. It also attracts luck and prosperity. This stone enhances psychic abilities, especially clairvoyance, and aids in interpreting prophetic messages. Associated with finding inner truth, it also aids in detecting deceit. Use it to stimulate creativity and to enhance business or job prospects. Additionally, emerald is instrumental in contacting spirits and fairies.

This stone is associated with the element earth and the deities Ceres, Isis, Mercury, Venus, and Vishnu. Its astrological influence comes from Jupiter, Venus, the fixed star Spica, and the zodiac constellations of Aries, Cancer, Gemini, Libra, Sagittarius, Taurus, and Virgo.

Epidote

Pronunciation: EP-ih-dote

E pidote is the name of a group of related minerals as well as the most prominent member of the group. Long mistaken for a variety of tourmaline, the French crystallographer René-Just Haüy distinguished epidote as a separate mineral in 1801.[86] The name of this stone was derived from the Greek *epidosis,* meaning "increased," in reference to one side of its crystal usually being wider than the others.[87]

Epidote was used in ancient pottery from the Neolithic through classical times in Europe and the Middle East and in pre-Columbian Central and South America. Sometimes used for jewelry, this stone is popular with mineral collectors for its elongated crystals.

Epidote is typically light green to dark blackish green, but it can also be gray or yellow. Ranging from transparent to opaque, it has a vitreous luster and a monoclinic inner structure. It is strongly trichroic, and twinning is common. Crystals can also be small and needlelike.

This stone awakens and expands awareness to receive messages and esoteric knowledge. Use it in spells to attract or increase something you desire in your life. Epidote is an amplifier of energy for magic. It is also instrumental for removing obstacles and warding off negativity. This stone functions well as a guardian for home and family. In addition, it provides supportive energy for setting goals and attaining success.

Epidote is associated with the elements earth and water. Its astrological influence comes from the zodiac constellation of Gemini.

86. Pierre Bariand and Michel Duchamp, eds., *Larousse Encyclopedia of Precious Gems* (New York: Van Nostrand Reinhold, 1991), 125.

87. Bonewitz, *Smithsonian Nature Guide: Rocks and Minerals,* 230.

Piemontite

Pronunciation: **PEE-mawn-tite or PEE-mon-tite**
Also known as piedmontite

Named for the Piedmont region of northern Italy, this variety of epidote ranges from a pinkish red to dark reddish brown. It sometimes has zonal patterns of color. This stone is an aid for love and all matters of the heart.

Pistacite

Pronunciation: **pi-STASH-uh-site or pi-STAH-shee-ite**

Although this name is sometimes used as a synonym for epidote, it is most often applied to this variety, which is a yellowish pistachio green. Some lighter-colored stones can exhibit a cat's-eye effect when cut en cabochon.

Feldspar

Pronunciation: **FELD-spar** *or* **FEL-spar**

Feldspar is a group that includes some of the most common minerals in the world. While a few types of feldspar are gem quality, most are used for manufacturing. One of the earliest-known applications was in Chinese porcelain. The presence of feldspar in the clay they used gave their porcelain a fine quality that Europeans could not duplicate for centuries. Feldspar is still used in making pottery, tile, and glass. This mineral group gets its name from the Swedish word *feldt,* meaning "field," and *spar,* an Anglo-Saxon word meaning "easily cleaved." [88] The gem-quality feldspars include amazonite, labradorite, moonstone, and sunstone, which are covered separately.

---

88. Jaroslav Bauer and Vladimir Bouška, *A Guide in Color to Precious & Semiprecious Stones* (Secaucus, NJ: Chartwell Books, 1992), 166.

Fluorite

Pronunciation: FLOHR-ite *or* FLAWR-ite

Also known as fluorspar

Used in metal processing as flux since ancient times, this mineral's name comes from the Latin *fluere*, meaning "to flow." [89] While the Egyptians carved fluorite mostly into statues and scarabs, the Chinese used it for a wide range of ornamental objects.

The term *fluorescence* was derived from this mineral because it was the first substance in which this light phenomenon—emitting light under ultraviolet light—was observed. Most types of fluorite exhibit a strong light blue or violet fluorescence. In addition, red and green fluorite become phosphorescent—glows in the dark—when heated. While fluorite is too soft to facet as a gemstone because of its cleavage planes, pieces are often tumbled for use in jewelry.

Ranging from colorless to almost all shades of the spectrum, this stone's colors are often distributed in zones. Fluorite has a vitreous luster, ranges from transparent to translucent, and has a cubic inner structure. Cruciform twinning is common.

Fluorite is a stone of the mind, helping to focus, analyze, or generally increase mental power. It strengthens willpower and self-discipline and stimulates motivation. Fluorite boosts the effects of other stones and helps to remove energy blocks. This stone helps to fine-tune intuition and is instrumental for divination, dreamwork, and astral travel. Its calming energy aids in emotional and spiritual healing. Fluorite helps to release things that we no longer need in our lives. This stone also aids in all forms of communication and in contacting fairies.

....

89. Oldershaw, *Firefly Guide to Gems*, 70.

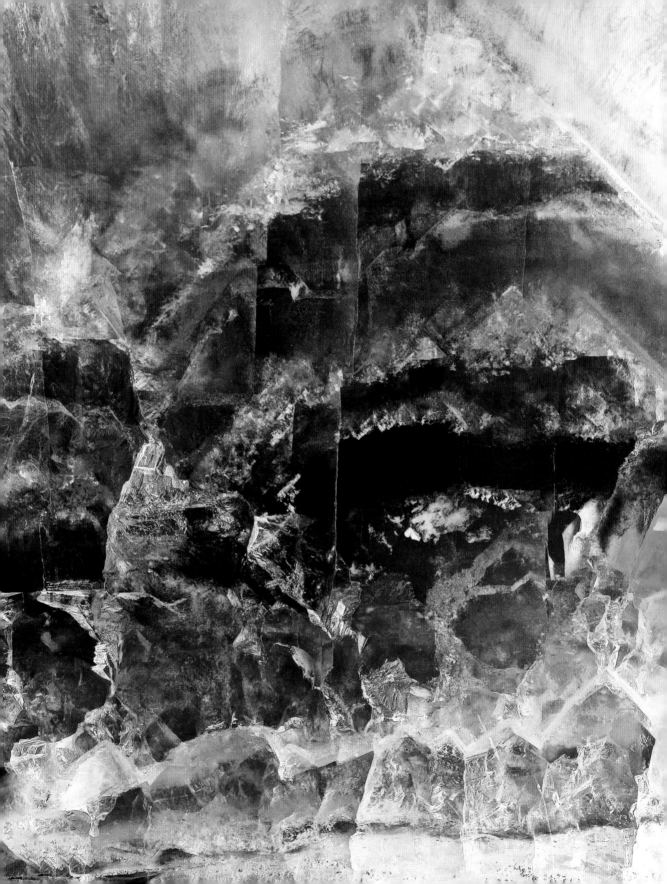

Fluorite is associated with the elements earth and water. Its astrological influence comes from Mercury, Neptune, and the zodiac constellations of Aquarius, Capricorn, Gemini, and Pisces.

Blue John
Also known as Derbyshire spar

This variety of fluorite has curved bands of blue, purple, violet, yellow, and white. Derived from the French *bleu et jaune,* meaning "blue and yellow," blue john is only found in Derbyshire, England.[90] English miners referred to the crystals as ore flowers. Blue john has been a prized ornamental stone since the time of the Romans who used it for vases and other ornamental objects. In fact, several blue john vases were found in the ruins of Pompeii. This stone remained popular through the eighteenth and nineteenth centuries. Blue john is a stone for getting things done. Use it when you need support for setting goals and attaining success.

90. Oldershaw, *Firefly Guide to Gems,* 71.

Garnet

Pronunciation: **GAHR-nit**

arnet is a group of minerals that have related chemical compositions. Although the name is applied to the entire group, originally it was used only for red stones. Garnet was one of the stones Pliny referred to as *carbuncle.* The name *garnet* was derived from the Latin *granatum,* meaning "grain" or "seed," in reference to red garnet pebbles resembling pomegranate seeds.[91] Favoring the dark red or reddish brown garnets, Egyptians used them as early as 3100 BCE for beads and other jewelry.[92] Mesopotamian garnet jewelry and cylinder seals date to approximately 2000 BCE.[93] The Mycenaeans of Greece also used these stones for jewelry. During the Middle Ages, garnet was believed to quell restlessness and aid sleep. Magically, it was believed to bring riches and honors and protect against evil spirits.

Garnets range from transparent to opaque and can have a greasy, resinous, or vitreous luster. They have a cubic inner structure. Garnets occur in almost every color except blue.

In general, garnets have strong supportive energy that strengthens personal power and helps to achieve goals. As a stone of emotional balance, garnet's calming energy brings patience and dissolves anger. It also fosters general well-being. This protective stone dispels negative energy and can be used for defense against nightmares. It is instrumental for

91. Grande and Augustyn, *Gems and Gemstones,* 170.

92. Ibid.

93. P. R. S. Moorey, *Ancient Mesopotamian Materials and Industries: The Archaeological Evidence* (Winona Lake, IN: Eisenbrauns, 1994), 83.

protection while traveling. Garnet also aids in remembering dreams and interpreting messages. Use this stone when seeking wisdom.

Most garnets are associated with the element fire. Their astrological influence comes from Mars, Pluto, and the zodiac constellations of Aquarius, Aries, Capricorn, Leo, and Virgo.

Almandine

Pronunciation: **AL-muhn-deen** *or* **AL-muhn-din**
Also known as almandite

This red stone has a violet or purplish tinge and can produce four- or six-rayed stars. Called *alabandicus* by Pliny and known as *alabandite* for centuries, it has been popular for jewelry since Roman times.[94] This stone has also been called almond stone and Ceylon ruby. It symbolizes courage, stability, and strength. Associated with lust and sexuality, it aids in attracting love. Use it to express devotion in a relationship. Its astrological influence comes from the zodiac constellation of Scorpio and the fixed stars Aldebaran and Regulus.

Grossularite

Pronunciation: **GROS-yuh-luh-rite**
Also known as grossular

While grossularite can occur in a wide range of colors, it is best known for its greens. The name of this variety comes from the Latin *grossularia,* meaning "gooseberry," in reference to its most common greenish color.[95] Grossularite can be brown, colorless, green, orange, or pink. It ranges from transparent to translucent with a vitreous or greasy luster. Grossularite is associated with fertility and fidelity. It aids in attracting friendship and engendering loyalty. It is especially effective for healing on many levels.

....

94. Robert Jameson, *A System of Mineralogy,* vol. 1, 3rd ed. (London: Hurst, Robinson & Company, 1820), 128.

95. Rapp, *Archaeomineralogy,* 98.

Hessonite

Pronunciation: HES-uh-nite

Also known as cinnamon stone

This stone ranges from orange to brownish orange and transparent to translucent. Hessonite has a vitreous or greasy luster. Its name comes from the Greek *esson,* meaning "inferior," because it is not as hard as other garnets.[96] The Greeks and Romans used this stone for cameos and intaglio work. When placed in a gold setting, hessonite was believed to be a powerful talisman. This stone provides emotional support and fosters courage to make important life changes. It also keeps energy grounded during times of change. Hessonite stimulates creativity and provides strong energy in matters of sexual attraction.

Melanite

Pronunciation: MEL-ahn-ite

This garnet is black and opaque. Its name comes from the Greek word meaning "black."[97] During the Victorian era, it was used extensively for mourning jewelry. This spiritual stone provides emotional support when dealing with grief and loss. Melanite is associated with the element earth.

Pyrope

Pronunciation: PIE-rope

Also known as bohemian garnet

A deep red color, pyrope often has a brownish tint. Its name comes from the Greek *pyropos,* meaning "fiery eyed."[98] Like almandine, it symbolizes courage, stability, and strength. Associated with lust and sexuality, it aids in attracting love. It stokes the power to change, bringing renewal and healing when needed. It also sparks creativity. Its astrological influence comes from the zodiac constellation of Scorpio and the fixed stars Aldebaran and Regulus.

Rhodolite

***Pronunciation:* RODE-uhl-ite**

Originally thought to be a type of almandine, this variety has a chemical composition that is between almandine and pyrope. It is pinkish red, purplish red, or rose colored. Its name was derived from the Greek *rhodon* and *lithos,* meaning "rose stone." [99] It is associated with lust and sexuality and aids in attracting love. Use it to express devotion in a relationship. Rhodolite is associated with the element earth. Its astrological influence comes from the zodiac constellation of Scorpio and the fixed stars Aldebaran and Regulus.

Spessartite

***Pronunciation:* SPES-er-tite**

Also known as mandarin garnet and spessartine

This stone ranges from orange to reddish orange and transparent to translucent. It was named for the Spessart Forest in Germany. [100] The energy of this stone exudes happiness and aids in attracting harmony to the home. It stimulates creativity and helps to keep energy grounded during times of change. Spessartite is helpful to focus the mind. This stone is associated with the elements earth and fire.

99. Grande and Augustyn, *Gems and Gemstones*, 176.

100. Schumann, *Gemstones of the World*, 120.

Tsavorite

Pronunciation: **TSAH-vuh-rite** *or* **SAH-vuh-rite**
Also known as tsavolite

Discovered in the 1960s in Tanzania and Kenya, this green to emerald-green garnet has become popular for jewelry.[101] It was named for the Tsavo National Game Park in Kenya. Tsavorite has grounding energy that fosters balance, harmony, and healing. Use it for introspection when seeking knowledge. Fostering fidelity and loyalty, it is helpful for communication, especially between lovers. It is also associated with fertility. This stone is associated with the elements fire and water. Its astrological influence comes from Mars, Pluto, Venus, and the zodiac constellations of Taurus and Virgo.

Uvarovite

Pronunciation: **oo-VAHR-uh-vite** *or* **yoo-VAHR-uh-vite**

With a vitreous luster, this stone is also green to emerald green. Named for Russian diplomat Count Uvarov (1765–1855), it is rarely used as a gem because its crystals are too small to facet. This stone fosters abundance and confidence and is instrumental in manifesting desires and goals. It is associated with fidelity, friendship, and loyalty. This stone also aids fertility and healing. Uvarovite is associated with the element earth.

101. John K. Warren, *Evaporites: A Geological Compendium*, 2nd ed. (New York: Springer, 2016), 1426.

Hawk's-Eye

Also known as blue tiger's-eye and falcon's-eye

This stone was once regarded as a pseudomorph, where one mineral replaces another over time. Although yet to be proven, newer theories regard hawk's-eye as an intergrowth of quartz and crocidolite (blue asbestos). The fibrous structure of the crocidolite produces the blue chatoyancy—cat's-eye effect. The effect can be seen in flat stones, but is more pronounced when the stone is cut en cabochon. Hawk's-eye is used for jewelry and small carvings.

Hawk's-eye is typically multicolored blue green or blue gray with stripes or wavy patterns. It ranges from semitranslucent to opaque. This stone has a vitreous or silky luster and a trigonal inner structure.

Hawk's-eye is especially powerful when working with animals, astral familiars, or magic that calls on the power of animals. It also aids in forming bonds with animals. Of course, it is particularly instrumental for bird magic. Hawk's-eye heightens awareness for astral travel and brings clarity to psychic work. It fosters insight that helps to bring all aspects of life into balance. With its help, we can get out of a rut and soar to new heights. In addition, this stone generates healing energy that wards off negativity and supports renewal.

Hawk's-eye is associated with the element air, the goddess Hathor, and the god Ra.

Hematite

Pronunciation: HEE-muh-tite *or* HEM-uh-tite

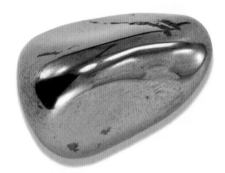

The name of this stone comes from the Greek *haima,* meaning "blood," which refers to its color when ground into a powder.[102] Known as *red ochre,* this pigment was used for Paleolithic cave paintings and Neolithic pottery. Symbolizing the power of the life-giving and regeneratrix aspects of the Great Mother Goddess, red was the color of rebirth and transformation. To emphasize this, Goddess figurines were often painted with red ochre. In Neolithic tombs dating to approximately 5000 BCE, corpses were often placed in the fetal position and sprinkled with the red powder.[103] Red ochre was also used by the Egyptians for tomb paintings.

In Babylon, hematite stones were used for cylinder seals. The Romans wore this stone as a talisman for a positive outcome in legal matters. In prehistoric North America, hematite was used for pendants and axes. In addition to burial rites, Native Americans used red ochre for ceremonial and war paints. Today, red ochre is a component in the metal polishing substance called jeweler's rouge. Although hematite is a heavy stone, it is used in jewelry for cameos and signet rings. Flat, intergrown crystals are called iron roses.

Hematite can be steel gray, black, or brownish red. It is opaque with a metallic or dull luster and has a trigonal inner structure.

Hematite is a stone of power that focuses strength for manifesting desires and goals. Although it aids in winning favors, this aspect should be used judiciously. This stone provides supportive energy for divination, dreamwork, and astral travel. It aids in grounding and

102. Eastaugh, et al., *Pigment Compendium*, 189.

103. Marija Gimbutas, *The Language of the Goddess* (New York: HarperCollins Publishers, 1991), 200.

centering energy after these practices. Use hematite at funerals for loved ones to send them into the afterlife and eventual rebirth. For the living, this stone aids in dealing with grief and supports adaptability. Hematite also aids in legal matters. This stone helps bring clarity for decision-making and problem-solving. Its calming energy reduces anxiety and aids the healing process. It also deflects negativity.

Hematite is associated with the elements earth and fire. Its astrological influence comes from Mars, Mercury, Saturn, and the zodiac constellations of Aquarius, Aries, and Capricorn.

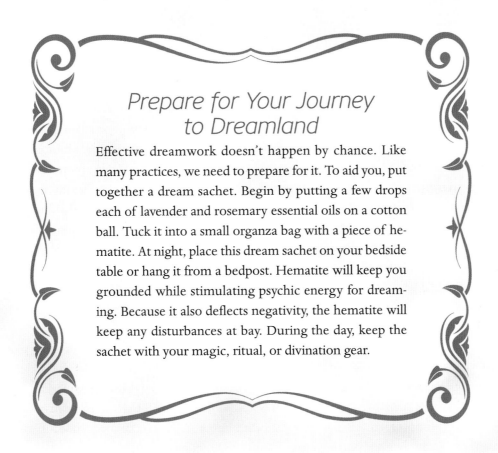

Prepare for Your Journey to Dreamland

Effective dreamwork doesn't happen by chance. Like many practices, we need to prepare for it. To aid you, put together a dream sachet. Begin by putting a few drops each of lavender and rosemary essential oils on a cotton ball. Tuck it into a small organza bag with a piece of hematite. At night, place this dream sachet on your bedside table or hang it from a bedpost. Hematite will keep you grounded while stimulating psychic energy for dreaming. Because it also deflects negativity, the hematite will keep any disturbances at bay. During the day, keep the sachet with your magic, ritual, or divination gear.

Herkimer Diamond

Pronunciation: HER-kuh-mer DYE-mund

Herkimer diamond is neither a unique species of mineral nor a diamond. It is the name given to doubly terminated, gem-quality clear quartz crystals found in Herkimer County, New York. Because of its brilliance, this stone was mistaken for diamond when it was first discovered in the late 1700s.[104] Although these crystals are found in several places around the world, only the ones from Herkimer County can claim this name.

Crystals that are naturally terminated in this manner are somewhat rare, making them popular with jewelry designers and mineral collectors. Because Herkimer diamonds tend to be small, they are usually wire wrapped for jewelry, but some are large enough to be faceted for more expensive pieces.

Although Herkimer diamond is colorless, it can be clear, cloudy, or slightly smoky. Occasionally it has inclusions or phantoms. This stone has a trigonal inner structure and its luster is vitreous or adamantine.

More than anything, Herkimer diamond is regarded as a dream crystal for receiving messages and for getting in touch with one's inner self. It is an aid for developing psychic abilities, especially clairvoyance. Because of its high level of spiritual energy, this stone is ideal to place on an altar for ritual, meditation, or whenever wisdom is sought. Use this stone in spells to attract luck and prosperity and to invite happiness into your life. Herkimer diamond is instrumental in reconciling and binding relationships and fostering fidelity.

Herkimer diamond is associated with the element fire. Its astrological influence comes from the moon, the sun, Uranus, and the zodiac constellations of Aries and Sagittarius.

---

104. Collings, *Gemlore*, 77.

Hiddenite

Pronunciation: HID-en-ite

Also known as green spodumene

Although this stone's name sounds as though it is associated with secrets, it has nothing to do with concealing anything. In 1881, this mineral was analyzed and named by chemist John Lawrence Smith (1818–1883) in honor of William Hidden (1853–1918), the geologist who discovered it while working for Thomas Edison.[105] The town near the mine where it was found was named after the mineral.

Hiddenite is one of two varieties of spodumene discovered around the turn of the twentieth century. The other is the pinkish lilac-colored kunzite, which is covered separately in this book. The name *spodumene* was derived from the Greek *spodumenos,* meaning "burned to ashes" or "ash colored," because most spodumene is grayish white like ash.[106]

....
105. John Sinkankas, *Gemstones of North America*, vol. 2 (New York: John Wiley & Sons, 1976), 433.

106. Schumann, *Gemstones of the World*, 130.

Hiddenite ranges from yellowish green to blue green and transparent to translucent. It has a vitreous luster and monoclinic inner structure. This stone is strongly trichroic. It fluoresces a weak reddish-yellow color. The emerald green variety called chrome hiddenite is relatively rare.

Hiddenite is a stone of nurturing and healing. It dispels all forms of negative energy, including thoughts that we may have about ourselves. Use it to restore confidence and self-worth. With highly spiritual vibrations, hiddenite aids in dealing with loss and grief. This stone also helps to maintain authenticity in a relationship. Hiddenite supports psychic development and divination practices. Use it to open the psyche for communicating with spirit guides.

Hiddenite is associated with the element water. Its astrological influence comes from the zodiac constellation of Taurus.

Be True to Yourself

The self-image that we have is often the result of listening to other people. Unfortunately, that self-image and feelings of self-worth are not always positive. With the help of two hiddenite crystals, we can remove negativity and cultivate a nurturing attitude toward ourselves. Hold a crystal in each hand, wrap your arms around yourself, and say three times:

I love you.

Repeat this exercise every day until you truly feel in your heart of hearts that you are a good and worthy person. It may feel awkward or uncomfortable at first, but stay with it. Self-healing is an empowering experience that can help us open our hearts and energy.

Howlite

Pronunciation: HOWL-ite *or* HOW-lite

Howlite was named for Canadian mineralogist and chemist Henry How (1828–1879), who discovered it in 1868.[107] Howlite is sometimes called white turquoise; however, this is a misleading name because this mineral is not related to turquoise. Because its veining pattern is similar to turquoise and it takes dye well, howlite is often passed off as the more expensive turquoise.

Mineral collectors are fond of howlite for the cauliflower-like clumps that it sometimes forms. This stone is used for beads, jewelry, and ornamental objects. It is often carved into the shape of a skull.

Howlite is white with fine gray or black veining that occasionally occurs in a web-like pattern. It has a monoclinic inner structure and is opaque with a dull or slightly vitreous luster. It fluoresces a brownish-yellow color.

This is a stone of the emotions. It is especially suited for reducing anger, stress, and anxiety. In addition, howlite provides support for showing emotions in a healthy manner. Howlite also stokes creativity and encourages the exploration of new mediums for creative expression. Its gentle energy fosters patience and compassion. As an aid to memory, this stone is a good choice for dreamwork to help remember and interpret dreams. Howlite also provides support for past-life work and contacting spirit guides.

Howlite is associated with the element air. Its astrological influence comes from the zodiac constellations of Gemini and Virgo.

....
107. Bonewitz, *Smithsonian Nature Guide: Rocks and Minerals*, 129.

Iolite

Pronunciation: EYE-uh-lite

Also known as blue cordierite, dichroite, and water sapphire

Iolite is the bluish gem-quality variety of the industrial mineral cordierite. Its name comes from the Greek *ion,* meaning "violet," and *lithos,* "stone." [108] Although its name dichroite hints that it exhibits two colors, it is actually trichroic, appearing yellow, dark blue to violet, or pale blue to almost clear from different angles. Even though iolite has been used as an alternative to sapphire, viewing it from the angle where it appears pale blue makes it look watery, hence its other name. However, the name water sapphire may also come from the fact that iolite is often found along streams and riverbeds.

The Romans used this stone for intaglio work and ornamental carvings. Although calcite was the "sunstone" of the Vikings, they also used thin slices of pale, transparent iolite as a light filter to help determine the position of the sun. While gem-quality stones are used for jewelry, tumbled and rough pieces of opaque iolite are popular, too.

Iolite can be blue, gray blue, or violet blue and range from transparent to opaque. It has an orthorhombic inner structure and a greasy or vitreous luster. Iolite can exhibit a star pattern.

This stone is an activator that stimulates spiritual growth and awakens new levels of faith. It also stirs up energy for ritual and spellwork. Iolite supports psychic work, visions, and astral travel. Although it can be used as a motivator to get things going, iolite is also calming and helps to stabilize emotions and situations. Use it when you need to let go of something in your life. As an aid for communication, this stone promotes cooperation.

Iolite is associated with the element water. Its astrological influence comes from the zodiac constellations of Libra, Sagittarius, and Taurus.

....

108. Joseph T. Shipley, *Dictionary of Word Origins* (New York: Dorset House, 1993), 136.

Jade

Pronunciation: jayd

While we may think of jade as only one type of stone, there are actually two types: jadeite and nephrite. The difference between the two was not determined until 1863.[109] Nephrite is the jade that was used in China as early as 3000 BCE for sacred and secular carvings. It is known as the "old" or "true" Chinese jade.[110] The Chinese people regarded jade as the stone of heaven and used it in burial rites. Jadeite was the type of jade in the Americas that the Olmec, Aztec, Maya, and Toltec valued more highly than gold. It was used to make tools and ceremonial objects, such as funerary masks. To the Maya, it symbolized the annual agricultural cycle and regeneration. Spanish explorers took jade back to Europe, where it was mostly unknown at the time. The name *jade* was derived from the Spanish *piedra de ijada,* meaning "hip stone," in reference to its use for protection against kidney disease.[111] Likewise, nephrite was derived from the Greek word for kidney. Today, jadeite is generally considered the "real" jade.

In addition to a wide range of greens, jadeite can be black, blue, brown, lavender, red, white, or yellow. It ranges from translucent to opaque. Nephrite can be pale to dark green, black, brown, gray, red, white, and yellow. It is opaque. Both jades have a monoclinic inner structure.

---

109. Oldershaw, *Firefly Guide to Gems,* 142.

110. Antoinette Matlins, *Colored Gemstones: The Antoinette Matlins Buying Guide,* 3rd ed. (Woodstock, VT: GemStone Press, 2010), 128.

111. Schumann, *Gemstones of the World,* 170.

Because of its receptive energy, jade is considered a good dream stone that provides guidance and inspiration. Use it in spells to attract abundance, prosperity, love, or luck. In addition to repelling negative energy, jade is effective for defensive magic and protection in general. Associated with the afterlife, use this stone at Samhain or whenever a loved one passes. It can also be used to contact spirits and attract fairies. Jade is instrumental for courage when asserting independence or when seeking justice. It fosters peace, harmony, and well-being. In addition to supporting fertility and growth, it helps when making decisions.

Jade is associated with the elements earth and water. Its astrological influence comes from Neptune, Venus, and the zodiac constellations of Aquarius, Aries, Gemini, Libra, Pisces, Taurus, and Virgo. It is also associated with the goddesses Athena, Chalchihuitlicue, Coatlicue, Kuan Yin, and Ma'at.

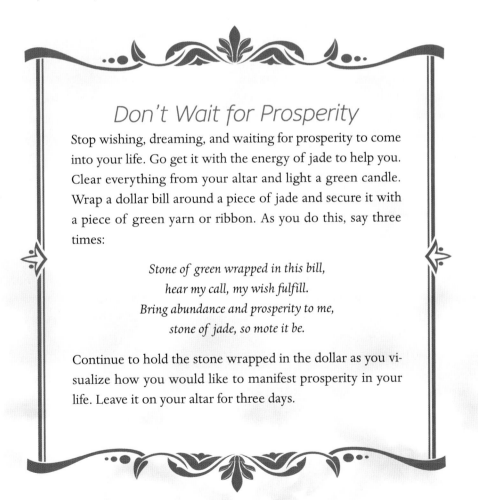

Don't Wait for Prosperity

Stop wishing, dreaming, and waiting for prosperity to come into your life. Go get it with the energy of jade to help you. Clear everything from your altar and light a green candle. Wrap a dollar bill around a piece of jade and secure it with a piece of green yarn or ribbon. As you do this, say three times:

> *Stone of green wrapped in this bill,*
> *hear my call, my wish fulfill.*
> *Bring abundance and prosperity to me,*
> *stone of jade, so mote it be.*

Continue to hold the stone wrapped in the dollar as you visualize how you would like to manifest prosperity in your life. Leave it on your altar for three days.

Jasper

Pronunciation: JAS-per

The ancient Egyptians, Greeks, and Romans used jasper for amulets and jewelry, seal stones, carvings, and mosaics. Sometimes found in huge masses, jasper was used for large vases and even pillars for buildings. The Egyptians used jasper for funeral scarabs. The name *jasper* was derived from its Greek and Latin name *iaspis,* meaning "spotted stone."[112] Jasper was also used in North America since prehistoric times for decorative and utilitarian objects. In Europe during the Middle Ages, it was believed to drive away evil spirits. Jasper was also considered an aid for keeping secrets.

Found in almost all colors, jaspers are generally multicolored with bands, spots, or patterns. They are usually referred to according to their pattern or predominant color. Banded or ribbon jasper has straight or swirling bands of color, orbicular jasper has orbs and swirls, and picture jasper contains scenic-like patterns. Jasper ranges from translucent to opaque and has a trigonal inner structure. Its luster can range from dull to waxy or vitreous.

Jasper is a stone of peace and wisdom. It is an aid during times of transition, providing stability and protection against negativity. This stone supports fortitude and perseverance. It also aids in keeping secrets. In addition, jasper helps when dealing with sexual issues and for accepting one's sexuality.

In general, jasper is associated with the element earth and the goddesses Athena and Isis. Its astrological influence comes from Mercury, Venus, the fixed star Arcturus, and the zodiac constellations of Leo, Libra, and Pisces.

112. Schumann, *Gemstones of the World*, 162.

Green Jasper

This jasper ranges from pale to dark green. While it can have a single color, it most often contains veining or patterns with other colors. It ranges from translucent to opaque. Its earliest use dates to approximately 4000 BCE in Egypt, where it was carved for amulets and beads.[113] Green jasper was commonly used for funerary scarabs. The Assyrians used it for jewelry, which was often buried with the dead. Phoenician scarabs depicted Isis and other deities. The Greeks and Etruscans commonly used this stone for seals.

Green jasper is a stone of compassion that promotes empathy and receptiveness. It fosters fertility and growth. This stone is instrumental in resolving problems. Use it in spells to attract luck, money, and wealth. It also facilitates sleep and supports well-being. Green jasper fosters the development of clairvoyant skills. This stone's astrological influence comes from Venus and the zodiac constellation of Gemini.

Leopard Skin Jasper

This stone is a variety of orbicular jasper that can be brown, gray, or sandy colored with tan or black spots. It was so named because the pattern often resembles the skin of a leopard. This stone is especially powerful for any type of work involving animals and in establishing bonds with familiars. It aids in connecting with animal energy and, when appropriate, using it to boost spells. This jasper is a stone of insight that supports shamanic work. It also aids mundane travel.

113. A. Lucas and J. R. Harris, *Ancient Egyptian Materials and Industries* (Mineola, NY: Dover Publications, 2012), 397.

Red Jasper

This variety of jasper runs from dull red to rich brick to brownish red. Although predominantly red, it is usually veined or mottled with other colors. Red jasper has been used for personal ornamentation since the Stone Age. Ancient carvings made with red jasper have been found throughout the Mediterranean region. To the Babylonians, it served as a symbol of childbirth. Like green jasper, its use in Egypt dates to predynastic times. The Etruscans and Romans used it for seals. Roman sites in England have yielded red jasper carvings of Isis. During the Middle Ages in Europe, it was used for altarpieces and in tombs.

Red jasper is especially effective for defensive magic and for warding off hexes. Use it for banishing rituals and spells of reversal. This stone helps to focus the mind for divination and supports astral work. It also attracts luck and engenders optimism. Use red jasper to kindle romance and spark love. This variety of jasper is associated with the element fire. Its astrological influence comes from Mars and the zodiac constellations of Aries, Scorpio, and Taurus.

Spider Web Jasper

This jasper can be black, brown, cream, green, or red overlaid with a crisscross pattern that frequently resembles a spider's web. It is used for jewelry, beads, and decorative items. Spider web jasper reminds us that we are responsible for weaving our own web of life. It is instrumental for binding spells and for raising protective energy or warding off negativity. This healing stone supports both our own personal growth and the health of our gardens. It is especially effective for accessing ancient wisdom.

Yellow Jasper

This jasper ranges from sandy to mustard yellow or brownish yellow. Frequently, it has subtle flow patterns or veining. It was used by the Egyptians for sculptures of royalty dating to approximately 1350 BCE.[114] Like other jaspers, it was used for scarabs. The Greeks and Romans also used it for carvings. A Greek seal stone dating to 200 CE bears a depiction of Athena.[115]

Yellow jasper attracts positive energy that supports healing. It is an aid for clearing the mind and knowing when to assert your willpower. This stone helps to keep a balanced perspective, especially for achieving success. It is also instrumental for connecting with the angelic realm. Yellow jasper's astrological influence comes from the zodiac constellation of Sagittarius.

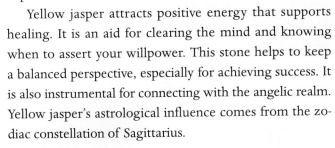

114. Lucas and Harris, *Ancient Egyptian Materials and Industries*, 398.

115. Jeffrey Spier, *Ancient Gems and Finger Rings* (Malibu, CA: The J. Paul Getty Museum, 1992), 127.

Jet

Also known as black amber

Jet is actually a type of coal formed from the fossilized wood of ancient conifers in the genus *Araucaria* that flourished 180 million years ago.[116] It has been used as beads for adornment since the Bronze Age. Its name comes from the Old French *jaiet*, which was derived from the Latin *gagates* after the town or river Gagas in Asia Minor, where it was mined.[117]

The Romans mined jet in northern England, beginning in approximately 1500 BCE, and valued it as a trade item.[118] Believing in jet's magical power, especially to guard against nightmares and witchcraft, the Romans used it for protective amulets. They also enjoyed it for simple jewelry, as evidenced by the rings found on the fingers of skeletons in the catacombs of Rome. During medieval times, large flat pieces were polished and used as scrying mirrors. In the eighteenth and nineteenth centuries, jet was favored for jewelry and made more popular by Queen Victoria when she went into mourning after the death of her beloved husband, Prince Albert.

Jet is black and opaque with a greasy luster. With no internal structure, it is classified as amorphous.

This stone is associated with the afterlife and helps bring emotional balance after grieving. In addition, jet has healing energy that soothes the emotions and the soul. It is an aid for dealing with fears, especially for children, and for dispelling nightmares. Use this stone

116. Oldershaw, *Firefly Guide to Gems*, 204.

117. Rapp, *Archaeomineralogy*, 118.

118. Ibid., 113.

for binding spells and for breaking or warding off hexes. Its protective energy also shields against black magic. Jet is instrumental as a good luck charm, especially in legal matters and for winning favors. This stone also supports divination practices and boosts psychic abilities.

Jet is associated with the elements earth and water. Its astrological influence comes from Pluto, Saturn, and the zodiac constellation of Capricorn. Jet is also associated with the deities Cybele, Dôn, Njord, and Pan.

Jettison Hexes with Jet

If you are concerned about hexes, black magic, or any negative energy intentionally sent your way, use jet to ward off anything unwanted. Prepare at least four pieces of jet by passing them through the smoke of burning mugwort and lavender. As you do this, say three times:

Powerful crystals, stones of black,
reverse negativity, send it back.
With your energy, power wield,
protect all within your shield.

Place one stone at each corner of your property or house and visualize their energy rising and connecting above the roof, creating a dome around you and your home. Any other pieces of jet that were prepared can be carried as talismans.

Kunzite

Pronunciation: KOONTS-ite

Also known as pink spodumene

Discovered in the early twentieth century, kunzite is a gem-quality variety of the industrial mineral spodumene. Unable to discern what it was, a sample was sent to mineralogist George Kunz (1856–1932) in New York, who recognized it as a new variety of spodumene. This mineral was named Kunzite in his honor. Queen Alexandra (1844–1925) of England made it popular during the Edwardian years because of her love for pink jewels. Kunzite earned the nickname evening stone because of the suggestion that it should be worn only in the evening to avoid strong sunlight, which can cause the stone's color to fade.

Kunzite is pinkish violet or light violet with a vitreous luster. It ranges from transparent to translucent and has a monoclinic inner structure. This stone is strongly dichroic, appearing a deep pink or amethyst from one direction and colorless from another. It has a strong fluorescence ranging from yellowish red to orange.

Kunzite opens the heart, fostering gentleness and deep compassion. Its energy is nurturing and calming, which provides emotional support. This stone removes negativity and obstacles that may impede personal growth. It fosters unconditional love and facilitates communication for reconciling relationship issues. Along with healing, kunzite brings peace and harmony to a household. Kunzite gently awakens spiritual energy for introspection and guidance.

Kunzite is associated with the element earth. Its astrological influence comes from Pluto, Venus, and the zodiac constellations of Leo, Libra, Scorpio, and Taurus.

Kyanite

Pronunciation: **KY-uh-nite** *or* **KAY-uh-nite**

Also known as disthene

First described by German chemist and mineralogist Abraham Werner in 1774, this mineral's name comes from the Greek *kyanos,* meaning "blue," in reference to its most common color.[119] The name *disthene* was derived from the Greek *di* and *sthenos* meaning "two strengths." [120] This refers to the unusual characteristic of unequal hardness within a single stone. In the past, the name kyanite was also spelled cyanite. Although kyanite has the same chemical composition as andalusite, their different crystal structures produce two different stones.

Kyanite is mainly used for manufacturing ceramics, electronic components, and a number of heat-resistant materials for a range of industries. While it is not one of the most glamorous stones, its use in jewelry is increasing. Mineral collectors and those of us who enjoy working with raw stones like kyanite for its flat, bladelike crystals.

Kyanite is found in a range of blues, blue green, brown, colorless, or gray. Its color is often uneven, blotchy, or streaked. This stone has a vitreous or pearly luster and a triclinic inner structure. It ranges from transparent to translucent. Kyanite is trichroic and fluoresces a weak red color.

....

119. Milos Kužvart, *Industrial Minerals and Rocks* (New York: Elsevier, 1984), 122.

120. Ibid.

This stone is especially useful for adding magic and enchantment to dreamwork, giving it more depth and fullness. Kyanite activates energy and provides focus to enhance and expand creative skills. Use it to double the strength of your spells and to repel negativity. Kyanite provides guidance to bring spirituality into everyday life. The calming energy of this stone removes anger, stress, and anxiety. Wear it to maintain a sense of well-being. Fostering loyalty, it draws people closer together in community. Use it to bring clarity for all forms of communication. This stone also provides stability during life's big changes, especially the ones that result in renewal.

Kyanite is associated with the element water. Its astrological influence comes from the zodiac constellation Libra.

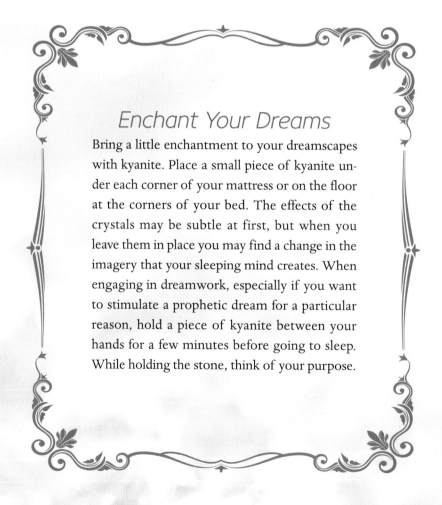

Enchant Your Dreams

Bring a little enchantment to your dreamscapes with kyanite. Place a small piece of kyanite under each corner of your mattress or on the floor at the corners of your bed. The effects of the crystals may be subtle at first, but when you leave them in place you may find a change in the imagery that your sleeping mind creates. When engaging in dreamwork, especially if you want to stimulate a prophetic dream for a particular reason, hold a piece of kyanite between your hands for a few minutes before going to sleep. While holding the stone, think of your purpose.

Labradorite

Pronunciation: **LAB-ruh-daw-rite** *or* **lab-ruh-DAWR-ite**

Also known as labrador spar and spectrolite

This stone is best known for its metallic, multicolored iridescence that was given the name labradorescence. While this iridescence is most often seen in peacock feather shades of blue, green, and gold, the effect can appear in almost any color of the spectrum. Labradorescence is more readily visible in tumbled or cut and polished stones; however, the effect is easily seen when a raw piece is moistened.

According to legend, labradorite was the source of the northern lights. As one version of the story goes, an Inuk shaman noticed the dance of color reflecting from some stones and pounded them with the handle of his spear to release the light. Not all of the light escaped, which is why the shimmering aurora borealis can be seen in some stones.

Labradorite was named for Labrador, Canada, where it was identified as a type of feldspar in the 1770s.[121] It became popular for jewelry in France and England. Also used for ornamental objects, large slabs of labradorite have been used as facings for office buildings. Labradorite found in Finland is called *spectrolite*.

Most often ranging from gray to gray black, labradorite can also be brownish or colorless. This opaque stone has a triclinic inner structure and a dull or vitreous luster. It fluoresces in yellowish striations. Dark stones with a pronounced blue labradorescence are sometimes called black moonstone and transparent stones with a wide spectrum of color in their labradorescence are sometimes called rainbow moonstone. However, these nicknames are not recognized as designated varieties of labradorite.

....

121. Oldershaw, *Firefly Guide to Gems*, 180.

Labradorite is instrumental in cultivating psychic abilities and stoking intuition. It is an aid for making contact with spirits and working with spirit guides. Labradorite is especially supportive for shamanic work. With strong powers of motivation and transformation, this stone raises awareness and ushers thoughts from inspiration to positive action. Labradorite reduces stress and brings personal energy into balance. Use it to boost the power of spells and when seeking wisdom. This stone also aids in connecting with animals.

Labradorite is associated with the element water. Its astrological influence comes from Neptune, Pluto, Uranus, and the zodiac constellations of Leo, Sagittarius, and Scorpio.

Connect with Plant Devas

If there is a plant in your garden where you suspect plant devas or other green world spirits live, here's a way to connect with them. Sit or kneel beside the plant while holding several pieces of labradorite against your chest. Let your heart energy flow into the stones, and then make a circle around the base of the plant with them. Hold the palm of your hands near the plant's flowers or leaves and visualize your energy connecting with the plant. Be alert for any subtle energy coming back to you. Have patience because it usually takes time for spirits to trust a human. After each session, leave a piece of labradorite as an offering.

Lapis Lazuli

Pronunciation: **LAP-is LAZ-oo-lee**

The name of this stone comes from the Latin *lapis* for "stone" and *lazulum* for "heaven," which was derived from the Persian *lazhward,* meaning "blue." [122] The use of lapis lazuli dates to approximately 6000 to 4000 BCE in India.[123] Technically, lapis lazuli is a rock that contains varying amounts of several minerals, mainly calcite with lazurite, haüyne, or sodalite, which are responsible for its blue color. It also contains pyrite, which adds gold speckles. Lazurite is relatively rare, and most lapis lazuli on the market contains haüyne.

In Mesopotamia, this stone was used for amulets, seals, and jewelry inlay, some of which had been inscribed with magical texts. A carved cup and a dagger hilt of lapis lazuli were found in an ancient royal tomb. Likewise, the Egyptians used this stone for jewelry and often for funeral scarabs. In addition, it was used for beads, amulets, small decorative objects, and statuettes. The goddess Hathor was sometimes referred to as the Mistress of Lapis Lazuli.

In addition to jewelry and seals, the Greeks and Romans gave this stone as gifts to reward bravery. Lapis lazuli was used medicinally in ancient and medieval times. Also like other gems, it was crushed and used as a pigment during the Middle Ages. Known as *ultramarine,* its name was a combination of the Latin *ultra,* "beyond," and the Spanish *mar,*

122. Oldershaw, *Firefly Guide to Gems,* 184.

123. Rapp, *Archaeomineralogy,* 105.

"sea." [124] Through the Renaissance, ultramarine was prized for paintings and illuminated manuscripts.

This stone can be deep blue or greenish blue, occasionally with a hint of violet. It is usually striated or veined and flecked with pyrite. It is opaque with a cubic inner structure and has a greasy or vitreous luster.

Lapis lazuli is a powerful stone of wisdom that strengthens intuition and psychic abilities. It is instrumental for divination, especially where enchantment or attracting love is involved. This stone also serves as a powerful amulet for protection when traveling or when seeking justice. Use it to bolster courage, ease shyness, and make friends. It also helps to heal heartbreak. Its high spiritual vibration aids in coping when a loved one passes beyond the veil. Lapis lazuli promotes peace and fidelity in relationships.

Lapis lazuli is associated with the element water. Its astrological influence comes from Neptune, Venus, and the zodiac constellations of Aries, Capricorn, Libra, Sagittarius, Taurus, and Virgo. This stone is also associated with the goddesses Hathor, Isis, Justinia, Nut, and Venus.

---

124. Eastaugh, et al., *Pigment Compendium*, 381.

Larimar

Pronunciation: LAR-uh-mar

Also known as blue pectolite and dolphin stone

While the mineral pectolite is found in various locations around the world, the blue variety is found only in the Dominican Republic. Known since the early 1900s, local Miguel Mendez and Peace Corps volunteer Norman Rilling rediscovered larimar and brought it to the world's attention in 1974.[125] Mendez coined the name *larimar* by combining his daughter's name, Larissa, and *mar,* the Spanish word for "sea."[126] This stone's white veining pattern on pale blue echoes the beauty and enchantment of clear Caribbean waters.

Larimar ranges from pale sky blue to deep cerulean often with gray or white spider veining patterns. When cut en cabochon, it may occasionally exhibit a faint cat's-eye effect. This stone ranges from translucent to opaque and has a vitreous or silky luster. Its inner structure is triclinic.

With its Caribbean Sea colors and patterns, larimar exudes peace and tranquility. Its calming energy dispels anger and fear and aids in healing. This stone is instrumental in releasing stress and removing any form of negativity. Larimar brings harmony to relationships and is effective for attracting love. It boosts confidence and aids in situations that require adaptability and acceptance. It also helps to let go of attachments in this life and

---

125. Katherine Tuider and Eval Caplan, *Other Places Travel Guide: Dominican Republic* (New York: Other Places Publishing, 2012), 340.

126. Collings, *Gemlore*, 94.

any past-life baggage that may have stayed with you. Use larimar to connect with merfolk, dolphins, or angels. It also supports creative expression.

Larimar is associated with the element water. Its astrological influence comes from the zodiac constellations of Leo and Scorpio.

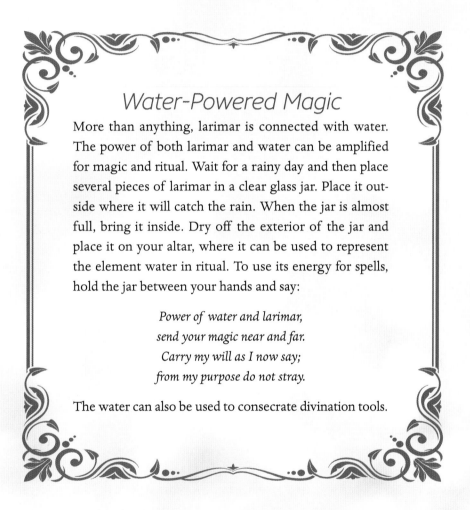

Water-Powered Magic

More than anything, larimar is connected with water. The power of both larimar and water can be amplified for magic and ritual. Wait for a rainy day and then place several pieces of larimar in a clear glass jar. Place it outside where it will catch the rain. When the jar is almost full, bring it inside. Dry off the exterior of the jar and place it on your altar, where it can be used to represent the element water in ritual. To use its energy for spells, hold the jar between your hands and say:

Power of water and larimar,
send your magic near and far.
Carry my will as I now say;
from my purpose do not stray.

The water can also be used to consecrate divination tools.

Lepidolite

Pronunciation: luh-PID-uh-lite *or* LEP-i-duh-lite

Also known as lithia mica

This member of the mica group of industrial minerals caught the eye of mineral collectors in the 1990s.[127] After that, it didn't take long for lepidolite to be used in jewelry and carved into small decorative objects. Meaning scale stone, its name comes from the Greek *lepis* and *lithos* in reference to the way it flakes into thin scales.[128] This mineral was first called *lilalite* because its whitish-pale colors were thought to resemble that of the lily. In the past, it was also called lilac stone. Industrially, lepidolite is a source of lithium carbonate, which is used in pharmaceuticals. This stone is also used in pottery glazes and in the manufacture of heat-resistant glass.

Lepidolite is usually colorless, pale lilac, pale pink, or white, and occasionally gray or yellowish. It is mottled or veined and often has sparkles from tiny flecks of mica. This stone ranges from transparent to opaque. It has a monoclinic inner structure and a pearly or vitreous luster. It fluoresces a beige, green, or yellow color.

This stone is known for its calm, peaceful energy that brings emotions into balance. In addition to relieving stress, it wards off negative energy and provides protection from nightmares. Use it when you need a change in perspective or help in lifting your mood. Lepidolite is instrumental in making changes that bring order and harmony. It also engenders patience. This stone helps to clear the mind and focus energy for psychic and shamanic

127. Oldershaw, *Firefly Guide to Gems*, 149.

128. Eastaugh, et al., *Pigment Compendium*, 236.

work. In spellwork, it aids in attracting love and luck. Also, use it to help manifest what you seek. Its spiritual energy purifies ritual space.

Lepidolite is associated with the element water. Its astrological influence comes from Jupiter, Neptune, and the zodiac constellation of Libra.

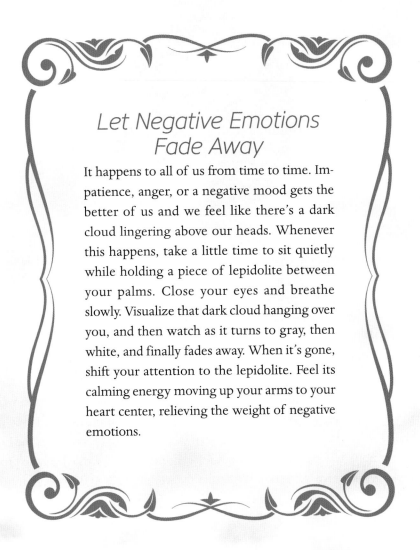

Let Negative Emotions Fade Away

It happens to all of us from time to time. Impatience, anger, or a negative mood gets the better of us and we feel like there's a dark cloud lingering above our heads. Whenever this happens, take a little time to sit quietly while holding a piece of lepidolite between your palms. Close your eyes and breathe slowly. Visualize that dark cloud hanging over you, and then watch as it turns to gray, then white, and finally fades away. When it's gone, shift your attention to the lepidolite. Feel its calming energy moving up your arms to your heart center, relieving the weight of negative emotions.

Lodestone

Pronunciation: LOHD-stone

Also known as magnetite

The earliest mention of lodestone and its magnetic properties was by Greek philosopher and mathematician Thales (c. 624–546 BCE). This stone was considered magical because of its ability to attract or repel pieces of iron. Despite charming stories about the shepherd Magnus, the name *magnetite* was derived from the Magnesia region on the eastern coast of Greece halfway between the cities of Athens and Thessaloniki, where an abundance of lodestone has been found.

While the Chinese used lodestone for a simple type of compass approximately 100 BCE, the first mention of such an invention in Europe did not occur until 1190.[129] In reference to its use for navigation, the name of this stone was derived from the Anglo-Saxon word *lode,* meaning "way" or "path." [130] It was also called way stone. A compass was believed to point north because of an attraction to the North Star, which came to be known as the Lodestar. In China, this stone was called *tzhu shih,* "loving stone," because its magnetic properties represented the powers of attraction.[131] During the Middle Ages in Europe, lodestone was

129. Ronald T. Merrill, Michael W. McElhinny, and Phillip L. McFadden, *The Magnetic Field of the Earth: Paleomagnetism, the Core, and the Deep Mantle* (San Diego, CA: Academic Press, 1998), 3.

130. Richard A. Muller, *Physics and Technology for Future Presidents: An Introduction to the Essential Physics Every World Leader Needs to Know* (Princeton, NJ: Princeton University Press, 2010), 213.

131. Ibid.

used to test a wife's fidelity. An unfaithful wife supposedly fell out of bed if it was placed under her pillow. In addition, lodestone was used medicinally for a range of maladies.

Lodestone is black, dark gray, or reddish brown with black streaks. It is opaque with a metallic or dull luster and has a cubic inner structure.

As expected, lodestone is especially effective when guidance is needed. Its energy is an aid for finding and fine-tuning one's spiritual path. Use it in spells to attract love, luck, or money. In addition, this stone aligns energy and boosts personal strength. Lodestone can be relied upon in situations that require forgiveness and reconciliation, particularly in marriage. It also fosters loyalty in all types of relationships and helps to bind people together. As a guardian, it provides protection no matter where you are—home or traveling. In addition to boosting motivation and confidence, lodestone helps achieve success in meaningful endeavors. With its grounding energy, this stone can provide stability when faced with challenging people or situations.

Lodestone is associated with the elements earth and water. Its astrological influence comes from Venus, the fixed star Polaris, and the zodiac constellation of Virgo. This stone is also associated with the goddess Juno.

Malachite

Pronunciation: MAL-uh-kite

It should come as no surprise that this vivid green stone has a long history of delighting people. The Egyptians were using it by 3000 BCE for jewelry and amulets.[132] They considered it effective as a charm to protect children from evil spirits. In addition to jewelry and amulets, the Greeks and Romans also used it for vases, sculptures, and other decorative objects. In classical and medieval literature, malachite was called chrysocolla, which has caused confusion down through the ages between these two stones. In the past, it was also called molochites.

Since the Bronze Age, powdered malachite has served as a pigment. Both the Egyptians and Assyrians used it for cosmetics. The Egyptians also used it for tomb paintings. As early as the ninth century CE, malachite pigment was used in Chinese paintings and Japanese scrolls and screens.[133] In Europe, it was used from the eighth to the sixteenth century for paintings and illuminated manuscripts.[134] While large slabs of malachite paneled rooms for the Russian tsars, small pieces were cut to make delicate furniture inlay. The name *malachite* was derived from the Greek *malache,* meaning "mallow," in reference to it resembling the color of mallow leaves.[135]

Malachite ranges from light to vivid green with blackish-green banding and from translucent to opaque. It has a monoclinic inner structure and a vitreous or dull luster. Malachite is a stone of communication that aids in personal and business success. Its power

132. Bonewitz, *Smithsonian Nature Guide: Rocks and Minerals*, 82.

133. Eastaugh, et al., *Pigment Compendium*, 249.

134. Ibid.

135. Oldershaw, *Firefly Guide to Gems*, 78.

encompasses everyday situations and spiritual growth. In the home, it brings peace and hope. It also aids in dealing with a death in the family. This stone is instrumental in banishing negativity, avoiding danger, and providing protection, especially for travel. It also aids in navigating life's setbacks and challenges, overcoming obstacles, and solving problems. Use it in spells to increase luck with money, prosperity, and wealth. Malachite aids in developing intuition and psychic skills. It also supports divination and dreamwork.

Malachite is associated with the element earth and the gods Mercury and Njord. Its astrological influence comes from Venus and the zodiac constellations of Capricorn, Libra, Scorpio, and Taurus.

Azurmalachite
Pronunciation: AZ-er-MAL-uh-kite
Also known as azure-malachite and azurite malachite
This stone is a blue and green mix of azurite and malachite. It brings the calming energy and insight of azurite to the power of malachite.

Eilat Stone
Pronunciation: ey-LAHT
This blue-green stone is a mixture of chrysocolla, turquoise, and malachite from the mines near Eilat in southern Israel. When working with it, you may find varying combinations of energy and power.

Peacock Eye
Also known as peacock stone
The banding in this variety of malachite forms patterns of concentric rings that resemble the eyelike markings on peacock feathers. This stone is especially supportive of psychic work and divination.

Moldavite

Pronunciation: MAWL-duh-vite *or* MOHL-duh-vite

Also known as moldovite

Moldavite is a form of natural glass called a tektite. It was once thought to be of extraterrestrial origin, but after intense scrutiny the scientific consensus is that tektites are formed from the melting and rapid cooling of terrestrial rocks that were vaporized by the high-energy impacts of meteorites. Tektites are named for the area where they are found. Discovered in 1787, moldavite was named for the River Moldau in the Czech Republic.[136]

Prized by mineral collectors, both faceted translucent stones and rough opaque ones have made their way into the jewelry market. It is sometimes marketed under the name bohemian chrysolite. In the past, it was called bottle stone because of its color.

Moldavite ranges from bottle green to brownish green and transparent to opaque. It has a vitreous luster. Without an inner structure, it is categorized as amorphous.

Because of its dramatic transformation by a meteorite, moldavite helps to tap into cosmic energy and consciousness for meditation or astral work. Also, use this stone to boost spells, enhance divination, and fine-tune psychic abilities. Moldavite is instrumental for purification, especially in rituals that commemorate any type of new beginning. Also, use this stone to bless and reconsecrate an altar or magic tools. In addition, moldavite aids in recovering from loss and letting go of attachments to things and people. Spiritually, it supports introspection for examining beliefs and fosters insight for finding deeper meaning.

Moldavite is associated with the elements air and fire.

....

136. Ibid., 191.

Moonstone

Also known as adularia moonstone

This gem-quality feldspar is a variety of adularia that exhibits a ghostly silvery or bluish sheen, which was given its own name of adularescence. Capturing the magic of the night sky with a shimmer that seems to move as the stone is rotated, moonstone was regarded as a sacred stone in ancient India. According to folklore, moonstone was used to arouse the passion of lovers. Not surprisingly, the Greeks and Romans associated this stone with lunar deities. French mineralogist and geologist Jean-Claude Delametherie (1743–1817) gave this mineral the name of *hecatolite* in reference to Hecate. In the past, moonstone from Sri Lanka was called Ceylon opal. This name is still used to pass moonstone off as a more expensive stone.

According to Roman legend, the brightness of this stone waxed and waned along with the phases of the moon. By the Middle Ages, moonstone was said to be most effective as a love charm on the waxing moon and to foretell the future on the waning moon. Although the Romans used it for jewelry, the popularity of moonstone soared to new heights in Art Nouveau jewelry during the early twentieth century.

The base color of moonstone can be blue, brown, colorless, green, orange, pink, white, or yellow. Moonstone has a monoclinic inner structure and a vitreous or dull luster. It ranges from transparent to translucent and has a weak bluish and orange fluorescence. Moonstone's ethereal adularescence is emphasized when cut en cabochon. This cut can sometimes bring out a cat's-eye effect or a two-rayed star.

As its name implies, moonstone is instrumental for working with lunar energy and magic. It aids in strengthening psychic skills, especially clairvoyance. It supports divination and dreamwork and is instrumental for contacting spirits. This stone is the perfect love charm because it also fosters friendship and loyalty. Use moonstone to overcome obstacles and to release what you no longer need. Its calming energy unites body, mind, and spirit, promoting healing and balance. When seeking wisdom, moonstone can provide guidance in all aspects of life. Use it to fine-tune intuition and to tap into your well of creativity. It is instrumental in spells for abundance and fertility.

Moonstone is associated with the element water. Its astrological influence comes from the moon and the zodiac constellations of Cancer, Gemini, Libra, Pisces, and Scorpio. This stone is also associated with the goddesses Arianrhod, Diana, Hecate, Isis, Luna, Rhiannon, and Selene.

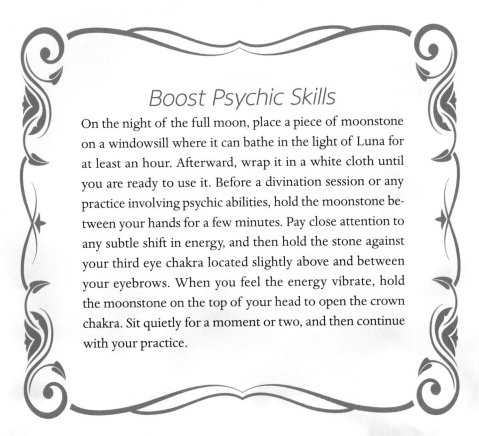

Boost Psychic Skills

On the night of the full moon, place a piece of moonstone on a windowsill where it can bathe in the light of Luna for at least an hour. Afterward, wrap it in a white cloth until you are ready to use it. Before a divination session or any practice involving psychic abilities, hold the moonstone between your hands for a few minutes. Pay close attention to any subtle shift in energy, and then hold the stone against your third eye chakra located slightly above and between your eyebrows. When you feel the energy vibrate, hold the moonstone on the top of your head to open the crown chakra. Sit quietly for a moment or two, and then continue with your practice.

Obsidian

Pronunciation: **ub-SID-ee-uhn**

Obsidian is a natural glass that forms when lava rapidly cools. It was valued during the Stone Age for utensils and weapons because of its hardness and for the razor-sharp edges that can be created when the stone is broken in a particular way. Around 10,000 BCE, it was an important trade item in early Neolithic cultures.[137] The Egyptians fashioned obsidian into knives and sickle-shaped blades. They also used it for beads, scarabs, cosmetic containers, and other small everyday objects. It was commonly used as inlay for the eyes of statues and death masks. Like the Egyptians, the Assyrians used obsidian for utilitarian tools, decorative objects, and jewelry.

Pliny is credited with naming this stone for fellow Roman Obsius, who reputedly brought pieces of obsidian home from his travels in Ethiopia. The Romans used this stone for amulets, jewelry, and other decorative objects. On the other side of the world, the Aztec used obsidian for sacrificial knives. Throughout Mexico, knives and arrowheads of obsidian were crafted well into the sixteenth century.[138] In Europe during the Middles Ages, flat slabs of highly polished obsidian were fashioned into scrying mirrors. John Dee reputedly used one from time to time.

Although usually black, obsidian can be brown, dark gray, green, or even reddish. It ranges from transparent to opaque and has a vitreous luster. Without an inner structure, it is classified as amorphous. Occasionally when cut en cabochon, obsidian can exhibit a cat's-eye effect.

....

137. Richard L. Smith, *Premodern Trade in World History* (New York: Routledge, 2009), 19.

138. Schumann, *Handbook of Rocks Minerals & Gemstones*, 238.

Obsidian is protective against aggressive people. Deeply associated with the emotions, it provides protection, especially when confronted with obstacles. This stone helps cultivate connections with other people and extend community relations. When appropriate, use obsidian in binding spells. Also, use it to attract luck and foster peace. In addition, obsidian is instrumental for developing magical skills. It brings clarity for divination and interpreting messages. This stone is an aid for keeping life in balance during the process of transformation.

Obsidian is associated with the element fire and the deities Athena, Felicitas, Lugh, the Morrigan, and Pele. Its astrological association comes from Pluto, Saturn, and the zodiac constellations of Capricorn, Sagittarius, and Scorpio.

Apache Tear

Pronunciation: **uh-PACH-ee teer**

This name is given to small, rounded pebbles of obsidian, which Native Americans used for jewelry and amulets. According to legend, apache tears are found where Native Americans died. Because of this association, this stone aids in dealing with the death of a loved one. Its grounding energy helps build good karma and protect anyone wearing it from negative energy and danger. Use it as a token of forgiveness to foster peace. Apache tear also supports psychic work. Its astrological influence comes from Saturn and the zodiac constellation of Aries.

Rainbow Obsidian

Also known as iris obsidian

The flowing bands of iridescent colors in this stone are created by inclusions that were oriented to the direction of lava flow as it cooled. These inclusions produce a unique rainbow effect, depending on the angle from which the stone is viewed. Expanding awareness and heightening the senses, this stone aids in connecting with the natural world. It also fosters connections with other people, helping to build healthy relationships and strong community. Rainbow obsidian is associated with the goddess Iris.

Snowflake Obsidian

Also known as flowering obsidian

Small, white cristobalite crystals trapped in the layers of lava as it cooled produce the snowflake-like patterns in this stone. Snowflake obsidian is especially effective for protection against people or situations that drain your energy. Use it to focus energy for magic work and to remove anything unwanted from your life.

Onyx

Pronunciation: ON-iks *or* OH-niks

Also known as true onyx

Confusion about onyx dates back to the conflicting information from ancient writers and continues today with the name often used only for completely black stones. Onyx actually consists of alternating layers of black and white. *Onyx* is a Greek word meaning "fingernail" or "claw." [139] Although the stone's resemblance to a fingernail is often mentioned, depending on how the stone is cut I think the white streaks on black resemble claws or claw marks more than fingernails.

Onyx beads have been found in Egyptian graves dating to approximately 3100 BCE.[140] This stone continued to be popular for a range of decorative objects throughout the Egyptian dynasties. A small piece of carved onyx found in the ruins of Knossos on Crete depicts the Goddess as a bee. The Greeks and Romans carved onyx into vases, bowls, cups, and jewelry. It was with onyx that the Romans brought cameo carving to a level of perfection. In addition, this stone was worn as a charm to gain favor. Although at one time it was believed that onyx caused discord between people because of the abrupt changes in color, this idea did not dampen the stone's popularity.

Onyx is black or blackish brown with straight, parallel bands of white. It ranges from translucent to opaque and has a vitreous or waxy luster. Its inner structure is trigonal.

....

139. Oldershaw, *Firefly Guide to Gems*, 167.

140. Rapp, *Archaeomineralogy*, 95.

With strong defensive energy, onyx provides protection against black magic and hexes. It also guards against negativity in relationships and strengthens bonds between people, especially in marriage. The energy of this stone supports decision-making and dealing with problems. While it is an aid for dreamwork, onyx also helps to ward off nightmares. Fostering personal growth, this stone builds confidence and provides support when facing fears. Use it to raise energy for ritual and in spells to bind. Onyx also strengthens willpower and discipline to manifest desires and goals.

Onyx is associated with the element fire and the deities Mars, the Morrigan, and Venus. Its astrological influence comes from Mars, Mercury, Saturn, the fixed star Ala Corvi, and the zodiac constellations of Aquarius, Capricorn, and Leo.

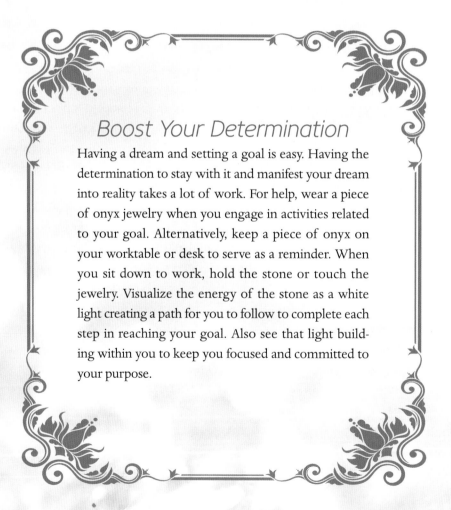

Boost Your Determination

Having a dream and setting a goal is easy. Having the determination to stay with it and manifest your dream into reality takes a lot of work. For help, wear a piece of onyx jewelry when you engage in activities related to your goal. Alternatively, keep a piece of onyx on your worktable or desk to serve as a reminder. When you sit down to work, hold the stone or touch the jewelry. Visualize the energy of the stone as a white light creating a path for you to follow to complete each step in reaching your goal. Also see that light building within you to keep you focused and committed to your purpose.

Opal

Pronunciation: OH-puhl

The earliest use of opal dates to approximately 4000 BCE as evidenced by artifacts found by famed archaeologist Louis Leakey.[141] Opal was highly prized by the Greeks and Romans, who valued it more than diamond. The Romans referred to white opal as *cupid paederos,* "cupid stone," and considered it a symbol of hope.[142] During the Middle Ages, some people regarded opal as lucky. However, according to other folklore this stone was considered bad luck because of a belief that if the appearance of an opal changed its owner would die. Containing up to 10 percent water, opals can change. In fact, heating or cracking can evaporate the water and change a transparent opal into opaque.

Over the centuries, opal drifted in and out of favor. Because of its fragile nature—which often resulted in stones being broken or cracked—it fell out of favor in the nineteenth century. Despite its reputation for bad luck, Queen Victoria wore opal jewelry. However, it is not recorded whether she continued to do so after an opal brooch caused a wardrobe malfunction.

Sources differ as to the origin of the Latin name *opalus.* According to some scholars, it was derived from the Sanskrit *upala,* meaning "precious stone." [143] According to others, it came from the Greek *opallios,* which had evolved from two root words, one meaning "seeing" (also the root of the English word optical) and the second meaning "other." [144] "Seeing

141. Allan W. Eckert, *The World of Opals* (New York: John Wiley & Sons, 1997), 53.

142. Grande and Augustyn, *Gems and Gemstones,* 232.

143. Thomas, *Gemstones,* 181.

144. Eckert, *The World of Opals,* 56.

other" could refer to the play of light that some opals exhibit. The nickname potch is an Australian mining term for common opals.

Opals can be nearly black, blue, brown, colorless, gray, green, orange, red, milky white, or yellow. They range from transparent to opaque with a vitreous, greasy, or occasionally pearly luster. Lacking an inner structure, they are classified as amorphous. There are three categories of opals: precious, fire, and common. Precious opals exhibit an effect called play of color, which is a rainbowlike iridescence that changes with the angle of view. Named for their rich hues, fire opals are colorful but do not exhibit a play of color. Usually opaque, common opals have their own special effect called opalescence, which is a slightly milky-blue or pearly appearance.

Opal is a stone of adaptability that aids in dealing with major obstacles and adjusting to changes. It also aids in keeping emotions balanced. This stone adds power to magic work by clearing the mind and focusing willpower. Use it in spells for love, luck, or prosperity. Opal also fosters hope. This stone supports psychic abilities and astral work. Use it for personal insight and when seeking wisdom.

Opal is associated with the elements air and water. Its astrological influence comes from Mercury, the moon, and the zodiac constellations of Aquarius, Cancer, Libra, Sagittarius, Scorpio, Taurus, and Virgo. This stone is also associated with the god Cupid.

Black Opal

This variety of precious opal can be dark gray, dark blue, dark green, or grayish black. It exhibits a play of color. Especially fine black opals can be as expensive as diamonds. Black opal enhances and strengthens spells by drawing down the energy of the moon. It also stimulates cosmic awareness. Use it in situations to assert authority as well as self-discipline.

Fire Opal

Named for its fiery colors, this stone can be brownish red, orange red, or yellowish red. It does not exhibit a play of color. This stone is instrumental for stirring energy and enhancing vitality. Use it in spells to stoke passion or attract money. Fire opal is associated with the element fire and its astrological influence comes from the zodiac constellation of Aries.

White Opal

Also known as milk opal and porcelain opal

This variety is one of the most plentiful of the opaque common opals. Opalescence is easily seen in this stone. Its soothing, calming energy is especially helpful when dealing with any type of change. The color of milk, white opal offers nurturing energy and growth.

Pearl

Pronunciation: **purl**

For thousands of years, pearls have been regarded as one of the most valuable gems. Along with mussel shells, they served as bling during the Paleolithic. Native Americans used freshwater pearls as evidenced in ancient burial mounds. By 2500 BCE, the pearl trade was well established in China.[145] The Chinese were the first to culture pearls in the twelfth or thirteenth century; however, it did not become a worldwide industry until the twentieth century.[146] While the most prized pearls come from oysters in the genus *Pinctada*, giant clams, giant conchs, and freshwater clams and mussels also produce them.

Pearls were seldom used in Egypt until Ptolemaic times, circa 300 BCE.[147] Although infrequently used for jewelry by the Greeks, an inscribed pearl pin was discovered, quite appropriately, in a temple of Aphrodite, who, according to legend, was born from the sea. In India, the statues of Hindu deities were often adorned with pearls because, according to legend, supreme god Vishnu created these precious gems. The Etruscans used pearls in jewelry, as did the Romans, but only for people of high rank. By the Renaissance, almost everyone was wearing them.

145. Schumann, *Gemstones of the World*, 263.

146. Oldershaw, *Firefly Guide to Gems*, 195.

147. Rapp, *Archaeomineralogy*, 107.

The name *pearl* was derived from either the Old French *perle* or the medieval Latin *perla*. The latter name could have had its roots in the earlier Latin *pera*, "stone," or *perna*, meaning "leg," in reference to the leglike appearance of a mollusk's extended foot.[148]

Though they are most often white, pearls can be bluish white, pinkish white, yellowish white, reddish, or blackish gray with a pearly luster, of course. Their shape can be round, oval, pear-shaped, or an irregular form. Pearls are translucent to opaque with an ortho-rhombic inner structure.

This gemstone is especially potent for attracting love and working moon magic. It is also instrumental for fertility, luck, and money spells. Pearls bring clarity to situations and provide guidance when meeting challenges. Use them when seeking peace, emotional balance, and of course, wisdom. Pearl stimulates creativity and supports spirituality. As a symbol of faith and purity, it aids in consecrating and purifying ritual space.

Pearl is associated with the element water. Its astrological influence comes from the moon, Venus, and the zodiac constellations of Aquarius, Cancer, Gemini, Pisces, and Scorpio. This gem is also associated with the deities Aphrodite, Diana, Freya, Hecate, Isis, Kuan Yin, Lakshmi, Neptune, Poseidon, Sarasvati, Venus, and Vishnu.

---

148. R. A. Donkin, *Beyond Price: Pearls and Pearl-fishing: Origins to the Age of Discoveries* (Philadelphia: The American Philosophical Society, 1998), 259.

Peridot

Pronunciation: **PER-ih-doh**

Also known as chrysolite and olivine

Born of fire from volcanoes and occasionally meteorites, peridot is a stone that min-eralogists do not agree upon. While some sources regard the name olivine as a syn-onym for peridot, others consider peridot a type of olivine. Likewise, the name chrysolite is sometimes regarded as a synonym for peridot and at other times a reference to a more yellowish-green olivine. In the past, the name chrysolite was commonly used for other stones of similar color. Even the name peridot has a couple of different potential sources. It may have come from the Old French *peritot,* meaning "gold," because its color can be somewhat golden.[149] Another contender is the Arabic *faridat,* meaning "gem." [150]

The Egyptians mined peridot from the volcanic Red Sea island of Zebirget—also known as Zabargad and St. John's Island—and used it for trade around the Mediterranean region. For themselves, the Egyptians used this stone for beads, pendants, and amulets. According to Pliny, Zebirget was known as *Topazos* and to the Romans peridot was known as *topazin.* In addition, peridot was sometimes referred to as evening emerald because it maintained its color and did not darken as the sunlight faded. This stone became popular in northern Europe when Christian crusaders took it home with them after their travels in the Middle East.

Peridot is usually found as irregularly shaped grains and rarely as crystals. It is yellowish green, olive green, or brownish green with a greasy or vitreous luster. It is transparent and

....

149. Oldershaw, *Firefly Guide to Gems*, 93.

150. Nicholson and Shaw, *Ancient Egyptian Materials and Technology*, 47.

has an orthorhombic inner structure. This stone is weakly trichroic. Although rare, peridot can exhibit a cat's-eye effect or a star.

Peridot stimulates and empowers psychic abilities, especially clairvoyance, and gives an added boost to spellwork. Use it for spells of prosperity that bring abundance and comfort to your life. Because of its fiery nature, this stone is ideal for purifying ritual space. It is instrumental to ward off negativity or purge whatever you want to remove from your life. Following this, it fosters growth and renewal. The calming energy of peridot is especially helpful for subduing anger and healing damaged relationships. Fostering patience, this stone brings peace and happiness. Also, use it to connect with the fairy folk.

Peridot is associated with the elements earth and fire. Its astrological influence comes from Mercury, the sun, Venus, the fixed star Vega, and the zodiac constellations of Leo, Sagittarius, Scorpio, and Virgo. This stone is also associated with the goddesses Banba, Brigid, and Pele.

Petrified Wood

Also known as fossilized wood

While petrified wood can appear dull and rough, it can be polished to an almost gemlike quality. Petrified wood is found worldwide, especially in areas where volcanoes have erupted. It is created when trees are quickly covered with sediment, which prevents the plant material from decaying. Over time, minerals such as calcite, chalcedony, or jasper preserve the shape and structure of the wood, right down to tree rings and wood grain.

During the Neolithic period, petrified wood was used as rough hammer stones. Although it was readily found in the Egyptian desert, petrified wood was not used for carvings during pharaonic times because it was too hard to cut. In North America, large pieces were used for building material. Smaller pieces were chipped and used for arrowheads and other tools. Ancient artifacts of petrified wood have also been found in Australia and Ireland.

With better tools for cutting, petrified wood was fashioned into jewelry and other ornaments in eighteenth-century Germany. Wood from the petrified forest near Chemnitz, Germany, came to be known as star stones because of the starlike pattern found in cross sections of tree trunks and branches.

Petrified wood can be various shades of blackish brown, bluish, brown, gray, reddish, or yellow. It is dull and opaque and has a trigonal inner structure.

The energy of petrified wood provides a connection with ancestors and aids in past-life work. It is also instrumental when seeking ancient wisdom. Use it to ground energy after ritual or magic work. In addition, use petrified wood in spells to help you reach your goals. It aids in surmounting obstacles and provides strength when dealing with problems. Petrified wood fosters harmony and helps bring people together as a community. This stone's healing energy reduces stress and supports renewal.

Petrified wood is associated with the element earth. Its astrological influence comes from the zodiac constellation of Leo.

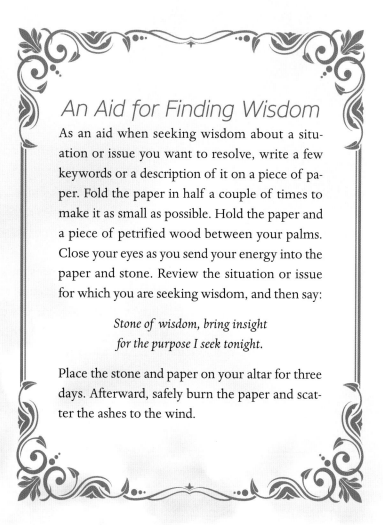

An Aid for Finding Wisdom

As an aid when seeking wisdom about a situation or issue you want to resolve, write a few keywords or a description of it on a piece of paper. Fold the paper in half a couple of times to make it as small as possible. Hold the paper and a piece of petrified wood between your palms. Close your eyes as you send your energy into the paper and stone. Review the situation or issue for which you are seeking wisdom, and then say:

Stone of wisdom, bring insight
for the purpose I seek tonight.

Place the stone and paper on your altar for three days. Afterward, safely burn the paper and scatter the ashes to the wind.

Phenacite

Pronunciation: **FEN-uh-site**

Also known as phenakite

Although it was recognized as a new mineral when it was discovered in 1811 in the Ural Mountains of southern Russia, phenacite was initially regarded as a variety of white tourmaline. Finnish mineralogist Nils Nordenskjold named it in 1833 from the Greek *phenakos,* meaning "deceiver," because it is so easily mistaken for quartz or white tourmaline.[151] It is mined mainly for its beryllium content; mineral collectors find this stone interesting for its intergrown twin crystals. Colorless phenacite is sometimes faceted into jewelry.

Usually colorless or white, phenacite can have a tinge of blue, brown, pink, or yellow. It ranges from transparent to translucent. This stone has a vitreous luster and a trigonal inner structure. Some translucent stones can exhibit a cat's-eye or four-rayed star when cut en cabochon. Phenacite is dichroic, appearing colorless or orange yellow from different angles. It fluoresces pale green to shades of blue.

Phenacite is instrumental for communicating and working with spirit guides. Its receptive energy aids in interpreting messages from them. Phenacite also helps to contact the fairy realm and angels. This stone is a powerful ally for dreamwork and psychic work. It also helps to fine-tune intuition and provides psychic protection. Use phenacite to cleanse the aura before astral work and as a talisman for guidance during mundane travel. This stone helps to activate and move energy for ritual and magic work. Also, use phenacite for introspection when seeking self-knowledge.

....

151. Richard C. Ropp, *Encyclopedia of the Alkaline Earth Compounds* (Oxford, England: Elsevier, 2013), 380.

Pyrite

Pronunciation: PIE-rite

Also known as fool's gold and monkey gold

Pyrite is one of the most common and widely distributed sulfide minerals. Frequently forming with gold, it is often mistaken for that valuable metal. In the past, it was smelted to extract gold and sulfur. Used to start fires since ancient times, its name means firestone from the Greek words *pyr,* meaning "fire," and the suffix *"ite"* from *lithos* "stone." [152] Centuries later, pyrite was used like flint in flintlock rifles to ignite gunpowder, which earned it the nickname of thunderbolts.

Pyrite beads have been found in ancient Egyptian and Iranian dwellings and graves. The Greeks and Romans used it for jewelry and amulets. Pyrite was included in Chinese mineral remedies as noted in the Shen Nong pharmacopeias that date to approximately 100–180 CE.[153]

In addition to jewelry and decorative mosaics, the Inca made polished plates of pyrite to use as mirrors. They also used pyrite in religious ceremonies and burials. Native Americans made amulets with it. From the Dark Ages to the Renaissance in Europe, pyrite was known as *marcasite,* the Arabic or Moorish name for a similar mineral. While the real marcasite has the same chemical composition as pyrite, it has a different crystal structure. Pyrite became popular for jewelry in Victorian times, but was still wrongly called marcasite.

Pyrite is opaque and brassy yellow with a metallic luster. It has a cubic inner structure. Twinning pyrite crystals are called iron crosses. This mineral sometimes occurs as

---

152. Charles A. Sorrell, *Rocks and Minerals: A Guide to Field Identification* (New York: St. Martin's Press, 2001), 6.

153. Rapp, *Archaeomineralogy,* 11.

inclusions in emeralds and opals, giving them a light golden sparkle. Lapis lazuli is usually streaked or flecked with pyrite.

This stone aids in focusing energy and keeping it grounded during divination and psychic work. Use pyrite in spells to strengthen your willpower and manifest intentions, especially where money is concerned. This stone is instrumental in discerning truth and provides protection from deceit. It is especially helpful to intuit appropriate information for making important decisions. Pyrite is also effective for tapping into deeply held memories.

Pyrite is associated with the element fire. Its astrological influence comes from Mars and the zodiac constellation of Taurus.

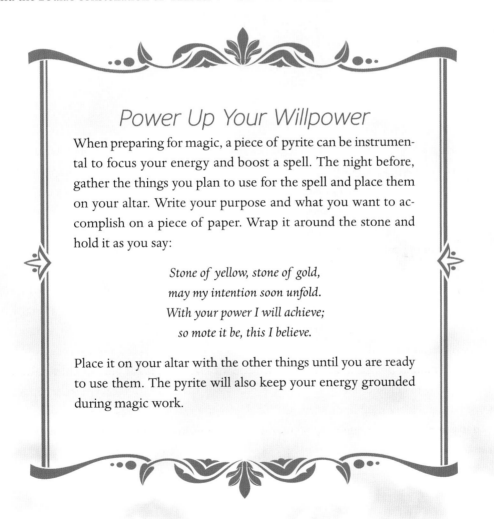

Power Up Your Willpower

When preparing for magic, a piece of pyrite can be instrumental to focus your energy and boost a spell. The night before, gather the things you plan to use for the spell and place them on your altar. Write your purpose and what you want to accomplish on a piece of paper. Wrap it around the stone and hold it as you say:

Stone of yellow, stone of gold,
may my intention soon unfold.
With your power I will achieve;
so mote it be, this I believe.

Place it on your altar with the other things until you are ready to use them. The pyrite will also keep your energy grounded during magic work.

Quartz

Pronunciation: **kwartz**

Quartz is one of the most common minerals—second only to feldspar—and it can be found almost everywhere on earth. There are two major varieties of quartz. The macrocrystalline quartz group includes the ones we usually think of as quartz such as amethyst, ametrine, citrine, hawk's-eye, smoky, rose, white, and tiger's-eye. This group also includes aventurine. The second group is called cryptocrystalline, which means the stones have microscopically small crystals. This group includes agate, chalcedony, carnelian, jasper, and sard.

The name of this mineral comes from *querkluftertz*, a German miner's term from the Middle Ages meaning "cross-vein ore," which was condensed to *quererz* and finally to quartz.[154] Use of quartz dates to the Paleolithic period, when it was employed as a tool to make tools. In North America, quartz was used for ritual purposes and everyday objects, such as projectile points. The Greeks and Romans used quartz for beads, seal stones, and decorative and ceremonial objects. In China, it was used for large carvings and spheres. Quartz was widely used during the Middle Ages for a range of things from sacred objects to secular items, such as gaming boards. Today it is an important mineral in the glass, ceramics, and electronics industries.

....
154. Richard V. Gaines, et al., *Dana's New Mineralogy*, 1573.

Quartz can be bluish white, brown, colorless, gray blue, green, pink, purple, rose, violet, white, or yellow. It ranges from transparent to opaque. Its inner structure is trigonal and it can have a greasy or vitreous luster. Single crystals are sometimes doubly terminated. While intergrown twins are common, quartz crystals more often form clusters.

Quartz is a strongly grounding stone that amplifies and focuses energy. It is helpful when dealing with issues because it brings clarity to the situation or problem at hand. Use it to maintain stability when making changes in your life and when seeking wisdom. Quartz amplifies energy for spells and psychic work. In addition, it is an aid for communication on all levels.

In general, quartz is associated with the elements fire and water. Its astrological influence comes from the moon, the sun, Uranus, and all of the zodiac constellations. Quartz is also associated with the goddess Hecate.

See separate entries for amethyst, ametrine, citrine, hawk's-eye, Herkimer diamond, rose quartz, smoky quartz, tiger's-eye, and white quartz.

Clear Quartz

Also known as rock crystal

As its name implies, clear quartz is colorless and transparent, although it can be translucent. It has a vitreous luster. In addition to being part of prehistoric tool kits, this variety of quartz has been associated with healing and divination for thousands of years. These crystals were integral to shamanism almost worldwide. Regarded as "living rock" or "solid light," they were power objects that represented the shaman's wisdom.[155]

The Mesopotamians used clear quartz for beads and cylinder seals, and the Assyrians carved large pieces into vessels and bowls. In medieval times, quartz crystal balls were believed to impart clairvoyance and other mystical powers. Through the Middle Ages and beyond, this stone was commonly used for carved ornaments, chandelier

155. James L. Pearson, *Shamanism and the Ancient Mind: A Cognitive Approach to Archaeology* (Walnut Creek, CA: Altamira Press, 2002), 142.

drops, and crystal balls. The popularity of crystal vessels surged in the late sixteenth century and gave rise to the name crystal for fine glassware.[156]

This quartz is a powerhouse for stimulating energy and boosting spells. It provides protection from hexes and enchantments. It is also effective in banishing spells to release unwanted spirits and any form of negative energy. Use it to foster receptive energy and to clear the mind for divination, dream and psychic work, and of course, shamanic work. This stone also aids in making decisions. Clear quartz is instrumental for any type of purification, including the aura, after which meaningful renewal can occur. It also raises awareness and lifts spiritual practice to a new level. This stone strengthens community, family bonds, and connection with departed ancestors. It is an offering welcomed by fairies. This stone is associated with the element air. Its astrological influence comes from the Pleiades fixed stars and the zodiac constellations of Aquarius, Aries, Cancer, Capricorn, and Gemini.

Rutilated Quartz

Pronunciation: ROO-tuh-lay-tid *or* ROOT-uh-lay-tid

Ranging from transparent to translucent, this variety of colorless, white, or sometimes smoky quartz has large inclusions of golden or red needles of the mineral rutile. In the past, stones with needles of rutile, tourmaline, or goethite crossing at 60-degree angles were called sagenite, from the Latin *sagena,* meaning "net." [157] Other old names for rutilated quartz include arrows of love, cupid's darts, needle stone, and Venus hair. Whenever hematite is included in a stone, the rutile needles radiate out from the center in a cross or star pattern. Such a gem is called star rutile.

Rutilated quartz is an energizer that increases and strengthens willpower. It also gives a boost to inspiration for creativity and finding the right outlet for talent. This stone aids in recognizing and overcoming fears. Rutilated quartz is associated with the element earth. Its astrological influence comes from the zodiac constellation of Scorpio.

156. Rapp, *Archaeomineralogy*, 90.

157. Robert L. Bates and Julia A. Jackson, eds., *Dictionary of Geological Terms* (New York: Anchor Press, 1984), 442.

Tourmalated Quartz

Pronunciation: TOOR-muh-lay-tid

Similar to its rutilated cousin, this stone is a variety of colorless or white quartz, but its inclusions are splinters or needlelike crystals of schorl (black tourmaline). Tourmalated quartz is instrumental for astral work because it keeps the physical body grounded and aids in returning to the mundane world. Use it for grounding energy when engaging in psychic work and after ritual. This stone fosters balance and helps us accept who we are—both light and dark sides. It also protects against negative energy. Tourmalated quartz is associated with the elements air and water. Its astrological influence comes from Pluto and the zodiac constellation of Capricorn.

Rhodochrosite

Pronunciation: **roe-duh-CROW-site**

Also known as Inca rose and raspberry spar

The name of this stone comes from the Greek *rhodon,* meaning "rose," and possibly *chroma,* "color," or *kirrós,* "orangy."[158] First described in 1813 by German mineralogist Johann Hausmann (1782–1859), rhodochrosite received little attention outside the mineralogy world.[159] However, when concentrically banded pieces called Inca rose were introduced to the public in the 1930s, it became popular as an ornamental stone for decorative objects and figurines.[160] The roselike pattern of Inca rose is revealed when a stalagmite or stalactite of rhodochrosite is cut in cross-section. These are only found in a silver mine in Argentina that the Inca abandoned in the thirteenth century.[161] Based on the word dialogue, this stone was formerly called dialogite because for a time its composition was so often debated among mineralogists. Rhodochrosite was also called manganese spar.

Although raspberry red and pink are the most common colors, rhodochrosite can be bright red, brownish or yellowish, salmon or light pink, or even orange red. It ranges from transparent to opaque. Rhodochrosite has a vitreous luster and a trigonal inner structure.

158. Oldershaw, *Firefly Guide to Gems,* 73; J. P. Mallory and D. Q. Adams, *The Oxford Introduction to Proto-Indo-European and the Proto-Indo-European World* (Oxford, England: Oxford University Press, 2013), 334.

159. Kimberly Knox and Bryan K. Lees, "The Gem Rhodochrosite from the Sweet Home Mine, Colorado," *Gems and Gemology,* vol. 33, no. 2 (Summer 1997): 122.

160. Oldershaw, *Firefly Guide to Gems,* 73.

161. Schumann, *Gemstones of the World,* 184.

Transparent crystals are rare and highly sought after by collectors. Inca rose is multicolored with marbled veins that often run in zigzag bands or concentric rings.

Because of its color, rhodochrosite has been associated with love. It engenders love on all levels and gently balances the emotions. When friendships hit a rough patch, this stone aids in fostering forgiveness and compassion. It also helps to rebuild fidelity. Rhodochrosite provides support and stability during times of transition. If you need to get energy moving in your home, use rhodochrosite to gently activate it. Use this stone in spells to invite abundance and comfort into your life. Rhodochrosite also fosters peace.

Rhodochrosite is associated with the element fire. Its astrological influence comes from Mars, Mercury, Venus, and the zodiac constellations of Leo and Scorpio.

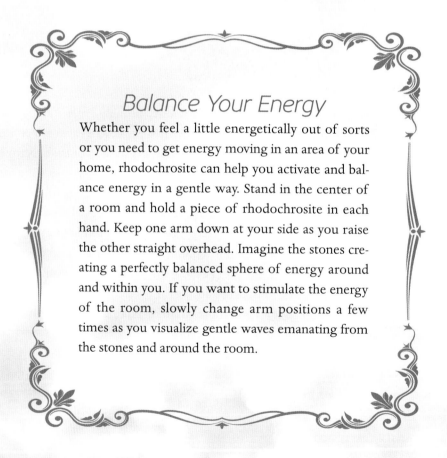

Balance Your Energy

Whether you feel a little energetically out of sorts or you need to get energy moving in an area of your home, rhodochrosite can help you activate and balance energy in a gentle way. Stand in the center of a room and hold a piece of rhodochrosite in each hand. Keep one arm down at your side as you raise the other straight overhead. Imagine the stones creating a perfectly balanced sphere of energy around and within you. If you want to stimulate the energy of the room, slowly change arm positions a few times as you visualize gentle waves emanating from the stones and around the room.

Rhodonite

Pronunciation: **ROE-duhn-ite** *or* **RODE-uhn-ite**

Like rhodochrosite, this stone takes its name from the Greek *rhodon,* meaning "rose," because of its color.[162] Although their names and colors are similar, rhodonite can be distinguished from rhodochrosite by black veining that forms weblike patterns. First discovered in 1795 in the Ural Mountains, it became one of the most popular decorative stones in Russia.[163] Rhodonite was used for jewelry boxes, bowls, furniture, and wall tiles. It was also carved into egg shapes and given as gifts at Easter. By 1830, rhodonite was also found in Massachusetts.[164] It has been called the stone of peace for its reputed healing properties.

Rhodonite is usually a mottled rose pink to dark red or orange red color. It is opaque with black veins called *dendrites,* which are created by inclusions that form branching, treelike patterns. Although rare, this mineral can produce transparent to semiopaque crystals with a deep red color that almost rivals ruby. Rhodonite has a triclinic inner structure and a pearly or vitreous luster.

Because of its rose color, rhodonite has been associated with love, fertility, and marriage. It is effective for drawing people closer together. This stone fosters patience, fidelity, and forgiveness. Its association with love also pertains to self-respect and confidence. It

162. Oldershaw, *Firefly Guide to Gems,* 73.

163. Joel A. Bartsch, *Kremlin Gold: 1000 Years of Russian Gems and Jewels* (New York: Abrams, 2000), 151.

164. Cristofono, *Rockhounding New England,* 7.

is well known for its healing properties. As a stone of peace, it attracts happiness to the home and cooperation in the community. This calming stone relieves anxiety and stress. Although its energy is gentle, rhodonite is effective to boost banishing spells. It can also help in meeting challenges.

Rhodonite is associated with the element fire. Its astrological influence comes from Mars and the zodiac constellation of Taurus.

Fowlerite

Pronunciation: **FOWL-er-ite**

This name is given to the brownish or yellowish variety of rhodonite. Use it to invite warmth and happiness to a relationship and stimulate renewal when needed. Fowlerite is especially helpful when recovering from a broken relationship.

Rose Quartz

This stone is the most popular variety of quartz. In early dynastic Egypt, approximately 3000 BCE, it was occasionally carved for funerary vessels.[165] Rose quartz beads were found in Assyrian tombs dating from 1400 to 1300 BCE.[166] The Assyrians used this stone for cylinder seals. One such seal from Babylon was inscribed to the supreme deity Enlil and his wife Ninlil. Rose quartz has been used for beads, figurines, vases, and a range of other decorative objects in Europe and China. According to geologist George Rapp, rose quartz may be the stone that Pliny called *anteros*, which also had the nickname Venus's eyelid.[167]

Rose quartz is usually a milky pale pink and often crackled. It may occasionally have a tinge of violet. This stone ranges from semitransparent to translucent. It has a greasy or vitreous luster and a trigonal inner structure. Because rose quartz is heat sensitive, its color can fade. Although weak, its fluorescence is dark violet. Stones with tiny rutile needles can produce a starlike effect when cut en cabochon. Crystal formations and almost colorless, semitransparent stones are rare.

Rose quartz is associated with romance, love, sex, and fertility. Its warmth aids in healing emotional turmoil and reconciling relationships. This stone dispels loneliness and opens the heart to compassion and friendship. It fosters acceptance and heals heartbreak. Use this stone to improve respect and self-image. Breaking through negative energy, rose

165. Tom Jackson, *What's that Rock or Mineral? A Beginners Guide* (New York: DK Publishing, 2001), 53.

166. Prudence O. Harper, et al., eds., *Assyrian Origins: Discoveries at Ashur on the Tigris* (New York: The Metropolitan Museum of Art, 1995), 97.

167. Rapp, *Archaeomineralogy*, 92.

quartz releases stress bringing comfort, happiness, and harmony. It aids in dealing with aggression. The calming energy of this stone relieves sorrow after the death of a loved one. It strengthens faith and brings us closer to the power and wisdom of the Divine.

Rose quartz is associated with the deities Angus, Enlil, Ninlil, and Venus. Its astrological influence comes from Venus and the zodiac constellations of Cancer, Capricorn, Libra, and Taurus.

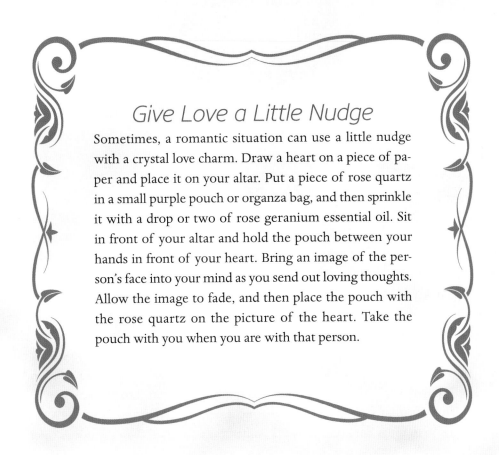

Give Love a Little Nudge

Sometimes, a romantic situation can use a little nudge with a crystal love charm. Draw a heart on a piece of paper and place it on your altar. Put a piece of rose quartz in a small purple pouch or organza bag, and then sprinkle it with a drop or two of rose geranium essential oil. Sit in front of your altar and hold the pouch between your hands in front of your heart. Bring an image of the person's face into your mind as you send out loving thoughts. Allow the image to fade, and then place the pouch with the rose quartz on the picture of the heart. Take the pouch with you when you are with that person.

Ruby

Pronunciation: ROO-bee

R uby is the red variety of corundum that takes its name from the Latin *ruber* meaning "red."[168] It was not until 1800 that ruby and sapphire were recognized as separate corundum species.[169] Rubies have been mined in Sri Lanka for more than two thousand years; however, the best stones come from Myanmar.

Ruby was known in India by the Sanskrit name *ratnaraj,* "king of gems," and in Myanmar as *ma naw ma ya,* "desire-fulfilling stone."[170] While the name carbunculus or carbuncle was used as a synonym for ruby, it also referred to red garnet and red spinel. In the past, ruby was also called oriental ruby, red corundum, red sapphire, rubine, and true ruby.

The Romans favored deep red garnets over rubies, presumably because they were easier to cut and carve—only diamond is harder than ruby. During the Middle Ages, rubies were highly regarded for their magical powers. They were used as amulets to prevent poisoning as well as the plague. Rubies were also believed to ward off curses. Also during this time, rubies were one of the most expensive luxury items traded from the East. Second to sapphire in popularity, by the late fourteenth century, ruby became top choice; however, a century later when the technology for diamond cutting was improved, ruby took second place again.[171] In today's market, flawless rubies are more rare than diamonds, making them more expensive. Non-gem quality rubies are used extensively in laser technology.

....

168. Clark, *Tropical Gems,* 10.

169. Schumann, *Gemstones of the World,* 98.

170. Clark, *Tropical Gems,* 12.

171. Colum P. Hourihane, ed., *The Grove Encyclopedia of Medieval Art and Architecture,* vol. 2 (New York: Oxford University Press, 2012), 494.

Ranging from transparent to opaque, rubies have a trigonal inner structure. Rough rubies have a dull or greasy luster, but when polished they are almost as brilliant as diamonds. The color of ruby ranges from various—and often intense—shades of red to brownish red, pinkish, or purplish. The most desirable rubies are deep red with a hint of blue and a silky luster. These stones are sometimes called pigeon blood ruby or Burma ruby. Because rubies fluoresce in natural daylight, they are often described as glowing from within, like red-hot coals. Inclusions are common and sometimes produce a six-rayed star or, more rare, a cat's-eye effect. Rubies exhibit a strong pleochroism, appearing yellowish red to deep red from different angles.

The color of passion, ruby has been a symbol of love, lust, and sexuality for centuries. Strengthening relationships, ruby engenders dedication and loyalty. It also fosters healing and compassion. Use it to attract wealth, inspire wisdom, and strengthen self-esteem. This stone dispels fear, builds courage, and provides protection from all forms of negativity, including hexes. The powerful energy of ruby spurs growth and creative expression. It supports intuitive abilities and psychic work. It also aids in interpreting information received through these practices.

Ruby is associated with the element fire and the deities Krishna and the Morrigan. Its astrological influence comes from Mars, the sun, the fixed star Aldebaran, and the zodiac constellations of Aries, Cancer, Capricorn, Leo, Sagittarius, Scorpio, and Taurus.

Salt

Also known as halite and rock salt

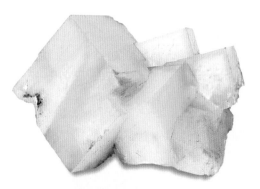

Mined from the ground and evaporated from seawater for thousands of years, salt has been a precious commodity since ancient times. It was vitally important for its cleansing properties and as a preservative for curing and storing food.

Beyond the mundane, salt was revered as mysterious. Important for religious ceremonies and magical charms, it became symbolic of wisdom, insight, and understanding. Medieval alchemists noted it as *sal sapientia,* "the salt of wisdom," and they considered it to have mystical properties when combined with sulfur.[172] It was believed that "whoever knows the salt, knows the secret of the ancient sages." [173]

Roman soldiers were originally given their pay in salt. Called *salarium,* it is the basis for our word salary.[174] Since ancient times, salt was also associated with fertility. While details vary by country, throughout Europe it has been traditional for bridal couples to carry salt with them to be married or to be given salt after the ceremony. This gift of salt symbolically purifies the couple's home and promotes a fertile union.

Salt is most often colorless or white but it can be bluish, brown, gray, pink, purple, or red. Ranging from transparent to translucent, it has a vitreous luster and a cubic inner structure.

---

172. C. G. Jung, *Mysterium Coniunctionis: An Inquiry into the Separation and Synthesis of Psychic Opposites in Alchemy* (Princeton, NJ: Princeton University Press, 1976), 242.

173. M. F. M. Van den Berk, *The Magic Flute: Die Zauberflöte, An Alchemical Allegory* (Boston: Brill, 2004), 144.

174. Shipley, *Dictionary of Word Origins,* 309.

As expected, salt has powerful cleansing and purification properties that are especially effective for ritual space, magical tools, and oneself. Use it to remove negative energy, break hexes, and bind oaths. It is also effective to banish unwelcomed spirits or anything unwanted from your life. This mineral is highly potent for protection, especially during psychic work. Use salt to bless your home, attract abundance and prosperity, or aid fertility. Salt provides supportive energy when seeking wisdom and is instrumental for initiating transformation. It is also a high-energy healer.

Mined salt is associated with the element earth and sea salt with water. Sea salt is associated with the deities Aphrodite, Neptune, and Poseidon.

Bind a Pledge

Sometimes when we give our word and make a pledge to someone we may want to emphasize its importance by putting extra energy into it. One way to increase its strength is by purifying it and binding it in fire. Write your pledge on a piece of paper, and then sprinkle a pinch of salt on it. Fold the paper to keep the salt within, hold it between your hands as you repeat your pledge, and then say:

Salt of wisdom, clean and pure,
with your strength, my words endure.

Place the bundle in your cauldron. As it burns, say:

Salt of wisdom and fire bright,
bind this pledge I make tonight.

Sapphire

Pronunciation: SA-fire

As previously mentioned, sapphire and ruby are the two gem-quality varieties of corundum. It was not until 1800 that these minerals were distinguished as separate corundum species.[175] Initially, sapphire only referred to blue corundum. Today, that name applies to any gem-quality corundum that is not red. Colors other than blue are sometimes called fancy sapphires.

Prized as a gem since at least 800 BCE, sapphire was frequently used as a talisman for travel.[176] According to Persian legend, the world rested on a magnificent sapphire and its reflection gave the sky its blue color. European folklore noted that colorless or pale sapphires were unripe rubies that would eventually turn red. The Franciscan monk Bartholomew Anglicus (c. 1203–1272), who wrote a compendium of natural sciences, claimed that sapphire was a favorite of witches. His reason for this is unknown.

Although the exact origin of this stone's name is not known, it is generally thought to have come from the Sanskrit *sauriratna,* meaning "sacred to Saturn."[177] Although the Greeks called it *sappheiros* and the Romans *sapphirus,* these names were also applied to a variety of blue stones.[178]

Known mostly for its shades of blue, sapphire can be black, colorless, green, orange, pink, purple, or yellow. It has a trigonal inner structure, a vitreous luster, and ranges from

175. Schumann, *Gemstones of the World*, 98.

176. Oldershaw, *Firefly Guide to Gems*, 61.

177. Clark, *Tropical Gems*, 14.

178. Lee Andrew Groat, ed., *The Geology of Gem Deposits* (Quebec, Canada: Mineralogical Association of Canada, 2007), 23.

transparent to opaque. This stone is most famous for its six-rayed stars, which are created by inclusions of tiny rutile needles that also give the stone a silky sheen. Although rare, black sapphires can produce twelve-rayed stars. Blue, green, purple, and yellow sapphires exhibit strong pleochroism in varying hues of their respective colors.

Sapphire is a gemstone of prophetic wisdom that boosts psychic abilities and enhances dreamwork. It also aids in subduing nightmares and fears in general. This stone is famous for its association with love, dedication, and fidelity. It enhances sexual relationships, dispels envy, and heals bruised emotions after quarrels. Sapphire fine-tunes intuitive abilities and aids in contacting spirits. It stokes the imagination for setting and working toward goals and dealing with problems. Use this stone when seeking fairness and justice and for defensive magic. It also supports astral work.

Sapphire is associated with the element water. Its astrological influence comes from the moon, Neptune, Saturn, Venus, the fixed star Capella, and the zodiac constellations of Aquarius, Cancer, Gemini, Leo, Libra, Pisces, Taurus, and Virgo. It is also associated with the deities Angus, Apollo, Hecate, Justitia, and Lugh.

Star sapphire is associated with the goddess Isis. Its astrological influence comes from Jupiter and the zodiac constellations of Capricorn and Sagittarius.

Sard

Pronunciation: sahrd

Also known as sard stone

Used for engraved jewelry since antiquity, sard is a reddish brown variety of carnelian. Both sard and carnelian were called sardion until the Middle Ages. The Greeks called this stone *sardios* and the Romans *sarda*. These names were derived from the city of Sardis, the Greek capital of ancient Lydia, located in what is now the western part of present-day Turkey. Located on the great royal road of the Persian Empire, Sardis was one of the richest cities of its time from 700 to 600 BCE.[179] Another potential source for this stone's name is the Persian word *sered*, which means "yellowish-red."[180]

Although sard may have been named for Sardis, it was used long before this city existed. Sard was carved into beads, seals, and small sculptures by the Mycenaeans and Assyrians, and farther afield in Pakistan by the Harappans, Bronze Age people of the Indus Valley. The Egyptians used it as early as 3100 BCE.[181] Sard was a favorite of Etruscan gem cutters who used it for cameos depicting deities, warriors, and the mythical sphinx. In the Middle Ages, a piece of sard jewelry was believed to protect the wearer against sorcery. The Victorians used it for cameos and intaglios.

179. Dana Facaros and Michael Pauls, *Turkey* (London: Cadogan Guides, 2000), 239.

180. E. H. Warmington, *The Commerce between the Roman Empire and India* (Cambridge, England: Cambridge University Press, 2014), 237.

181. Rapp, *Archaeomineralogy*, 93.

The reddish-brown color of sard often varies from light to dark brown. Ranging from transparent to translucent, it has a trigonal inner structure and a vitreous or waxy luster.

As a stone of courage, sard fosters dignity and respect for oneself and others. It aids in setting goals and having the determination to manifest them into reality. This stone also helps in meeting challenges and solving problems. While it protects against danger, it also stimulates intuition to remain mindful and alert when in a dicey situation. Sard aids in making friends and building community. It is also effective to bind a pledge.

Sard is associated with the element fire. Its astrological influence comes from Mars and the zodiac constellation of Aries.

Find Where You Fit In

While moving to a new town or taking a new job is exciting, there may be some challenging aspects, especially if it takes you away from old friends and colleagues. Fitting into any new situation takes effort and time. For a little help, wear sard jewelry or carry a piece of sard in your pocket or purse. Before putting on the jewelry or the stone in your pocket, hold it between your palms. Close your eyes and visualize your new situation and a successful outcome. Sard aids in making new friends, and, as a stone of courage, it helps to overcome any initial shyness.

Sardonyx

Pronunciation: sahr-DON-iks

Also known as sard stone

Although the name of this stone may suggest that it is a combination of sard and onyx, it is a layered mix of sard and white chalcedony that resembles onyx. Like sard, it is also known as sard stone. For centuries, sard and sardonyx have been two of the most widely used stones for engraved jewelry. Sardonyx was mined in India for millennia. The Egyptians carved sardonyx scarabs for use as protective talismans. Both the Egyptians and Romans carved vessels and decorative pieces from this stone.

For courage in battle, Roman soldiers carried or wore sardonyx engraved with images or symbols of Mars, the god of war. Widely worn in classical Greece and Rome, sardonyx cameos continued to be popular for many centuries. It was also used for beads and small figurines. During the Renaissance, this stone's power to bestow eloquence made it a favorite for public speakers to carry or wear.

As mentioned, sardonyx consists of alternating bands of reddish brown sard and white chalcedony. It ranges from transparent to translucent and has a vitreous or waxy luster. Its inner structure is hexagonal.

Sardonyx aids in clear, focused thinking and enhances communication skills. This stone also helps in making decisions and meeting challenges. Use it for guidance when seeking wisdom. The energy of this stone is instrumental for cultivating self-discipline and strengthening courage. Sardonyx is also effective for protection. In addition, this stone helps when it comes to love and marriage. Use sardonyx to help you find that special someone and in spells for luck or to increase fertility. Generating a peaceful atmosphere, sardonyx fosters happiness.

Sardonyx is associated with the element fire and the god Mars. It astrological influence comes from Mars, Mercury, the fixed star Antares, and the zodiac constellations of Aries, Leo, and Virgo.

Reduce the Size of Your Challenge

Occasionally after we have made up our minds to do something, challenges arise and seem like barriers preventing us from accomplishing our plans. Instead of regarding a challenge as a barrier blocking your path, think of it as something you can simply step over. Write a few keywords about your challenge on a small piece of paper. Place it on your altar, and then put a piece of sardonyx on top of it. Close your eyes and visualize your challenge as a big block. Watch as the piece of sardonyx acts as a weight reducing the size of your challenge to nothing. Safely burn the paper and scatter the ashes outside.

Selenite

Pronunciation: SEL-uh-nite *or* si-LEE-nite

Selenite is a crystal-forming variety of gypsum. It gained worldwide attention when gigantic crystals were discovered in a cave in northern Mexico. Although calcite was "the" alabaster of ancient Egypt, fine-grained selenite was also sometimes called *alabaster*. Also called gypsum spar, selenite was ground into a powder and used in plasters and wall paint in Egypt and other areas around the Mediterranean.[182] Selenite was a component in the pigments called terra alba and mineral white.

Because its soft sheen is reminiscent of moonlight, the Greeks named it *selenites,* meaning "moon stone." [183] Selenite is not related to the more widely known feldspar called moonstone. The word *selene* was derived from *selas,* meaning "light" or "bright," just as the Latin *luna* was derived from *lux,* "light." [184]

Easily split into thin sheets, it was called spectacle stone, alluding to its transparency. The Romans used thin sheets of selenite to cover windows and diffuse light. The stone Pliny called *lapis specularis,* "window stone," may refer to selenite.[185] Dating to approximately 200–300 CE, tablets made of lead and selenite were discovered on the island of Cyprus in

182. Eastaugh, et al., *Pigment Compendium*, 342.

183. L. L. Y. Chang, R. A. Howie, and J. Zussman, *Rock-forming Minerals: Non-Silicates,* vol. 5B (Bath, England: The Geological Society Publishing House, 1998), 40.

184. Anonymous, *The Orphic Hymns,* translated by Apostolos N. Athanassakis and Benjamin M. Wolkow (Baltimore: The Johns Hopkins University Press, 2013), 90.

185. Eastaugh, et al., *Pigment Compendium*, 342.

the late nineteenth century.[186] Inscribed in Greek, the selenite tablets contained invocations to chthonic deities, curses, and calls for justice. Archaeologists regard this cache as one of the most substantial records of ancient magical practices.

Mostly colorless, selenite can also be bluish or pink. It ranges from transparent to opaque and has a vitreous, pearly, or silky luster. Its inner structure is monoclinic. Selenite's twinned swallowtail crystals and starlike formations are popular with mineral collectors.

This stone's strong lunar association makes it ideal for moon magic and esbat rituals. Use it to power love spells to spark romance. Selenite draws on the cyclic power of renewal, providing energy for new beginnings. It is effective for warding off negativity, particularly when seeking justice. This stone fosters inspiration and clarity for communication, especially when emotions are involved. Its calming energy engenders harmony and peace and reduces stress. Selenite is also instrumental for dreamwork and when making decisions.

Selenite is associated with the element water. Its astrological influence comes from the moon and the zodiac constellations of Cancer and Taurus. This stone is also associated with the goddesses Hecate, Luna, and Selene.

---

186. Andrew T. Wilburn, *Materia Magica: The Archaeology of Magic in Roman Egypt, Cyprus, and Spain* (Ann Arbor, MI: University of Michigan Press, 2012), 209.

Serpentine

Pronunciation: SUR-pen-teen *or* SUR-pen-tine

Serpentine is a group of related minerals that are generally divided into two structural and economic groups. The antigorite group, also called precious serpentine, has a flaky structure. It is used as an ornamental stone and is the variety discussed here. The chrysotile group, also called fibrous serpentine because of its structure, is used mainly as a source of asbestos. Serpentinite is a rock that consists of several serpentine minerals.

Serpentine was so named because its coloring often resembles snakeskin. From the Latin *serpens,* meaning "snake," it was called *serpentium* by the Romans.[187] Just a side note about another name: The fibrous serpentine variety called lizardite has nothing to do with reptiles. Instead, it was named for Lizard, a town and peninsula in Cornwall, England, where it is found.

Serpentine has been prized for thousands of years and made into bowls, vases, figurines, and other household items. Some of these date to 7000 BCE in Greece and 2100 BCE in Mesopotamia.[188] The Mesopotamians also used it for cylinder seals, beads, and amulets. Serpentine cylinder seals made by the Assyrians often depicted heraldic-style lions. Dating to 3500 BCE, the Egyptians used this stone for vessels, amulets, statues, and small funerary

....

187. Rapp, *Archaeomineralogy*, 118.

188. Ibid.

objects, such as heart scarabs.[189] A range of carved objects found on Crete date to Minoan times. Through the Middle Ages, serpentine was widely used as a protective amulet against snakebites.

The coloring of green serpentine often resembles jade, which may be the reason it was popular with the ancient Chinese, Olmec, and Maya, who were especially fond of that stone. Serpentine has been marketed under the misleading names of Korean jade and new jade.

Serpentine can be brown, grayish green, green, or yellow. Its luster can be greasy, resinous, silky, or dull. Ranging from translucent to opaque, it has a monoclinic inner structure.

Serpentine's association with serpents extends to its ability to draw kundalini energy—often depicted as snakelike—through the body to augment meditation, sexuality, and spellwork. This energy also connects us with the cycles of nature and animals. This stone is instrumental for stimulating energy and getting motivated. It fosters inspiration and stokes creativity. Serpentine is also a stone of protection. Use it as a symbol or offering on your altar when you give thanks for your blessings.

Serpentine is associated with the element fire. Its astrological influence comes from Saturn and the zodiac constellation of Gemini.

Bowenite

Pronunciation: **BOE-en-ite**

This popular stone is a pale green variety of precious serpentine that resembles translucent jade. It was named for mineralogist George Bowen (1803–1828) who first described it. Bowenite is particularly effective to encourage renewal and growth.

---

189. Nicholson and Shaw, *Ancient Egyptian Materials and Technology,* 56.

Smithsonite

Pronunciation: **SMITH-suh-nite**

Also known as bonamite

Smithsonite is one of the most common zinc minerals and in the past it was called zinc spar. The Romans used it in their production of brass. Likewise, during the Tang Dynasty in China (618–907 CE), smithsonite was used to smelt brass for ornaments and coins.[190] From ancient through medieval times, this mineral was used medicinally to treat typhoid and skin problems. Known as *lapis calaminaris* during the Middle Ages, it was called calamine in Britain until geologist James Smithson (1765–1829) differentiated the two minerals that shared this name. His work led to this mineral being named for him. Smithson is most well known for leaving his fortune to found the Smithsonian Institution.

Rarely forming crystals, smithsonite is a soft stone that is not widely used for jewelry. However, collectors love it for its rounded shapes that look like clusters of bubbles or grapes.

Smithsonite can be blue, apple green, blue green, brown, green, gray, lilac, pink, white, or yellow. Occasionally it has a faint banding of color. It ranges from translucent to opaque and has a vitreous or pearly luster. Smithsonite has a trigonal inner structure. Depending on the color of the stone, it may fluoresce bluish white, pink, or brown.

Smithsonite is instrumental for developing and fine-tuning psychic skills. It is especially helpful to keep the mind alert and intuition engaged during any type of psychic work. Smithsonite is also effective for dreamwork. A stone of the emotions, it aids in aligning the

190. Ying-hsing Sung, *Chinese Technology in the Seventeenth Century,* translated by E-tu Zen Sun and Shiou-chuan Sun (Mineola, NY: Dover Publications, 1997), 258.

heart and mind to bring balance. Its healing energy blocks negativity and increases compassion and kindness. Smithsonite supports personal growth and relationships on all levels. Use this stone to aid in work with spirit guides.

Smithsonite is associated with the element water. Its astrological influence comes from Neptune and the zodiac constellations of Pisces and Virgo.

Bonamite
Pronunciation: **baw-nuh-MEE-ite**
While this name is most often applied to apple green stones, it is also used as a synonym for smithsonite. Frequently cut en cabochon, bonamite is the trade name given to this stone by the Goodfriend Brothers jewelers in New York. Intended as a play on words, the name was derived from the French *bon ami,* meaning "good friend." [191] This stone's calming energy soothes anger and relieves stress and anxiety.

191. Webster, *Gems,* 286.

Smoky Quartz

This variety of quartz has been used since ancient times for jewelry and ornamental objects. While it was used for seal stones throughout the Mediterranean region, the Egyptians used it for beads and a range of carved objects. Smoky quartz was popular for intaglio work with the Romans who knew it as *mormorion*, the name ascribed to it by Pliny.[192] As remarkable as it may sound, the Chinese made an early form of sunglasses in the thirteenth century from thin pieces of smoky quartz.

This stone ranges from smoky gray to brown and black. The color can vary within a stone. Crystals with black and gray banding are affectionately referred to as raccoon-tail quartz. The color of smoky quartz is produced by mineral impurities and exposure to natural radiation. It sometimes includes rutile needles. Ranging from transparent to opaque, smoky quartz has a trigonal inner structure and a vitreous or greasy luster. It is dichroic, appearing different hues from different angles.

Smoky quartz is a powerhouse of energy. Use it before ritual or magic work to cleanse an area and afterward to ground and center your energy. This stone aids in raising awareness for psychic work and for opening a channel to tap into subconscious wisdom. When used for introspection, it enhances creative expression and dreamwork. The energy of smoky quartz can also give your sex life a boost. It is instrumental for building community

....

192. Bonewitz, *Smithsonian Nature Guide: Gems*, 98.

and unity among people in general. Use this stone in spells to attract luck and abundance to the home. Its potent energy provides protection and removes negativity and obstacles.

Smoky quartz is associated with the elements earth and fire. Its astrological influence comes from the zodiac constellations of Capricorn and Libra.

Morian

Pronunciation: **MAWR-ee-on**

This opaque variety of smoky quartz is very dark and almost black. Its name was either derived from or misinterpreted from the Roman name for smoky quartz, *mormorion*.[193] This stone is effective for dealing with grief, sorrow, and loss. It supports introspection during difficult times to ultimately restore normalcy.

193. Rapp, *Archaeomineralogy*, 92.

Sodalite

Pronunciation: SOHD-uhl-ite

S odalite is the name of a mineral and a group of three related minerals that are called feldspathoids because they are chemically and structurally similar to the feldspar group. In this book, sodalite refers to the individual mineral of that name.

Most commonly blue, sodalite is reminiscent of lapis lazuli, which is not surprising, as sodalite is sometimes a component of that stone. Even though it is often used as a substitute for lapis lazuli, sodalite does not have the same glittery appearance because it lacks pyrite inclusions. Sodalite is a component of the pigment called French ultramarine. It is also used for jewelry, ornamental objects, and inlay work. This stone's name refers to its sodium content.

Sodalite was used for beads in Mesoamerica but was unknown in Europe until deposits were found in Greenland. Originally thought to be a regular feldspar mineral, it was described and named in 1811 by Scottish mineralogist and professor Thomas Thomson (1773–1852).[194] Sodalite crystals have since been found in the lava beds on Mount Vesuvius in Italy.

Sodalite can be blue, colorless, gray white, greenish, pink, reddish, or yellowish. In addition to sometimes having white veins of calcite, blue sodalite can have a tinge of violet coloring. Sodalite ranges from transparent to opaque. It has a vitreous or greasy luster and a cubic inner structure.

This stone aids in quieting the mind to draw peace and happiness into your life. It is especially helpful for dreamwork when seeking guidance. Sodalite heightens awareness

----

194. Nickel and Nichols, *Mineral Reference Manual*, 194.

and insight. It is particularly useful when developing intuitive and psychic skills. This stone helps clarify one's purpose and direction in life and supports the pursuit of knowledge. Sodalite enhances community relations, supports adaptability, and aids in logically resolving problems. Its calming energy aids in meeting emotional challenges, restoring balance, and releasing stress. It supports determination for successfully achieving goals. This stone also dispels fear.

Sodalite is associated with the elements air and water. Its astrological influence comes from Mercury, Venus, and the zodiac constellation of Sagittarius.

Hackmanite

Pronunciation: HACK-muh-nite

This variety of sodalite appears pink when freshly fractured or cut, but it fades when exposed to light. The color returns when the stone is kept in the dark. This unusual property is called photochromism. Magically, hackmanite aids in holding secrets and supports shamanic work.

Sphene

Pronunciation: sfeen

Also known as titanite

While titanite is the accepted mineral name for this stone, the jewelry trade uses the name sphene. It was derived from the Greek word *sphen,* meaning "wedge," in reference to this stone's wedge-shaped crystals.[195] Sphene was briefly known as menachanite for the Menachan Valley in Cornwall, England, where it was found by amateur mineralogist William Gregor (1761–1817). In 1795, German chemist Martin Klaproth (1743–1817) renamed the mineral titanite because of its titanium content.[196] Klaproth had previously discovered the metal titanium and named it in honor of the Titans of Greek mythology.

Sphene is one of the few stones with a luster and fire to match diamond; however, because it is too soft to use for rings it is not considered a top-notch gem. It is mostly used for earrings, brooches, and pendants. Industrially, it is used as a pigment for ceramics and occasionally mined for titanium. Mineral collectors like this stone for its fishtail-shaped twinning of crystals.

....

195. Oliver Cummings Farrington, *Gems and Gem Minerals* (Chicago: A. W. Mumford Publishing, 1903), 138.

196. Per Enghag, *Encyclopedia of the Elements: Technical Data, History, Processing, Applications* (Weinheim, Germany: Wiley-VCH Verlag, 2004), 498.

Sphene can be brown, green, reddish, or yellow. Ranging from transparent to opaque, it has an adamantine or greasy luster and a monoclinic inner structure. Sphene is strongly trichroic, appearing different hues from three different angles.

This is a stone of the mind and mental power, helping to make decisions and think things through. This goes hand in hand with its energy, which fosters knowledge and learning. Sphene also provides stability for everyday endeavors while it supports the cultivation of the spiritual aspect of life.

Sphene is associated with the element air. Its astrological influence comes from Mercury and the zodiac constellation of Sagittarius.

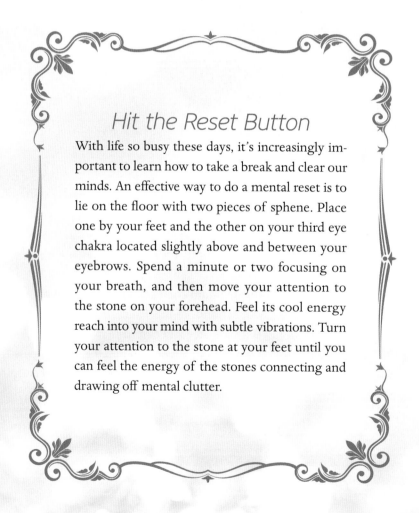

Hit the Reset Button

With life so busy these days, it's increasingly important to learn how to take a break and clear our minds. An effective way to do a mental reset is to lie on the floor with two pieces of sphene. Place one by your feet and the other on your third eye chakra located slightly above and between your eyebrows. Spend a minute or two focusing on your breath, and then move your attention to the stone on your forehead. Feel its cool energy reach into your mind with subtle vibrations. Turn your attention to the stone at your feet until you can feel the energy of the stones connecting and drawing off mental clutter.

Spinel

Pronunciation: **spuh-NEL** *or* **SPIN-el**

Spinel is the name of a group of minerals and an individual mineral. Red spinel was originally thought to be a type of ruby because of its resemblance to that stone and the fact that it is often found with rubies and sapphires. French mineralogist Jean Baptiste Louis Romé de l'Isle (1736–1797) is credited with making the distinction between spinel and ruby in 1783.[197] The name *spinel* comes from the Latin *spina,* meaning "spine" or "thorn," in reference to its crystals that are sometimes sharply pointed.[198]

This stone has been popular for jewelry from the days of ancient Greece and Rome through the nineteenth century. During the Middle Ages, it was used for lavish decorative objects. Myanmar has been a major source of spinel since ancient times. According to folklore, perfect spinel crystals were cut and polished by spirits.

Spinel can be black, blue, brown, colorless, green, orange, purple, red, violet, or yellow. Colorless and blue stones are extremely rare. Ranging from transparent to opaque, it has a vitreous luster and a cubic inner structure. This mineral occasionally exhibits a four- or six-rayed star. Crystals are frequently twinned.

Spinel helps to meet challenges and overcome the obstacles that life puts in the way. The stimulating energy of this stone propels us to success in whatever we choose to pursue. Use it in spells when seeking wealth or for protection. By fostering cooperation, spinel

197. Paul E. Desautels, *The Gem Kingdom* (New York: Random House, 1977), 119.

198. Oldershaw, *Firefly Guide to Gems,* 54.

is an aid to maintaining healthy relationships. In addition, it provides support when dealing with grief and sorrow.

In general, spinel is associated with the element fire. Its astrological influence comes from Pluto and the zodiac constellations of Aries and Sagittarius.

Balas Spinel

Pronunciation: BAL-uhs
Also known as red spinel and ruby spinel

This spinel ranges from pink to pale red. Like ruby, it fluoresces in daylight, making it look like a smoldering ember. During the Middle Ages, it was called balas ruby for the Balascia (now Badakhshan) region in Afghanistan, which was a source for this stone. Because of the confusion over this mineral, a number of famous rubies, including several in the British crown jewels, are actually red spinel. As a stone of wisdom, balas spinel is instrumental in bringing insight and finding truth. Although it is also a stone of passion—creative and sexual—when necessary it fosters balance to keep enthusiasm in check. Balas spinel also supports the emotions and bolsters courage.

Flame Spinel

Flame spinel is the trade name for orange spinel that ranges from yellowish to orange red. Its old name, *rubicelle,* was derived from the Latin *ruber* for "red." [199] Flame spinel is especially effective for sparking passion and romance. Like balas spinel, it is a stone of passion—creative and sexual—that also helps to keep enthusiasm in check and balanced.

199. Michael Weinstein, *Precious and Semi-Precious Stones* (Redditch, England: Read Books, 2013), 89.

Pleonaste

Pronunciation: PLEE-uh-nast
Also known as black spinel

Originally called *ceylonite* for its earliest known source in Ceylon (now Sri Lanka), its current name was derived from the Greek *pleonastos,* meaning "abundant," in reference to its various crystal forms.[200] This opaque variety of spinel ranges from very dark green to black. During the Victorian era, it was used for mourning jewelry. Pleonaste is a stone of determination that helps keep us on course to follow our path and purpose in life. Use it for support when a loved one passes.

200. Alexander Senning, *Elsevier's Dictionary of Chemoetymology: The Whys and Whences of Chemical Nomenclature and Terminology* (Oxford, England: Elsevier, 2007), 313.

Staurolite

Pronunciation: STAWR-uh-lite

Also known as cross stone, fairy cross, and fairy stone

The name of this mineral comes from the Greek *stauros*, meaning "cross," and *lithos*, "stone."[201] Intergrown twin crystals frequently form two types of crosses. In one type, the crystals cross at a 90-degree angle and in the other they cross obliquely at 60 degrees, forming an X shape. Although rare, three crystals growing together in the configuration of both crosses form a starlike shape. In the past, staurolite was also called *lapis crucifer* and twin stone.

According to legend, staurolite crosses form where a fairy's tear has touched the ground. For centuries, it was regarded as a good luck charm and worn as an amulet. Christians used staurolite crosses as protection against witchery. During the Middle Ages, these crosses became a common feature on baptismal fonts. Also during this time, schist was quarried for use as millstones when it contained staurolite inclusions because of the rough surface the staurolite provided. Today, industrial-grade staurolite is used for pressure (sand) blasting.

Staurolite can be brownish black, dark reddish brown, or yellowish brown. Ranging from transparent to opaque, it can have a vitreous, greasy, or dull luster. Its inner structure is monoclinic. The rare transparent stones are faceted for jewelry. This mineral produces

---

201. Oldershaw, *Firefly Guide to Gems*, 113.

fairly equal amounts of single crystals and crossed twins. Staurolite is trichroic, appearing nearly colorless, reddish brown, or yellowish from different angles.

The association of staurolite with fairies makes it the perfect stone to use in rituals to honor them or to leave as an offering. As a stone of protection, it can guard against fairy mischief. Staurolite also brings protection and security to the home. This stone is good for grounding energy before and after ritual or magic work and any time you need to bring your energy into balance. Staurolite is also instrumental for working in the astral realm and traveling in the mundane world. Use it in spells for luck or money. This stone helps to initiate changes that bring about transformation. It also aids in spiritual guidance.

Staurolite is associated with all four elements and with fairies. Its astrological influence comes from the zodiac constellation of Pisces.

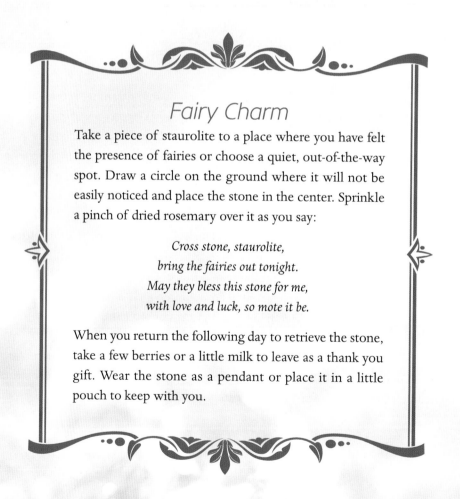

Fairy Charm

Take a piece of staurolite to a place where you have felt the presence of fairies or choose a quiet, out-of-the-way spot. Draw a circle on the ground where it will not be easily noticed and place the stone in the center. Sprinkle a pinch of dried rosemary over it as you say:

Cross stone, staurolite,
bring the fairies out tonight.
May they bless this stone for me,
with love and luck, so mote it be.

When you return the following day to retrieve the stone, take a few berries or a little milk to leave as a thank you gift. Wear the stone as a pendant or place it in a little pouch to keep with you.

Sugilite

Pronunciation: SOO-guh-lite *or* soo-GEE-lite

Also known as lavulite, luvulite, and royal azel

This stone was named in honor of geologist Ken-ichi Sugi, who discovered it in Japan in 1944. However, it was not determined to be a unique mineral until 1976 after deposits of spectacular stones were discovered in South Africa.[202] Sugilite from South Africa became enormously popular as soon as it hit the jewelry market. It was sold under the name royal azel, which was a combined reference to the dark royal purple colors and the town of Hotazel near where it was found. Sugilite has been found in other locations around the world.

This stone has also been called lavulite for its shades of lavender. The spelling of this name is apparently altered to luvulite to emphasize its association with love (luv). Sugilite is usually cut en cabochon or into beads for jewelry. It is also used for inlay.

Sugilite ranges from deep purple to lavender and violet to reddish violet. It is often mottled or veined. Most often opaque, it is frequently translucent. Transparent crystals are very rare. Sugilite has a hexagonal inner structure and its luster can be vitreous, resinous, or greasy.

This stone helps to release attachments and instill a sense of freedom that invites growth. Sugilite is an aid when developing psychic skills and when seeking wisdom. It also

---

202. Anna Fischel, ed., *Smithsonian Gem: The Definitive Visual Guide* (New York: DK Publishing, 2016), 221.

aids in contacting spirits. This stone is instrumental for emotional balance and healing, especially when dealing with anger or jealousy. It fosters a sense of well-being and is an aid to spiritual growth and transformation. Use it to attract a lover or to tap into the energy of universal love and peace. Sugilite also strengthens memory and willpower.

Sugilite is associated with the elements earth and water. Its astrological influence comes from Jupiter and the zodiac constellations of Pisces, Sagittarius, and Virgo.

Time to Let Go

Every now and then, we come to the conclusion that we need to make changes and let go of certain things in our lives. For whatever reason, that something to let go of can be a person. For this spell you will need two small pieces of paper, a short length of thread, and a piece of sugilite. Light a white candle on your altar. Use one slip of paper to write your name and the second paper for the other person's name. Poke a small hole in each paper, tie the ends of the thread to them, and then place it on your altar. As you position the sugilite in the middle of the string, visualize your connection with the person dissolving.

Sunstone

Also known as oligoclase sunstone

Like aventurine, sunstone has inclusions that produce glittering reflections called aventurescence. In sunstone, sparkly flakes of hematite and/or goethite are responsible for the metallic sheen. First described and called heliolite by French mineralogist Jean-Claude Delametherie (1743–1817), German chemist and mineralogist Theodor Scheerer (1813–1873) shortly afterward classified it as a feldspar and named it aventurine feldspar.[203]

Regardless of its scientific designation, this mineral's most common name remained sunstone, *sonnenstein* (German), *pierre de soleil* (French), and *heliolite* (Greek) because of its warm, sunny colors.[204] However, this simple name has caused some confusion, because other stones have been known as sunstone. The magic jewel of Hindu folklore called the *syamantaka sunstone* is generally accepted to have been a ruby or a diamond. In addition, the famed sunstone used as a navigational aid by the Vikings was actually the light-polarizing calcite.

Sunstone is usually cut en cabochon for jewelry to emphasize its spangled appearance. Industrially, it is used for ceramic glazes.

Sunstone can be orange, reddish brown, or pale yellow. Occasionally the glittery sheen has a blue or green tinge. Sunstone ranges from translucent to opaque and has a dull or vitreous luster. Its inner structure is triclinic. This stone fluoresces a dark brownish-red color.

....

203. Tom F. W. Barth, *Feldspars* (New York: John Wiley and Sons, 1969), 241.

204. Ibid.

Because of its name and sparkly appearance, this stone is instrumental in drawing on the strength and energy of the sun for magic and ritual. Not surprisingly, it is a stone of optimism, warmth, and healing. It also aids in personal growth and well-being. Use sunstone to stimulate action, bolster determination, and bring success. This stone offers protection and helps to dispel fear. It also attracts luck.

Sunstone is associated with the element fire. Its astrological influence comes from the sun and the zodiac constellations of Leo and Libra. It is also associated with the gods Lugh and Ra.

Solar-Powered Magic

Give your spells, divination practices, or rituals a boost with energy from the sun. Place several pieces of sunstone on a windowsill where they will catch the daylight. As you do this say:

Shining sun, our daystar bright,
fill this stone with magic and light.

Whether or not it's a bright sunny day, the stone's connection with the sun will be activated. After an hour or so, individually wrap the stones in yellow cloth until you are ready to use them. These stones can also be used on a rainy day to brighten the energy of a room.

Tiger's-Eye

Like hawk's-eye, this stone was once regarded as a pseudomorph where one mineral replaces another. Although yet to be proven, newer theories regard tiger's-eye as an intergrowth of quartz and crocidolite (blue asbestos). The fibrous structure of the crocidolite produces the cat's-eye effect in this stone. Unlike its cousin hawk's-eye, tiger's-eye undergoes the process of oxidation, becoming coated with iron oxides and hydroxides, which are responsible for its brown coloring.

The ancient Egyptians used tiger's-eye for amulets, often in the form of scarabs. Roman soldiers wore this stone as a protective amulet for battle. Tiger's-eye was an important trade commodity for the Chinese, who used it for decorative objects. Through the ages, this stone has been used for beads and engraved jewelry. Tiger's-eye was especially popular in late Victorian and early Art Nouveau jewelry. In addition, slabs of tiger's-eye were occasionally used for small decorative tabletops. In the past, it was called African cat's-eye and wood cat's-eye.

Tiger's-eye is typically multicolored brown, golden yellow, or reddish brown in stripes or wavy patterns. It is opaque with a silky luster and has a trigonal inner structure. Light reflecting off the surface of tiger's-eye produces a golden silky sheen. The rays of tiger's-eye are smaller than the cat's-eye and less dramatic.

As expected, tiger's-eye is instrumental for working and communicating with animals—mundane or otherwise—especially cats. It empowers psychic abilities and, through insight and introspection, it can reveal unexpected talents. This stone supports learning and developing skills. It is an aid to divination, especially when seeking truth and wisdom. Providing protection and security, tiger's-eye helps to avoid danger. It also fosters strength and confidence. It is instrumental where money is concerned, especially in recovering what is

owed. This stone provides a boost to inspiration by accessing a flow of creative energy. Use it in spells for luck and success, particularly for a new job or a business venture. The calm strength of tiger's-eye helps to overcome fear. It is also an aid for all aspects of sexuality.

Tiger's-eye is associated with the deities Bast, Ra, and Sekhmet. Its astrological influence comes from the sun and the zodiac constellations of Gemini and Leo.

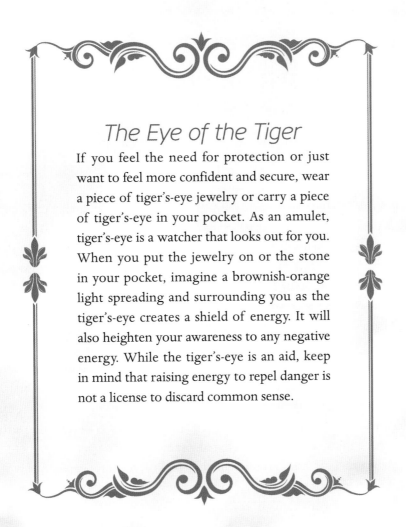

The Eye of the Tiger

If you feel the need for protection or just want to feel more confident and secure, wear a piece of tiger's-eye jewelry or carry a piece of tiger's-eye in your pocket. As an amulet, tiger's-eye is a watcher that looks out for you. When you put the jewelry on or the stone in your pocket, imagine a brownish-orange light spreading and surrounding you as the tiger's-eye creates a shield of energy. It will also heighten your awareness to any negative energy. While the tiger's-eye is an aid, keep in mind that raising energy to repel danger is not a license to discard common sense.

Topaz

Pronunciation: TOE-paz

Called *topazion* by ancient Greeks, Pliny noted that *topazius* came from Topazos, an island in the Red Sea—now called Zebirget, Zabargad, and St. John's Island. Although the name was applied to a number of yellowish stones, the topazion from this island was actually peridot. Another theory as to the origin of the name *topaz* is that it was derived from the Sanskrit *tapas,* meaning "fire," in reference to its color or brilliance.[205] Along with peridot and chrysoberyl, topaz was sometimes called chrysolite.

Rare and highly prized during the Middle Ages, topaz was credited with reflecting images like a mirror. In addition, the power of topaz was believed to wax and wane with the phases of the moon. Found in Brazil in 1740, the large diamond used in the Portuguese royal crown turned out to be a colorless topaz.[206] Acquired from the Ural Mountains in the nineteenth century, a rare pink variety was called imperial topaz to honor the czar.[207] By the mid-nineteenth century it was highly valued and expensive. Nowadays the term *imperial topaz* is applied to stones that are sherry red, orange red, and pink.

Topaz can be pale blue, colorless, green, pink, pinkish red, orange, orange red, sherry red, reddish brown, red, or yellow. The most common color is yellow with a brownish or reddish tint. Purely red stones are extremely rare. Topaz ranges from transparent to trans-

205. Federman, *Modern Jeweler's Consumer Guide to Colored Gemstones,* 227.

206. Oldershaw, *Firefly Guide to Gems,* 116.

207. Federman, *Modern Jeweler's Consumer Guide to Colored Gemstones,* 232.

lucent. It has a vitreous luster and an orthorhombic inner structure. This stone is known for its well-formed crystals. Like amber and tourmaline, it can become electrically charged, attracting dust and other small particles. Yellow topaz is dichroic, appearing honey lemon or straw yellow from different angles.

This is a stone of power that boosts the energy of rituals and magic. Use it in spells to attract luck and money. It also works well to subdue fear and acts as a powerfully protective amulet for avoiding danger. Topaz fosters insight and introspection that can lead to a new level of wisdom. The sunny color of this stone brings renewal and blessings and aids in dealing with the death of a loved one. Topaz also brings clarity and inspiration for divination and aids shamanic work. Associated with sex and love, topaz heightens passion and strengthens fidelity. In addition, the energy of this stone fosters adaptability to carry you through the changing situations of life.

Topaz is associated with the element fire. Its astrological influence comes from Mercury, the sun, the fixed stars Alphecca and Vega, and the zodiac constellations of Gemini, Leo, Sagittarius, Scorpio, and Taurus. Topaz is also associated with the gods Jupiter, Lugh, and Ra.

Blue Topaz

This variety of topaz is pale blue or sometimes a light greenish blue that can be mistaken for aquamarine. Blue topaz is weakly dichroic, appearing light or dark blue from different angles. This stone fosters peace and harmony in the home, opening the channels of communication for better understanding among family members. Supporting emotions, it smooths the way to forgiveness. This stone's calming energy is especially effective for warding off nightmares and enhancing sleep. Use it to purify ritual space or in spells to release whatever is unwanted in your life. Blue topaz is associated with the elements air and water.

Tourmaline

Pronunciation: TOOR-muh-leen *or* TOOR-muh-lin

Tourmaline encompasses a group of minerals with the same crystal structure but variable chemical compositions. The first documented use of tourmaline comes from Greece after Alexander the Great (356–323 BCE) returned with it from the East. However, tourmaline received little attention in the rest of Europe until 1703 when the Dutch imported it from Sri Lanka.[208] In Sinhalese—a language spoken in Sri Lanka—the name for this stone, *thoramalli,* was derived from a plant they called *thora* and the word *mal,* "flower."[209] The tourmaline popular at the time resembled the yellowish-brown color of the plant's flower. The Chinese also used tourmaline and liked to combine red tourmaline with jade in jewelry and carvings.

Tourmaline can be black, blue, brown, colorless, green, pink, red, or yellow. Most are usually multicolored and crystals often have different colors at opposite ends. Ranging from transparent to opaque, tourmaline has a vitreous or greasy luster and a trigonal inner structure. Like amber and topaz, it can become electrically charged, attracting dust and other small particles.

This stone is known for getting energy moving and helps stir it up for ritual and magic work. On a personal level, tourmaline helps to build inner strength and self-confidence. It supports self-reliance and independence and fosters acceptance. It also helps to fine-tune psychic skills and develop creative talents. Use it to find a guardian spirit when guidance is needed.

In general, the astrological influence for tourmaline comes from Pluto and the zodiac constellation of Scorpio.

....

208. Schumann, *Gemstones of the World,* 126.

209. Staff Writer, *Sri Lanka Mineral & Mining Sector Investment and Business Guide,* vol. 1 (Washington, DC: International Business Publications USA, 2013), 54.

Dravite

Pronunciation: DRAH-vite
Also known as brown tourmaline

This variety of tourmaline is yellowish brown to dark brown. It is pleochroic, appearing dark or light brown from different angles. Faceted for jewelry, transparent light brown stones are often called champagne tourmaline. Dravite was named for a district along the Drava River in Austria where it is found. The Romans used dravite for seal stones and signet rings.

This is a stone of courage that aids in defense where justice is called for. Its peaceful energy supports the spiritual aspects of life, bringing healing and emotional balance. Use it to keep energy grounded during ritual and magic work. Dravite is associated with the element earth.

Indicolite

Pronunciation: in-DIK-uh-lite
Also known as blue tourmaline and indigolite

This variety of tourmaline can be deep blue or neon blue and many shades in between. It is strongly dichroic, appearing light blue and dark blue from different angles. This stone may also exhibit a cat's-eye effect. It was named for the color indigo.

Indicolite is a stone that stokes inspiration and creativity and supports the quest for learning. It fosters introspection that brings clarity and insight for self-knowledge. This stone is an aid for overcoming obstacles. Use it for support in psychic work. Indicolite is associated with the elements air and water. Its astrological influence comes from Venus and the zodiac constellations of Libra and Taurus.

Rubellite

Pronunciation: **ROO-buh-lite** *or* **roo-BEL-ite**
Also known as red tourmaline

With its name from the Latin *ruber,* meaning "red," this stone ranges from pink to red, sometimes with a violet tinge.[210] It is dichroic, appearing different hues from two different angles. It may exhibit a cat's-eye effect. Dark red stones can be stunning enough to rival ruby and red spinel.

This tourmaline supports and balances the emotions. As a symbol of dedication and devotion, it is instrumental for attracting love and romance. It is also a stone of action, helping to manifest your desires. Pink shades are associated with the element water. Their astrological influence comes from Venus and the zodiac constellation of Libra. Red shades are associated with the element fire. Their astrological influence comes from Mars and the zodiac constellation of Sagittarius.

Schorl

Pronunciation: **shor'l** *or* **shawrl**
Also known as black tourmaline

This black, opaque variety is the most abundant type of tourmaline. Its name comes from *schrul,* a German mining term for black stones that were discarded after washing mined ores.[211] During the Victorian period, black tourmaline was commonly used for mourning jewelry. Thin, needlelike crystals of schorl form tourmalated quartz.

This stone is instrumental for protection and for grounding negativity. Its supportive energy fosters happiness and dispels fear. Schorl is associated with the elements earth and water. Its astrological influence comes from Saturn, the sun, and the zodiac constellations of Capricorn, Libra, Pisces, and Sagittarius.

210. Schumann, *Gemstones of the World,* 126.

211. Cairncross, *Field Guide to Rocks & Minerals of Southern Africa,* 212.

Verdelite

Pronunciation: VER-duh-lite
Also known as green tourmaline

The name *verdelite* was derived from the Latin *verde,* meaning "green," and the Greek *lithos,* "stone." [212] The color of this tourmaline includes various shades of green. It is dichroic, appearing light green or yellow green from different angles. Bright emerald green stones are often called chrome tourmaline.

Verdelite amplifies energy for ritual and magic work. It also aids in grounding and realigning energy to maintain balance. Use it for spells of abundance or rituals of renewal. Associated with willpower, this stone helps to retain money and prosperity. In addition, verdelite supports adaptability and encourages personal growth. This stone is associated with the element earth. Its astrological influence comes from Venus and the zodiac constellations of Capricorn and Sagittarius.

Watermelon Tourmaline

This variety is the most dramatic of tourmalines. With a pink core progressing to a white and green rim, it resembles a slice of watermelon. This is a fun stone of abundance and harmony that supports relationships. Watermelon tourmaline is associated with the elements earth and water. Its astrological influence comes from Mars, Venus, and the zodiac constellations of Gemini and Virgo.

....
212. Grande and Augustyn, *Gems and Gemstones,* 144.

Turquoise

Pronunciation: TUR-koyz

Also known as kallaite

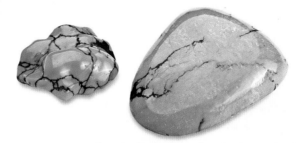

The name *turquoise* comes from the Old French *turque,* meaning "Turkish," in reference to the trade route that passed through Turkey.[213] The name *kallaite* comes from its more ancient name *callais,* which was derived from the Greek *kallos,* "beautiful," and *lithos,* "stone."[214] Found and valued worldwide, turquoise is one of the oldest-known talismanic gemstones. Mined on the Sinai Peninsula since approximately 8000 BCE, this stone was used by the Mesopotamians, Greeks, and Egyptians.[215] Inscriptions in a temple to Hathor on the Sinai Peninsula referred to her as the Lady of the Turquoise Country. Turquoise was sacred to her because its color represented fertility and rebirth.

Mining turquoise for thousands of years, the Chinese perfected its use for carvings and inlay work. In Tibet and Nepal, turquoise was used for a range of sacred and secular objects. On the other side of the world, mines in the American Southwest were worked in prehistoric times, and by 1000 BCE, turquoise was a major trade item in Mexico.[216] The Zuni and Navajo used it extensively for jewelry. The Aztec and other people of South America used turquoise for a number of religious and everyday items. Worldwide, the

213. Douglas M. Considine, ed., *Van Nostrand's Scientific Encyclopedia,* vol. 2, 8th ed. (New York: John Wiley & Sons, 1995), 3116.

214. Bariand and Duchamp, *Larousse Encyclopedia of Precious Gems,* 225.

215. Joe Dan Lowry and Joe P. Lowry, *Turquoise: The World Story of a Fascinating Gemstone* (Layton, UT: Gibbs Smith, 2010), 45.

216. Rapp, *Archaeomineralogy,* 109.

popularity of this stone has not waned and continues to be used for jewelry and decorative objects.

This stone can be blue green, greenish gray, or sky blue. It is often mottled with small veins of brown or black. Ranging from translucent to opaque, turquoise has a vitreous, waxy, or dull luster and a triclinic inner structure. It also has a weak fluorescence of greenish yellow and light blue.

Turquoise is a spiritual stone that aids in reaching a profoundly deep level. Use it for guidance and when seeking truth and wisdom. This stone fine-tunes intuition and is instrumental for dreamwork. Use it to manifest ideas into reality and achieve success. It brings clarity to communications and sparks creative expression. Turquoise attunes the emotions, opening the heart for compassion and empathy. This stone also fosters happiness for the wearer or the household when placed around the home. Use it as an aid for fertility and renewal on any level. In addition, turquoise is a protector that wards off all forms of negativity and is especially helpful for travel.

Turquoise is associated with the elements earth and water. Its astrological influence comes from Jupiter, the moon, Neptune, Venus, and the zodiac constellations of Aquarius, Pisces, Sagittarius, Scorpio, Taurus, and Virgo. This stone is also associated with the deities Chalchihuitlicue, Hathor, Kuan Yin, Ma'at, Manannan, and Ogma.

Eilat Stone

***Pronunciation:* ey-LAHT**

This blue-green stone is a mixture of chrysocolla, turquoise, and malachite from the mines near Eilat in southern Israel. When working with this stone you may find varying combinations of energy and power.

White Quartz

Also known as milky quartz and snowy quartz

In addition to being used for tools since ancient times, this variety of quartz has had great significance beyond the mundane. Dating to approximately 3100 BCE, the Egyptians were using white quartz for furniture inlay and beads and carving it into pendants and funerary vessels.[217] They also used this stone in the ceremony called "opening the mouth" to symbolically revive the deceased so he or she could speak, eat, and drink in the afterlife.

Throughout the British Isles and parts of France, white quartz has been found in association with standing stone circles and wedge tombs. At the famous passage tomb of New-grange in Ireland, it was used for the facade of the entrance wall. White quartz pebbles covered the tops of some burial mounds, while at others the stones were placed inside the mounds. In some individual burials in England, white quartz pebbles had been placed in the mouths of the deceased, seemingly to echo the Egyptian practice. In addition, white quartz pebbles have been found in ancient graves in China. The practice of placing this stone in graves continued into Christian medieval burials in Europe.

As the color of bone, white has been associated with death since Paleolithic times. However, death was only part of the cycle of life/death/rebirth, and so ancient symbols of death were usually accompanied by symbols of regeneration. It was perhaps the greatest power of the Goddess to not only give and take life, but to bring it back. White symbolized this power, making white quartz an especially important stone.

....

217. Nicholson and Shaw, *Ancient Egyptian Materials and Technology*, 52.

This quartz is a soft white color with a vitreous luster and a trigonal inner structure. When cut en cabochon, it can resemble opal. Occasionally, white quartz occurs as a phantom crystal inside clear quartz.

As its ancient use suggests, white quartz is associated with death and the afterlife. It aids in connecting with loved ones who have passed as well as ancestors. It is effective for past-life work and healing, especially from grief and loss as this stone offers hope and renewal. Although white quartz connects us with the past, it also connects us with living family members. This stone provides inspiration for initiating changes when seeking transformation. In addition, white quartz is a stone of inspiration that stokes creativity. White quartz is associated with moon goddesses.

Stoke Your Creativity

White quartz is instrumental in getting your creative energy flowing. Hold a stone in each hand for a few minutes, and then raise your arms out to the sides to shoulder height. Slowly turn in a circle three times as you say:

Milky stone, shine and glow;
stir my energy, make it flow.
Kindle within me a creative fire;
with your power, my mind inspire.

Lower your arms and take a few minutes to think about the creative work or project you want to accomplish. Place the stones on your desk or table where you work on creative projects.

Zircon

Pronunciation: ZER-kahn

Named from the Arabic *zarqun*, meaning "golden color," zircon may be the stone Pliny called *melichrysus*.[218] Although zircon has been mined in Sri Lanka and used throughout Asia and the Middle East for more than two thousand years, it did not become popular in the West until the 1920s.[219] Because the synthetic stone called zirconia—which is often passed off as diamond—has a similar name, zircon is sometimes regarded as a cheap imitation despite the fact that it is second only to diamond in refracting and dispersing light.

Industrially, this mineral is a source of the metal zirconium, which is used in the manufacture of nuclear reactors. Most stones, particularly the green ones, contain a trace of radioactive uranium or thorium; however, these are rarely in the gem trade. Zircon is also used in the manufacture of ceramics.

Zircon can be blue, brown, colorless, green, orange, red, violet, or yellow. It has an adamantine or greasy luster and a tetragonal inner structure. Ranging mostly from transparent to translucent, occasionally it is opaque. Bipyramidal terminations and twinning are common. Zircon occasionally exhibits a cat's-eye effect.

This is a stone of motivation that aids in successfully attaining goals. Use it for inspiration when making plans for the future. Zircon is also a protector, especially for the home. It fosters peace, harmony, and unity for the family. Use it in spells to attract love or abundance. Zircon is also effective for purifying ritual and magic space. Yellow zircon is a stone

218. Rapp, *Archaeomineralogy*, 104.

219. Oldershaw, *Firefly Guide to Gems*, 99.

of peace and happiness that provides supportive energy when encouragement is needed. It also stimulates sexual energy.

In general, zircon is associated with the element fire and the deities Danu and the Dagda. Its astrological influence comes from the sun and the zodiac constellations of Leo, Scorpio, and Taurus. The astrological influence for yellow zircon comes from the zodiac constellation of Capricorn.

Red Zircon

This variety of zircon can be red, reddish brown, or brownish orange. One of its former names, hyacinth, actually referred to stones that were yellow, yellow red, or reddish brown. In addition, this name and variations of it have been used for some varieties of beryl, garnet, quartz, and spinel. In the past it was also known as jachant and jacinth.

In ancient times, red zircon was popular with the Greeks for intaglio work. German abbess Hildegard of Bingen (1098–1179) recommended its use for breaking spells. During the Middle Ages, this stone was believed to bring a restful sleep when worn as a ring. In addition, it was regarded as a powerful talisman and used for scrying.

Red zircon is an energizer. Use it to activate energy in the home or to stimulate ideas. Also, use it to add power to magic work. This stone builds strength for healing and well-being and helps to bring emotions into balance. Red zircon builds confidence and fosters acceptance, too. Its astrological influence comes from Jupiter, Mars, and the zodiac constellations of Aquarius, Cancer, Libra, Sagittarius, and Virgo.

Zoisite

*Pronunciation: ZOE-ee-site *or* ZOY-sit*

Also known as saualpite

This mineral was named for Austrian scientist Sigmund von Zois (1747–1819), who discovered it and originally named it in 1805 for the Sau Alp Mountains in Austria.[220] The most well-known variety of zoisite, tanzanite, was discovered in 1967 while a prospector was searching for sapphire near Mount Kilimanjaro in Tanzania.[221] For a time, it was only available through Tiffany & Company.

Zoisite can be blue, brown, colorless, gray, green, pink, or yellowish. It is transparent with a vitreous or pearly luster. Zoisite has an orthorhombic inner structure.

This is a stone of love, fertility, and growth. Its energy supports all forms of beginnings and renewals from relationships to projects to a new home. Zoisite also supports the emotions, releasing fear, building confidence, and fostering optimism. It is helpful when developing psychic abilities.

Anyolite

Pronunciation: en-EE-uh-lite
Also known as ruby zoisite

Anyolite is actually a rock containing green zoisite with veins of black hornblende and red inclusions that are often opaque rubies. Discovered in Tanzania in 1954, its name comes from the

220. Schumann, *Gemstones of the World*, 176.

221. Thomas Thompson, "Tanzania to Tiffany's," *Life Magazine*, vol. 66, no. 18 (May 9, 1969): 71.

Maasai word *anyoli*, which means "green." [222] Anyolite is used for ornamental objects. This is a stone of motivation and trust that aids in finding the right path in life. It also fosters happiness.

Thulite

Pronunciation: THOO-lite *or* TOO-lite
Also known as rosaline

This variety of zoisite is opaque and ranges from light pink to rose red, usually with mottled coloring. Occasionally it may have a hint of green. It was discovered in Norway in the early 1800s and named for the legendary island Ultima Thule, the ancient Greek name for Norway. [223] Thulite is used for beads, jewelry, and ornamental objects. When it comes to relationships, thulite supports good communication and insight. Use it to kindle or rekindle passion in a sexual relationship. This stone also adds a spark to creative energy.

Tanzanite

Pronunciation: TAN-zuh-nite
Also known as blue zoisite

The color of this variety of zoisite ranges from lilac to sapphire blue to violet. It is strongly trichroic, appearing in hues of purple, blue, or brownish yellow from different angles. Although rare, it can exhibit a cat's-eye effect.

Tanzanite is instrumental for love charms; however, because it is also a stone of truth, it should be used wisely in matters of romance. It is also a stone of willpower and protection that strengthens determination and aids in solving problems. Use it to manifest the changes you want to make in your life. It also gives a boost to psychic abilities and helps when seeking guidance.

....

222. Thomas, *Gemstones*, 123.

223. Grande and Augustyn, *Gems and Gemstones*, 226.

SUMMARY

As we have seen, the use of crystals and gemstones dates to very ancient times when they served as bling and so much more. Through the millennia, crystals have been used as symbols of power and wealth, beauty and prestige, and tokens of love.

Like other areas of the natural world, gemstones offer depth to ritual and magic. While it is easy to work with crystals on a superficial level, we have seen that with a little more knowledge we can tap into the deeper power and wisdom of the mineral kingdom.

While some gemstones attract our attention with rich colors, others seem to play with the light or shine from within. Regardless of their beauty, we are also attracted to certain crystals because of their energy. Crystals are simple and effective because they are formed by dynamic processes—the powerful creative and destructive forces of the earth.

Knowing about the optical characteristics and the historical and cultural backgrounds of stones rounds out our knowledge base and aids in the more effective selection and use of crystals. In addition, the shape of a stone's inner structure provides us with a unique and powerful type of crystal grid.

When we take time to explore and learn as much as we can about the natural world and the tools it offers, we follow in the footsteps of the wise women and men who developed a working knowledge of the world around them. Be informed and inspired as you explore the magic that surrounds you.

Appendix A
MAGICAL CORRESPONDENCES

Following is a quick reference list to help you find crystals for particular situations and circumstances.

Abundance / comfort: Agate, apatite, calcite, chrysoberyl, chrysoprase, citrine, diamond, dioptase, dolomite, garnet, jade, moonstone, peridot, rhodochrosite, rose quartz, salt, smoky quartz, tourmaline, zircon

Acceptance: Angelite, apatite, aragonite, beryl, chalcedony, charoite, jasper, larimar, quartz, rose quartz, tourmaline, zircon

Action / activate / stimulate: Agate, amethyst, calcite, charoite, danburite, dumortierite, emerald, epidote, fluorite, iolite, kunzite, kyanite, labradorite, opal, pearl, peridot, phenacite, quartz, rhodochrosite, rhodonite, sard, serpentine, spinel, sunstone, tourmaline, zircon

Adaptability: Alexandrite, bloodstone, chrysoprase, hematite, larimar, opal, sodalite, topaz, tourmaline

Aggression: Bloodstone, carnelian, obsidian, rose quartz

Angels: Angelite, barite, beryl, blue lace agate, celestine, danburite, jasper, larimar, phenacite

Anger (to subdue, avert): Blue lace agate, chalcedony, chrysoprase, dolomite, garnet, howlite, kyanite, larimar, peridot, smithsonite, sugilite

Animals (to work with): Agate, cat's-eye, diopside, hawk's-eye, jasper, labradorite, serpentine, tiger's-eye

Anxiety (to relieve): Angelite, azurite, celestine, cuprite, hematite, howlite, kyanite, rhodonite, smithsonite

Astral travel / work: Alexandrite, apophyllite, barite, calcite, carnelian, celestine, cerussite, fluorite, hawk's-eye, hematite, iolite, jasper, moldavite, opal, phenacite, quartz, sapphire, staurolite

Awareness / consciousness: Amethyst, ametrine, angelite, azurite, calcite, cat's-eye, celestine, cerussite, chrysocolla, danburite, epidote, hawk's-eye, labradorite, moldavite, obsidian, opal, quartz, smoky quartz, sodalite, topaz

Balance: Agate, ametrine, apophyllite, aragonite, calcite chalcedony, chrysoprase, danburite, desert rose, diopside, dioptase, dolomite, garnet, hawk's-eye, jasper, jet, labradorite, lepidolite, moonstone, obsidian, opal, pearl, quartz, rhodochrosite, smithsonite, sodalite, spinel, staurolite, sugilite, tourmaline, zircon

Banish: Aquamarine, beryl, bloodstone, chrysoprase, cuprite, dioptase, jasper, malachite, rhodonite, quartz, salt

Bind: Herkimer diamond, jasper, jet, lodestone, obsidian, onyx, salt, sard

Business / employment: Bloodstone, emerald, malachite, tiger's-eye

Calm / soothe: Amber, amethyst, ametrine, aragonite, aventurine, azurite, beryl, blue lace agate, celestine, chrysocolla, diamond, dolomite, dumortierite, fluorite, garnet, hematite, iolite, kunzite, kyanite, larimar, lepidolite, moonstone, opal, peridot, rhodonite, rose quartz, selenite, smithsonite, sodalite, tiger's-eye, topaz

Challenges / difficulties (to deal with): Azurite, beryl, carnelian, diamond, lodestone, malachite, pearl, rhodonite, sard, sardonyx, smoky quartz, sodalite, spinel

Changes / transitions (to deal with, initiate): Amber, andalusite, amethyst, aventurine, blue lace agate, cerussite, chrysocolla, citrine, garnet, jasper, kyanite, lepidolite, opal, quartz, rhodochrosite, staurolite, topaz, white quartz, zoisite

Clarity: Amber, ametrine, apophyllite, aquamarine, aventurine, beryl, blue lace agate, calcite, celestine, cerussite, chrysoberyl, citrine, danburite, diamond, dumortierite, hawk's-eye, hematite, kyanite, labradorite, obsidian, pearl, quartz, sardonyx, selenite, sodalite, topaz, tourmaline, turquoise

Communication: Amazonite, amethyst, angelite, apatite, aquamarine, azurite, beryl, blue lace agate, calcite, carnelian, celestine, cerussite, chalcedony, danburite, dumortierite, fluorite, garnet, hiddenite, iolite, kunzite, kyanite, malachite, phenacite, quartz, sardonyx, selenite, tiger's-eye, topaz, turquoise, zoisite

Community: Aventurine, charoite, citrine, diopside, kyanite, obsidian, petrified wood, quartz, rhodonite, sard, smoky quartz, sodalite

Compassion: Angelite, aragonite, aventurine, celestine, chrysoberyl, chrysoprase, cuprite, dolomite, howlite, jasper, kunzite, rhodochrosite, rose quartz, ruby, smithsonite, turquoise

Confidence: Agate, aragonite, aventurine, bloodstone, blue lace agate, calcite, carnelian, chrysoberyl, diamond, garnet, hiddenite, labradorite, larimar, lodestone, onyx, rhodonite, tiger's-eye, tourmaline, zircon, zoisite

Courage / fortitude: Agate, aventurine, beryl, calcite, carnelian, danburite, diamond, garnet, jade, jasper, labradorite, lapis lazuli, ruby, sard, sardonyx, spinel, tourmaline

Creativity: Agate, amber, amethyst, apatite, aquamarine, aventurine, calcite, carnelian, cat's-eye, chrysocolla, citrine, cuprite, dumortierite, emerald, garnet, howlite, kyanite, larimar, moonstone, pearl, quartz, ruby, sapphire, serpentine, smoky quartz, spinel, staurolite, tiger's-eye, tourmaline, turquoise, white quartz, zoisite

Danger (to avoid): Agate, malachite, obsidian, sard, tiger's-eye, topaz

Death / ancestors / the afterlife: Amber, amazonite, carnelian, hematite, jade, jet, lapis lazuli, malachite, obsidian, petrified wood, quartz, rose quartz, topaz, white quartz

Decisions: Ametrine, aventurine, azurite, barite, bloodstone, carnelian, hematite, jade, onyx, pyrite, quartz, sardonyx, selenite, sphene

Dedication / devotion / commitment: Charoite, diamond, diopside, garnet, ruby, sapphire, tourmaline

Determination / perseverance / discipline: Agate, andalusite, dumortierite, garnet, jasper, onyx, opal, sard, sardonyx, sodalite, spinel, sunstone, zoisite

Divination: Amethyst, apatite, azurite, bloodstone, calcite, charoite, diopside, fluorite, hematite, hiddenite, jasper, jet, lapis lazuli, malachite, moldavite, moonstone, obsidian, pyrite, quartz, tiger's-eye, topaz

Dreamwork: Alexandrite, amethyst, andalusite, angelite, azurite, barite, calcite, chalcedony, chrysocolla, citrine, desert rose, dumortierite, fluorite, garnet, hematite, Herkimer diamond, howlite, jade, kyanite, malachite, moonstone, onyx, phenacite, quartz, sapphire, selenite, smithsonite, smoky quartz, sodalite, turquoise

Emotions: Agate, amazonite, ametrine, aventurine, azurite, beryl, calcite, celestine, chalcedony, chrysoberyl, chrysoprase, cuprite, diamond, dioptase, dolomite, emerald, fluorite, garnet, howlite, iolite, jet, kunzite, lepidolite, obsidian, opal, pearl, rhodochrosite, rose quartz, sapphire, selenite, smithsonite, sodalite, spinel, sugilite, topaz, tourmaline, turquoise, zircon, zoisite

Envy / jealousy (to deal with): Chrysoprase, emerald, sapphire, sugilite

Fairies (to contact): Amber, andalusite, danburite, diopside, emerald, fluorite, jade, peridot, phenacite, quartz, staurolite

Faith: Alexandrite, bloodstone, diamond, iolite, pearl, rose quartz

Fear (to deal with, subdue): Blue lace agate, calcite, charoite, cuprite, dolomite, jet, larimar, onyx, quartz, ruby, sapphire, sodalite, sunstone, tiger's-eye, topaz, tourmaline, zoisite

Fertility: Amazonite, carnelian, diamond, garnet, jade, jasper, moonstone, pearl, rhodonite, rose quartz, salt, sardonyx, turquoise, zoisite

Fidelity: Diamond, garnet, Herkimer diamond, lapis lazuli, rhodochrosite, rhodonite, sapphire, topaz

Focus / concentrate: Amazonite, amethyst, ametrine, andalusite, apatite, beryl, calcite, fluorite, garnet, jasper, kyanite, lepidolite, obsidian, opal, pyrite, quartz, sardonyx

Forgiveness: Angelite, chrysoberyl, diopside, dioptase, lodestone, obsidian, rhodochrosite, rhodonite, topaz

Friendship: Aventurine, blue lace agate, chrysoprase, garnet, lapis lazuli, lodestone, moonstone, rhodochrosite, rose quartz, sard, smithsonite

Goals: Agate, amazonite, amethyst, calcite, citrine, epidote, fluorite, garnet, hematite, onyx, petrified wood, sapphire, sard, sodalite, staurolite, zircon

Grief / sorrow (to deal with): Amber, apatite, aquamarine, carnelian, dolomite, garnet, hematite, hiddenite, jet, lapis lazuli, malachite, rose quartz, smoky quartz, spinel, topaz, white quartz

Ground and center energy: Agate, amazonite, amethyst, andalusite, aragonite, blue lace agate, calcite, cerussite, chrysocolla, cuprite, diopside, dolomite, garnet, hematite, lodestone, obsidian, petrified wood, pyrite, quartz, smoky quartz, staurolite, tourmaline

Growth: Agate, amazonite, amethyst, ametrine, apophyllite, aragonite, azurite, beryl, calcite, cat's-eye, celestine, charoite, chrysoprase, citrine, danburite, diopside, iolite, jade, jasper, kunzite, malachite, onyx, opal, peridot, ruby, serpentine, smithsonite, sugilite, sunstone, tourmaline, zoisite

Guidance: Amethyst, ametrine, aquamarine, aragonite, barite, beryl, calcite, citrine, danburite, jade, kunzite, kyanite, lodestone, malachite, moonstone, pearl, phenacite, sardonyx, sodalite, staurolite, tourmaline, turquoise, zoisite

Happiness / joy: Alexandrite, apophyllite, aquamarine, aventurine, blue lace agate, cat's-eye, chrysoprase, citrine, garnet, Herkimer diamond, peridot, rhodonite, rose quartz, sardonyx, sodalite, tourmaline, turquoise, zircon, zoisite

Harmony: Agate, amazonite, amethyst, ametrine, apatite, blue lace agate, celestine, citrine, garnet, jade, kunzite, larimar, lepidolite, petrified wood, rose quartz, selenite, topaz, tourmaline, zircon

Healing: Agate, amber, amethyst, ametrine, apatite, aquamarine, aragonite, aventurine, beryl, bloodstone, blue lace agate, calcite, celestine, chalcedony, chrysoberyl, danburite, diamond, diopside, dioptase, fluorite, garnet, hawk's-eye, hematite, hiddenite, jasper, jet, kunzite, lapis lazuli, larimar, moonstone, peridot, petrified wood, rhodonite, rose quartz, ruby, salt, sapphire, smithsonite, sugilite, sunstone, tourmaline, white quartz, zircon

Heartbreak (to recover from): Aventurine, beryl, calcite, chrysocolla, lapis lazuli, rhodonite, rose quartz

Hexes (to break, avoid): Emerald, jasper, jet, onyx, quartz, ruby, salt

Home / family: Agate, amazonite, apatite, apophyllite, blue lace agate, calcite, celestine, citrine, epidote, garnet, kunzite, lodestone, malachite, quartz, rhodochrosite, rhodonite, salt, smoky quartz, staurolite, topaz, turquoise, white quartz, zircon, zoisite

Hope: Agate, amazonite, blue lace agate, citrine, malachite, opal, white quartz

Independence: Aquamarine, aventurine, jade, tourmaline

Insight / illumination: Agate, amber, aventurine, azurite, calcite, cat's-eye, dumortierite, hawk's-eye, jasper, moldavite, opal, sodalite, spinel, tiger's-eye, topaz, tourmaline, zoisite

Inspiration: Amazonite, amethyst, apatite, aquamarine, blue lace agate, calcite, carnelian, cuprite, jade, labradorite, quartz, ruby, selenite, serpentine, tiger's-eye, topaz, tourmaline, white quartz, zircon

Introspection: Ametrine, calcite, garnet, kunzite, moldavite, phenacite, smoky quartz, tiger's-eye, topaz, tourmaline

Intuition: Agate, amazonite, amethyst, apophyllite, aragonite, azurite, calcite, cat's-eye, diopside, fluorite, labradorite, lapis lazuli, malachite, moonstone, phenacite, pyrite, ruby, sapphire, sard, smithsonite, sodalite, turquoise

Justice / legal matters: Amethyst, aventurine, bloodstone, diamond, hematite, jade, jet, lapis lazuli, sapphire, selenite, tourmaline

Knowledge / learning: Apatite, apophyllite, beryl, cat's-eye, charoite, dumortierite, epidote, garnet, phenacite, sodalite, sphene, tiger's-eye, tourmaline

Loss (to deal with): Ametrine, aquamarine, garnet, hiddenite, malachite, moldavite, rose quartz, smoky quartz, topaz, white quartz

Love / romance: Agate, alexandrite, amethyst, apatite, aquamarine, beryl, calcite, chrysocolla, danburite, desert rose, diamond, diopside, dioptase, emerald, epidote, garnet, jade, jasper, kunzite, lapis lazuli, larimar, lepidolite, lodestone, moonstone, opal, pearl, rhodochrosite, rhodonite, rose quartz, ruby, sapphire, sardonyx, selenite, sugilite, topaz, tourmaline, zircon, zoisite

Loyalty: Barite, garnet, kyanite, lodestone, moonstone, ruby, spinel

Luck: Agate, alexandrite, amazonite, andalusite, aventurine, bloodstone, cat's-eye, chrysoprase, citrine, diamond, emerald, Herkimer diamond, jade, jasper, jet, lepidolite, lodestone, malachite, obsidian, opal, pearl, sardonyx, smoky quartz, staurolite, sunstone, tiger's-eye, topaz

Manifestation: Amazonite, amber, amethyst, andalusite, blue lace agate, calcite, citrine, garnet, hematite, lepidolite, onyx, pyrite, sard, tourmaline, turquoise, zoisite

Marriage: Aquamarine, beryl, lodestone, onyx, rhodonite, rose quartz, sardonyx

Memory / memories: Andalusite, barite, chalcedony, dumortierite, howlite, pyrite, sugilite

Messages / omens (to receive, interpret): Angelite, barite, calcite, chalcedony, citrine, dumortierite, emerald, epidote, garnet, Herkimer diamond, howlite, obsidian, phenacite, ruby

Money: Agate, aventurine, bloodstone, calcite, jasper, lodestone, malachite, opal, pearl, pyrite, staurolite, tiger's-eye, topaz, tourmaline

Motivation: Amber, calcite, celestine, fluorite, labradorite, lodestone, serpentine, zircon, zoisite

Negativity (to dispel, avert): Amazonite, ametrine, andalusite, azurite, carnelian, charoite, dolomite, epidote, garnet, hawk's-eye, hematite, hiddenite, jade, jasper, kunzite, kyanite, larimar, lepidolite, malachite, obsidian, onyx, peridot, quartz, rose quartz, ruby, salt, selenite, smithsonite, smoky quartz, tourmaline, turquoise

Nightmares (to subdue, ward off): Chrysoprase, garnet, jet, lepidolite, onyx, sapphire, topaz

Obstacles (to overcome, remove): Agate, azurite, barite, bloodstone, blue lace agate, diamond, epidote, fluorite, kunzite, malachite, moonstone, obsidian, opal, petrified wood, smoky quartz, spinel, tourmaline

Optimism: Agate, beryl, cat's-eye, chrysoberyl, citrine, dolomite, jasper, sunstone, zoisite

Past-life work: Andalusite, chalcedony, cuprite, desert rose, dumortierite, howlite, larimar, petrified wood, white quartz

Patience: Blue lace agate, danburite, dumortierite, garnet, howlite, lepidolite, peridot, rhodonite

Peace / tranquility: Amethyst, aquamarine, blue lace agate, celestine, chalcedony, chryso-beryl, chrysocolla, chrysoprase, danburite, desert rose, jade, jasper, kunzite, lapis lazuli, larimar, lepidolite, malachite, obsidian, pearl, peridot, rhodochrosite, rhodonite, sard-onyx, selenite, sodalite, sugilite, topaz, tourmaline, zircon

Problems (to deal with, solve): Agate, aventurine, barite, chrysocolla, citrine, cuprite, he-matite, jasper, malachite, onyx, petrified wood, quartz, rhodochrosite, sapphire, sard, sodalite, zoisite

Prosperity / wealth: Agate, alexandrite, aventurine, calcite, cat's-eye, diamond, dioptase, emerald, Herkimer diamond, jade, jasper, malachite, opal, peridot, ruby, salt, spinel, tiger's-eye, tourmaline

Protection / defense: Agate, amber, amethyst, andalusite, angelite, aquamarine, aventurine, calcite, carnelian, cat's-eye, charoite, citrine, cuprite, diamond, emerald, epidote, garnet, jade, jasper, jet, lapis lazuli, lepidolite, lodestone, malachite, obsidian, onyx, phenacite, pyrite, quartz, ruby, salt, sapphire, sard, sardonyx, serpentine, smoky quartz, spinel, staurolite, sunstone, tiger's-eye, topaz, tourmaline, turquoise, zircon, zoisite

Psychic abilities / work: Alexandrite, amethyst, angelite, apatite, aquamarine, aragonite, azurite, barite, beryl, calcite, chalcedony, charoite, citrine, danburite, desert rose, dia-mond, dumortierite, emerald, hawk's-eye, Herkimer diamond, hiddenite, iolite, jasper, jet, labradorite, lapis lazuli, lepidolite, malachite, moldavite, moonstone, obsidian, opal, peridot, phenacite, pyrite, quartz, ruby, salt, sapphire, smithsonite, smoky quartz, soda-lite, sugilite, tiger's-eye, tourmaline, zoisite

Purification / cleanse: Amber, amethyst, ametrine, apophyllite, aquamarine, aragonite, cal-cite, charoite, lepidolite, moldavite, pearl, peridot, phenacite, quartz, salt, smoky quartz, topaz, zircon

Reconciliation: Apatite, beryl, diamond, Herkimer diamond, kunzite, lodestone, rose quartz

Relationships: Amazonite, amber, apatite, aquamarine, barite, beryl, chrysocolla, cuprite, garnet, Herkimer diamond, hiddenite, kunzite, lapis lazuli, larimar, lodestone, obsidian, onyx, peridot, rhodochrosite, rhodonite, rose quartz, ruby, sapphire, sardonyx, smith-sonite, sodalite, spinel, tourmaline, zoisite

Remove / release: Agate, apatite, aventurine, carnelian, cuprite, dolomite, fluorite, iolite, kunzite, larimar, moldavite, moonstone, obsidian, peridot, quartz, rose quartz, salt, su-gilite, topaz

Renewal / rebirth / new beginnings: Ametrine, aquamarine, bloodstone, calcite, carnelian, chrysoberyl, citrine, garnet, hawk's-eye, hematite, kyanite, moldavite, peridot, petrified wood, quartz, rhodonite, selenite, serpentine, topaz, tourmaline, turquoise, white quartz, zoisite

Respect: Alexandrite, cerussite, chrysoberyl, dioptase, rhodonite, rose quartz, sard

Self: Agate, alexandrite, angelite, apatite, apophyllite, aragonite, blue lace agate, celestine, charoite, chrysoberyl, chrysoprase, danburite, dioptase, dumortierite, emerald, fluorite, Herkimer diamond, hiddenite, jasper, kunzite, onyx, opal, phenacite, rhodonite, rose quartz, ruby, sard, sardonyx, tourmaline

Sex / sexuality: Agate, cuprite, garnet, jasper, rose quartz, ruby, sapphire, serpentine, smoky quartz, spinel, tiger's-eye, topaz, zircon, zoisite

Shamanic work: Chrysocolla, jasper, labradorite, lepidolite, quartz, sodalite, topaz

Spirits / spirit guides: Amethyst, ametrine, azurite, barite, bloodstone, diopside, dumortierite, emerald, hiddenite, howlite, jade, labradorite, moonstone, phenacite, quartz, salt, sapphire, smithsonite, sugilite, tourmaline

Spirituality: Alexandrite, amethyst, ametrine, andalusite, apatite, apophyllite, azurite, barite, beryl, bloodstone, blue lace agate, calcite, celestine, charoite, citrine, danburite, desert rose, diamond, diopside, dolomite, fluorite, garnet, Herkimer diamond, hiddenite, iolite, kunzite, kyanite, lapis lazuli, lepidolite, lodestone, malachite, moldavite, pearl, quartz, rose quartz, sphene, staurolite, sugilite, tourmaline, turquoise

Stability: Amazonite, amber, amethyst, ametrine, azurite, calcite, celestine, chrysocolla, cuprite, dolomite, garnet, iolite, jasper, kyanite, lodestone, quartz, rhodochrosite, sphene

Strength: Agate, alexandrite, amazonite, amethyst, ametrine, aventurine, bloodstone, charoite, diamond, garnet, hematite, kyanite, lodestone, moonstone, opal, petrified wood, pyrite, quartz, rose quartz, ruby, sardonyx, tiger's-eye, tourmaline, zircon

Stress (to relieve): Agate, angelite, apophyllite, aragonite, beryl, blue lace agate, celestine, diamond, dioptase, dolomite, howlite, kyanite, labradorite, larimar, lepidolite, petrified wood, rhodonite, rose quartz, selenite, smithsonite, sodalite

Success: Agate, alexandrite, amazonite, amber, amethyst, andalusite, aventurine, bloodstone, calcite, carnelian, chrysoprase, citrine, epidote, fluorite, garnet, jasper, labradorite, lodestone, malachite, sodalite, spinel, staurolite, sunstone, tiger's-eye, turquoise, zircon

Transformation: Alexandrite, amethyst, angelite, apophyllite, azurite, blue lace agate, cat's-eye, cerussite, chrysocolla, labradorite, moldavite, obsidian, salt, staurolite, sugilite, white quartz

Travel: Aquamarine, beryl, emerald, garnet, jasper, lapis lazuli, lodestone, malachite, phenacite, staurolite, turquoise

Trust: Amazonite, apophyllite, blue lace agate, charoite, diamond, zoisite

Truth: Aragonite, danburite, dioptase, emerald, pyrite, spinel, tiger's-eye, turquoise, zoisite

Unity: Amazonite, charoite, diamond, smoky quartz, zircon

Well-being: Agate, aventurine, beryl, calcite, dioptase, garnet, jade, jasper, kyanite, sugilite, sunstone, zircon

Willpower: Beryl, cat's-eye, chrysoprase, citrine, fluorite, jasper, onyx, opal, pyrite, quartz, sugilite, tourmaline, zoisite

Wisdom: Agate, amber, amethyst, apophyllite, aquamarine, beryl, blue lace agate, carnelian, chrysocolla, chrysoprase, desert rose, dioptase, garnet, Herkimer diamond, jasper, labradorite, lapis lazuli, moonstone, opal, pearl, petrified wood, quartz, rose quartz, ruby, salt, sapphire, sardonyx, smoky quartz, spinel, sugilite, tiger's-eye, topaz, turquoise

Appendix B

DEITIES

This list will help you find crystals that are associated with particular deities.

Angus: Rose quartz, sapphire
Aphrodite: Pearl, salt
Apollo: Amber, sapphire
Arianrhod: Moonstone
Asclepius: Agate
Athena: Celestine, jade, jasper, obsidian
Bacchus: Amethyst
Badb: Bloodstone
Banba: Peridot
Bast: Cat's-eye, tiger's-eye
Brigid: Azurite, peridot
Ceres: Emerald
Chalchihuitlicue: Jade, turquoise
Coatlicue: Jade
Cupid: Opal
Cybele: Jet
The Dagda: Diamond, zircon
Danu: Amber, diamond, zircon
Diana: Amethyst, moonstone, pearl
Dionysus: Amethyst
Dôn: Jet

Enlil: Rose quartz

Epona: Azurite

Felicitas: Obsidian

Freya: Amber, pearl

Hathor: Hawk's-eye, lapis lazuli, turquoise

Hecate: Moonstone, pearl, quartz, sapphire, selenite

The Heliades: Amber

Helios: Amber, heliodor beryl

Iris: Rainbow obsidian

Isis: Carnelian, emerald, jasper, lapis lazuli, moonstone, pearl, star sapphire

Juno: Lodestone

Jupiter: Topaz

Justitia: Amethyst, lapis lazuli, sapphire

Krishna: Ruby

Kuan Yin: Jade, pearl, turquoise

Lakshmi: Pearl

Lugh: Obsidian, sapphire, sunstone, topaz

Luna: Moonstone, selenite, white quartz

Ma'at: Jade, turquoise

Manannan: Azurite, turquoise

Mars: Onyx, sardonyx

Mercury: Emerald, malachite

The Morrigan: Red agate, bloodstone, obsidian, onyx, ruby

Neptune: Beryl, pearl, salt

Ninlil: Rose quartz

Njord: Amber, jet, malachite

Nut: Lapis lazuli

Odin: Carnelian

Ogma: Azurite, turquoise

Pan: Jet

Pele: Obsidian, peridot

Poseidon: Beryl, pearl, salt

Ra: Hawk's eye, sunstone, tiger's-eye, topaz

Rhiannon: Moonstone

Sarasvati: Pearl

Sekhmet: Tiger's-eye

Selene: Moonstone, selenite, white quartz

Tiamat: Beryl

Venus: Amethyst, emerald, lapis lazuli, onyx, pearl, rose quartz

Vesta: Chrysoprase

Vishnu: Emerald

MINERALOGICAL GLOSSARY

Adamantine luster: The effect of light reflecting off the surface of a stone when it sparkles like a diamond or lead crystal glass. This is also called a diamond luster.

Adularescence: The optical effect of a bluish-white, ethereal reflection. It is most pronounced in adularia and moonstone. The name of the stone and optical effect were derived from Adula, a name used in antiquity for the Gotthard area of Switzerland now commonly known as the Adula Alps.[224]

Amorphous crystal system: Although not a true crystal system, this term is used to denote a lack of specific internal structure.

Asterism: A star pattern that is formed by tiny needlelike inclusions arranged at varying angles within a stone.

Aventurescence: The colorful play of glittering reflections from inclusions within the mineral aventurine. This effect is also seen in sunstone.

Banding: The effect of different colors that are clearly layered into stripes or bands.

Bipyramidal: A type of doubly terminated crystal that has a pyramid shape at both ends.

Brilliant cut: A style of cutting gemstones into a round shape with facets (flat planes) that maximize a stone's brilliance and fire. It is also called a diamond cut.

Cabochon: A method of cutting a gemstone so it is smooth, domed, and without facets. It emphasizes and enhances the cat's-eye effect. A stone cut in this manor is referred to as being cut en cabochon.

Cameo: A method of cutting a stone so that one layer is carved with a design and raised above a background layer.

----

224. Philippe Roth, *Minerals First Discovered in Switzerland and Minerals Named After Swiss Individuals* (Charlottesville, VA: Excalibur Mineral Corporation, 2007), 219.

Carbuncle: An old term used since ancient times through the Victorian era referring to translucent red stones. It is believed to most often refer to almandine garnet or ruby.

Cat's-eye: An effect created by parallel fibers, needles, or channels within a stone that produce a luminous line resembling the slit of the cat's-eye. The line seems to move as the stone is rotated. This effect is also called chatoyancy.

Chatoyancy: From the French *chat*, "cat," and *oeil*, "eye," this term is another name for the cat's-eye effect.

Cleavage: The predictable manner in which a stone can be smoothly broken.

Cluster: A dense growth of crystals.

Color change phenomenon: A stone that appears different colors depending on the type of light (natural or artificial, for example) in which it is viewed.

Cryptocrystalline: A rock made up of crystals that are so tiny they cannot be seen with the unaided eye.

Crystal symmetry: The degree of regularity in the arrangement of atoms in a crystal structure.

Crystal system: One of seven categories of crystal structures based on the symmetry or regularity of its internal pattern.

Cubic crystal system: The most symmetrical crystal system with a square inner structure. Exterior shapes include the cube, octahedron, and rhombic dodecahedron. It is also called the isometric crystal system.

Dendrite: A mineral inclusion that forms a branching, treelike pattern.

Diamond luster: The effect of light reflecting off the surface of a stone when it sparkles like a diamond or lead crystal glass. This is also called an adamantine luster.

Dichroic: The effect where a stone appears two different colors or hues when viewed from different angles.

Double refraction: The effect when light does not pass straight through a stone but is split in two and each ray is bent (refracted) at different angles. This causes a stone to appear extra sparkly.

Doubly terminated: The description of a crystal that has complete terminations (not broken) at both ends.

Emerald cut: A style of cutting a stone into an eight-sided, octagonal shape. This cut is intended to bring out the depth of color rather than the sparkle as in the diamond cut.

Face: A flat plane or side of a crystal; also called a crystal face.

Facet: A flat, polished surface of a cut gemstone.

Fibrous: A mineral that is made up of fine, parallel threads.

Fishtail: A type of twinning where two crystals are attached on one side and grow as mirror images of each other creating a V-shape.

Flawless: A gemstone that has no inclusions or cracks.

Fluorescence: A light phenomenon whereby a stone emits a different color or multiple colors under ultraviolet light. This is most pronounced and named for the mineral fluorite.

Glassy luster: The effect that occurs when light reflects off the surface of a stone, making it appear shiny like a freshly washed glass. This is also called a vitreous luster.

Greasy luster: The effect of light reflecting off a stone's surface, making it appear shiny like an ink or grease spot on paper. It is not as shiny as the glassy/vitreous luster.

Hardness: The measure of how resistant a stone is to scratching.

Hexagonal crystal system: This system has a hexagon shape as its inner structure. Exterior shapes include four-sided prisms and pyramids, twelve-sided pyramids, and double pyramids.

Inclusion: An imperfection within a stone that can be in the form of a solid, liquid, or gas.

Intaglio: A method where an image is engraved or etched into a stone, unlike a cameo where a carved image is raised above a background layer.

Intergrown crystals: The growth pattern of two or more crystals that penetrate each other.

Iridescence: The optical effect when a stone displays rainbowlike colors from different angles.

Isometric: Another name for the cubic crystal system.

Labradorescence: A metallic iridescence that is especially pronounced and named for the mineral labradorite.

Luminescence: A light phenomenon whereby a stone gives off light under certain conditions. For example, barite becomes bright under a light source and then retains some of its brightness for a time in the dark. Fluorescence is another example of a type of luminescence.

Luster: The visual effect of light reflected off the surface of a stone.

Metallic luster: The effect of light reflecting off a stone's surface, giving it a polished metal sheen.

Mineral group: A recognized selection of minerals that are similar in structure and/or chemical composition.

Monoclinic crystal system: This system has a parallelogram-shaped inner structure. Exterior shapes include prisms with inclined end faces.

Opalescence: The optical effect when a stone displays a milky-blue or pearly appearance. This is most pronounced in common opals.

Organic gemstone: A non-mineral gemstone such as amber or pearl.

Orthorhombic crystal system: This system has a diamond-shaped inner structure. Exterior shapes include single and double pyramids, and rhombic prisms.

Piezoelectric effect: The phenomenon whereby an electrical charge occurs when a stone is heated, compressed, or vibrated.

Play of color: A description of the rainbowlike iridescence that changes with the angle of view. This occurs in precious opals.

Pleochroism: The appearance of different colors or hues when a stone is viewed from different angles. Dichroic exhibits two colors or hues, and trichroic exhibits three.

Photochromism: A phenomenon where a stone's color fades when exposed to light but returns after the stone is kept in the dark.

Pseudomorph: The process through which one mineral replaces another.

Refraction: The bending of white light and splitting it into colors of the spectrum.

Rock-forming mineral: A mineral that is abundant and common in the earth's crust.

Sixling: A sixfold structure formed by six intergrown crystals.

Tektite: A rock that is formed from the melting and rapid cooling of terrestrial rocks that were vaporized by the high-energy impacts of meteorites and comets.

Tetragonal crystal system: This system has a rectangular inner structure. Exterior shapes include four- and eight-sided pyramids and prisms.

Transparency: A description of the amount of light that passes through a crystal.

Trichroic: The appearance of three different colors or hues when viewed from different angles.

Triclinic crystal system: This system has a trapezium-shaped inner structure. Exterior shapes usually have paired faces.

Trigonal crystal system: This system has a triangular inner structure. Exterior shapes include three-sided prism and pyramids and rhombohedron. It is considered a subsystem of the hexagonal crystal system.

Trilling: A sixfold structure formed by three intergrown twinned crystals.

Twinning: Twinning is the process of two crystals that grow together in a mirrored pattern.

Vitreous luster: The effect that occurs when light reflects off the surface of a stone making it look shiny like a freshly washed glass. This is also called a glassy luster.

BIBLIOGRAPHY

Addison, Julia de Wolf Gibbs. *Arts and Crafts in the Middle Ages*. Boston: L. C. Page & Company, 1908.

Agnew, Neville, ed. *Conservation of Ancient Sites on the Silk Road*. Los Angeles: Getty Publications, 2010.

Alexander, Pramod O. *A Handbook of Minerals, Crystals, Rocks and Ores*. New Delhi, India: New India Publishing Agency, 2009.

Altman, Jen. *Gem and Stone: Jewels of Earth, Sea, and Sky*. San Francisco: Chronicle Books, 2012.

Anderson, Dale. *Ancient China*. Chicago: Raintree, 2005.

Anonymous. *The Orphic Hymns*. Translated by Apostolos N. Athanassakis and Benjamin M. Wolkow. Baltimore: Johns Hopkins University Press, 2013.

Bangert, Andrea. "Introduction to Mineralogy: A Collection of Copper Minerals." University of California, Santa Cruz, accessed January 8, 2016 at http://dave.ucsc.edu/myrtreia/specimens.html#Chrysocolla.

Bariand, Pierre, and Michel Duchamp, eds. *Larousse Encyclopedia of Precious Gems*. New York: Van Nostrand Reinhold, 1991.

Barth, Tom F. W. *Feldspars*. New York: John Wiley and Sons, 1969.

Bartsch, Joel A. *Kremlin Gold: 1000 Years of Russian Gems and Jewels*. New York: Abrams, 2000.

Bates, Robert L., and Julia A. Jackson, eds. *Dictionary of Geological Terms*. New York: Anchor Press, 1984.

Bauer, Jaroslav, and Vladimir Bouška. *A Guide in Color to Precious & Semiprecious Stones*. Secaucus, NJ: Chartwell Books, 1992.

Bergslien, Elisa. *An Introduction to Forensic Geoscience*. Hoboken, NJ: Wiley-Blackwell, 2012.

Bishop, A. C., A. R. Woolley, and W. R. Hamilton. *Cambridge Guide to Minerals, Rocks and Fossils,* 2nd ed. New York: University of Cambridge Press, 2001.

Bonewitz, Ronald Louis. *Smithsonian Nature Guide: Gems*. New York: DK Publishing, 2013.

_____ . *Smithsonian Nature Guide: Rocks and Minerals*. New York: DK Publishing, 2012.

Bristow, Henry William. *A Glossary of Mineralogy*. London: Longman, Green, Longman, and Roberts, 1861.

Bunson, Margaret R. *Encyclopedia of Ancient Egypt,* rev. ed. New York: Facts on File, 2002.

Burnie, David. *Light*. New York: Dorling Kindersley Publishing, 1999.

Cairncross, Bruce. *Field Guide to Rocks & Minerals of Southern Africa*. Cape Town, South Africa: New Struik Publishers, 2004.

_____ . *First Field Guide to Gemstones of Southern Africa*. Cape Town, South Africa: Struik Publishers, 2001.

Causey, Faya. *Amber and the Ancient World*. Los Angeles: Getty Publications, 2011.

Chang, L. L. Y., R. A. Howie, and J. Zussman. *Rock-forming Minerals: Non-Silicates,* vol. 5B. Bath, England: Geological Society Publishing House, 1998.

Cirillo, Dexter. *Southwestern Indian Jewelry*. New York: Abbeville Press, 1992.

Clark, Carol. *Handy Pocket Guide to Asian Gemstones*. Hong Kong: Periplus Editions (HK), 2004.

_____ . *Tropical Gemstones*. Hong Kong: Periplus Editions (HK), 1998.

Clucas, Stephen, ed. *John Dee: Interdisciplinary Studies in English Renaissance Thought*. Dordrecht, The Netherlands: Springer, 2006.

Collings, Michael R. *Gemlore: An Introduction to Precious and Semi-Precious Stones,* 2nd ed. Rockville, MD: The Borgo Press, 2009.

Collon, Dominique. *Ancient Near Eastern Art*. Los Angeles: University of California Press, 1995.

Considine, Douglas M., ed. *Van Nostrand's Scientific Encyclopedia,* vol. 2, 8th ed. New York: John Wiley & Sons, 1995.

Cristofono, Peter. *Rockhounding New England: A Guide to 100 of the Region's Best Rockhounding Sites*. Guilford, CT: Morris Book Publishing, 2014.

Cunningham, Scott. *Cunningham's Encyclopedia of Crystal, Gem & Metal Magic*. St. Paul: Llewellyn Publications, 2001.

De Puma, Richard Daniel. *Etruscan Art in the Metropolitan Museum of Art*. New York: The Metropolitan Museum of Art, 2013.

Dennis, Geoffrey W. *The Encyclopedia of Jewish Myth, Magic and Mysticism*, 2nd ed. Woodbury, MN: Llewellyn Publications, 2016.

Desautels, Paul E. *The Gem Kingdom*. New York: Random House, 1977.

Donkin, R. A. *Beyond Price: Pearls and Pearl-fishing: Origins to the Age of Discoveries*. Philadelphia: The American Philosophical Society, 1998.

Driscoll, Killian. *Understanding Quartz Technology in Early Prehistoric Ireland*, vol. 1. University College Dublin, January 2010. Accessed February 15, 2016, at http://www.lithicsireland.ie/.

Eastaugh, Nicholas, Valentine Walsh, Tracey Chaplin, and Ruth Siddall. *Pigment Compendium: A Dictionary and Optical Microscopy of Historical Pigments*. Burlington, MA: Butterworth-Heinemann, 2008.

Eckert, Allan W. *The World of Opals*. New York: John Wiley & Sons, 1997.

Editors of Encyclopedia Britannica. "Tektite." Encyclopedia Britannica Online. Accessed January 29, 2016, at http://www.britannica.com/science/tektite.

Edwards, Ron, and Lisa Dickie. *Diamonds and Gemstones*. New York: Crabtree Publishing Company, 2004.

Efraim Lev, and Zohar Amar. *Practical Materia Medica of the Medieval Eastern Mediterranean According to the Cairo Genizah*. Leiden, The Netherlands: Koninklijke Brill NV, 2008.

Egleston, T., ed. "Bulletin of the United States National Museum," no. 33: *Catalogue of Minerals and Synonyms*. Washington, DC: Government Printing Office, 1887.

Enghag, Per. *Encyclopedia of the Elements: Technical Data, History, Processing, Applications*. Weinheim, Germany: Wiley-VCH Verlag, 2004.

Evdokimov, Mikhail D. "Charoite: A Unique Mineral from a Unique Occurrence." *Gems and Gemology*, vol. 33, no. 1 (Spring 1997), 74.

Facaros, Dana, and Michael Pauls. *Turkey*. London: Cadogan Guides, 2000.

Farrington, Oliver Cummings. *Gems and Gem Minerals*. Chicago: A. W. Mumford Publishing, 1903.

Federman, David. *Modern Jeweler's Consumer Guide to Colored Gemstones*. New York: Van Nostrand Reinhold, 1990.

Finlay, Victoria. *Jewels: A Secret History*. New York: Random House, 2007.

Fischel, Anna, ed. *Smithsonian Gem: The Definitive Visual Guide*. New York: DK Publishing, 2016.

Freeman, Tom. *Environmental Geology Laboratory*. New York: John Wiley & Sons, 2004.

Friedman, John Block, and Kristen Mossler Figg, eds. *Trade, Travel, and Exploration in the Middle Ages: An Encyclopedia*. New York: Routledge, 2000.

Frondel, Clifford, ed. *Dana's The System of Mineralogy*, 7th ed., vol. 3: *Silica Minerals*. New York: John Wiley & Sons, 1962.

Gaines, Richard V., H. Catherine W. Skinner, Eugene E. Foord, Brian Mason, and Abraham Rosenzweig. *Dana's New Mineralogy: The System of Mineralogy of James Dwight Dana and Edward Salisbury Dana*, 8th ed. New York: John Wiley & Sons, 1997.

Gee, Lionel C. E., ed. *A Short Review of Mining Operations in the state of South Australia*, Issue 16. Adelaide, Australia: R.E.E. Rogers, 1912.

Gimbutas, Marija. *The Language of the Goddess*. New York: HarperCollins, 1991.

Grande, Lance, and Allison Augustyn. *Gems and Gemstones: Timeless Natural Beauty of the Mineral World*. Chicago: The University of Chicago Press, 2009.

Green, Miranda J. *Celtic Myths*, 2nd ed. Austin TX: University of Texas Press, 1995.

Groat, Lee Andrew, ed. *The Geology of Gem Deposits*. Quebec, Canada: Mineralogical Association of Canada, 2007.

Hamer, Frank, and Janet Hamer. *The Potter's Dictionary of Materials and Techniques*, 5th ed. Philadelphia: University of Pennsylvania Press, 2004.

Hansen, Valerie, and Kenneth R. Curtis. *Voyages in World History*, 2nd ed., vol. 1: to 1600. Boston: Wadsworth Cengage Learning, 2014.

Harper, Prudence O., Evelyn Klengel-Brandt, Joan Aruz, and Kim Benzel, eds. *Assyrian Origins: Discoveries at Ashur on the Tigris*. New York: Metropolitan Museum of Art, 1995.

Hayes, William C. *The Scepter of Egypt: A Background for the Study of the Egyptian Antiquities in the Metropolitan Museum of Art*. New York: Metropolitan Museum of Art, 1990.

Hekster, Olivier, Sebastien Schmidt-Hofner, and Christian Witschel, eds. *Ritual Dynamics and Religious Change in the Roman Empire*. Leiden, The Netherlands: Koninklijke Brill, NV, 2009.

Hesse, Rayner W., Jr. *Jewelrymaking Through History: An Encyclopedia*. Westport, CT: Greenwood Press, 2007.

Hourihane, Colum P., ed. *The Grove Encyclopedia of Medieval Art and Architecture*, vol. 2. New York: Oxford University Press, 2012.

Howard, Michael C. *Transnationalism in Ancient and Medieval Societies: The Role of Cross-Border Trade and Travel*. Jefferson, NC: McFarland & Company, 2012.

Hranicky, William Jack. *Archaeological Concepts, Techniques, and Terminology for American Prehistoric Lithic Technology*. Bloomington, IN: AuthorHouse, 2013.

Hunter, Dana. "Tiger's Eye: A Deceptive Delight," *Rosetta Stones*, Scientific American, July 29, 2015, https://blogs.scientificamerican.com/rosetta-stones/tiger-s-eye-a-deceptive-delight/, accessed 10/21/16.

Jackson, Tom. *What's that Rock or Mineral? A Beginners Guide*. New York: DK Publishing, 2014.

Jameson, Robert. *A System of Mineralogy*, vol. 1, 3rd ed. London: Hurst, Robinson & Company, 1820.

Johns, Catherine. *The Jewellry of Roman Britain: Celtic and Classical Traditions*. New York: Routledge, 1996.

Jolly, Karen, Catharina Raudvere, and Edward Peters. *Witchcraft and Magic in Europe*, vol. 3: *The Middle Ages*. London: The Athlone Press, 2002.

Jones, Cindy. *The Illustrated Dictionary of Geology*. New Delhi, India: Lotus Press, 2006.

Jung, C. G. *Mysterium Coniunctionis: An Inquiry into the Separation and Synthesis of Psychic Opposites in Alchemy*. Princeton, NJ: Princeton University Press, 1976.

King, Charles William. *Antique Gems: Their Origin, Uses, and Value*, 2nd ed. London: John Murray, 1866.

Koehler, Cheryl Angelina. *Touring the Sierra Nevada*. Reno, NV: University of Nevada Press, 2007.

Kogel, Jessica Elzea, Nikhil C. Trivedi, James M. Barker, and Stanley T. Krukowski, eds. *Industrial Minerals & Rocks: Commodities, Markets, and Uses*, 7th ed. Littleton, CO: Society for Mining, Metallurgy, and Exploration, 2006.

Knox, Kimberly, and Bryan K. Lees. "The Gem Rhodochrosite from the Sweet Home Mine, Colorado" *Gems and Gemology*, vol. 33, no. 2 (Summer 1997): 122.

Kunz, George Frederick. *The Curious Lore of Precious Stones*. Mineola, NY: Dover Publications, 1997.

Kurlansky, Mark. *Salt: A World History*. New York: Penguin Group, 2002.

Kužvart, Milos. *Industrial Minerals and Rocks*. New York: Elsevier, 1984.

Lambdin, Laura Cooner, and Robert Thomas Lambdin, eds. *A Companion to Old and Middle English Literature*. Westport, CT: Greenwood Press, 2002.

Linsell, Gavin. *Gems TV: Guide to Gems & Jewelry*. Doncaster, England: Insignia Books, 2009.

Loomis, Frederick Brewster. *Field Book of Common Rocks and Minerals*. New York: G. P. Putnam's Sons, 1948.

Lowry, Joe Dan, and Joe P. Lowry. *Turquoise: The World Story of a Fascinating Gemstone*. Layton, UT: Gibbs Smith, 2010.

Lucas, A., and J. R. Harris. *Ancient Egyptian Materials and Industries*. Mineola, NY: Dover Publications, 2012.

Mach, Ernst. *The Principles of Physical Optics: An Historical and Philosophical Treatment*. Translated by John S. Anderson and A. F. A. Young. Mineola, NY: Dover Publications, 2003.

Magnusson, Magnus. *Scotland: The Story of a Nation*. New York: Grove Press, 2000.

Maitra, K. K. *Encyclopaedic Dictionary of Clothing and Textiles, Part One*. New Delhi, India: Mittal Publications, 2007.

Mallory, J. P., and D. Q. Adams. *The Oxford Introduction to Proto-Indo-European and the Proto-Indo-European World*. Oxford, England: Oxford University Press, 2013.

Mallowan, Max. *Mallowan's Memoirs*. New York: Dodd, Mead & Company, 1977.

Mangathayaru, K. *Pharmacognosy: An Indian Perspective*. New Delhi, India: Pearson, 2013.

Manutchehr-Danai, Mohsen. *Dictionary of Gems and Gemology*. New York: Springer-Verlag, 2000.

Matlins, Antoinette. *Colored Gemstones: The Antoinette Matlins Buying Guide*, 3rd ed. Woodstock, VT: GemStone Press, 2010.

Matlins, Antoinette, and Antonio C. Bonanno. *Jewelry & Gems: The Buying Guide*, 7th ed. Woodstock, VT: GemStone Press, 2009.

McEwan, Colin, Andrew Middleton, Caroline Cartwright, and Rebecca Stacey. *Turquoise Mosaics from Mexico*. Durham, NC: Duke University Press, 2006.

McPherson, Alan. *State Geosymbols: Geological Symbols of the 50 United States*. Bloomington, IN: AuthorHouse, 2011.

Mercer, Ian F. *Crystals*. Cambridge, MA: Harvard University Press, 1990.

Merrill, Ronald T., Michael W. McElhinny, and Phillip L. McFadden. *The Magnetic Field of the Earth: Paleomagnetism, the Core, and the Deep Mantle*. San Diego, CA: Academic Press, 1998.

Miller, Anna M. *Illustrated Guide to Jewelry Appraising: Antique, Period, and Modern.* New York: Chapman & Hall, 1990.

Moorey, P. R. S. *Ancient Mesopotamian Materials and Industries: The Archaeological Evidence.* Winona Lake, IN: Eisenbrauns, 1994.

Morgan, William N. *Ancient Architecture of the Southwest.* Austin, TX: University of Texas Press, 1994.

Morris, Desmond. *Body Guards: Protective Amulets & Charms.* Shaftesbury, England: Element Books, 1999.

Moyer, Harold N., ed. *Medicine: A Monthly Journal of Medicine and Surgery,* vol. 3 January to December 1897. Detroit, MI: William M. Warren Publisher, 1898.

Muller, Richard A. *Physics and Technology for Future Presidents: An Introduction to the Essential Physics Every World Leader Needs to Know.* Princeton, NJ: Princeton University Press, 2010.

Neuendorf, Klaus K. E., James P. Mehl, Jr., and Julia A. Jackson, eds. *Glossary of Geology,* 5th ed. Alexandria, VA: American Geological Institute, 2005.

Nichols, Deborah L., and Christopher A. Pool, eds. *The Oxford Handbook of Mesoamerican Archaeology.* New York: Oxford University Press, 2012.

Nicholson, Paul T., and Ian Shaw, eds. *Ancient Egyptian Materials and Technology.* New York: Cambridge University Press, 2006.

Nickel, Ernest H., and Monte C. Nichols. *Mineral Reference Manual.* New York: Springer Science + Business Media, 1991.

Norris, Michael. *Medieval Art: A Resource for Educators.* New York: Metropolitan Museum of Art, 2005.

Northrup, Cynthia Clark, ed. *Encyclopedia of World Trade: From Ancient Times to the Present,* vol. 2. New York: Routledge, 2005.

O'Donoghue, Michael. *Gemstones.* New York: Chapman and Hall, 1988.

Ogden, Jack. *Ancient Jewelry: Interpreting the Past.* Berkeley, CA: University of California Press, 1992.

Oldershaw, Cally. *Firefly Guide to Gems.* Toronto, Canada: Firefly Books, 2003.

Ostrooumov, Mikhail. *Amazonite: Mineralogy, Crystal Chemistry, and Typomorphism.* Waltham, MA: Elsevier, 2016.

Pearson, James L. *Shamanism and the Ancient Mind: A Cognitive Approach to Archaeology.* Walnut Creek, CA: Altamira Press, 2002.

Petersen G., Georg. *Mining and Metallurgy in Ancient Perú*. Translated by William E. Brooks. Boulder, CO: Geographical Society of America, 2010.

Piccolino, Marco, and Nicholas J. Wade. *Galileo's Visions: Piercing the Spheres of the Heavens by Eye and Mind*. New York: Oxford University Press, 2014.

Pliny the Elder. *The Natural History of Pliny*, vol. 6. Translated by John Bostock and H. T. Riley. London: George Bell and Sons, 1898.

Polk, Patti. *Collecting Agates and Jaspers of North America*. Iola, WI: Krause Publications, 2013.

_____ . *Collecting Rocks, Gems and Minerals: Identification, Values and Lapidary Uses*, 3rd ed. Iola, WI: Krause Publications, 2016.

Pough, Frederick H. *A Field Guide to Rocks and Minerals*, 5th ed. New York: Houghton Mifflin Company, 1988.

Proctor, Keith. "Chrysoberyl and Alexandrite from the Pegmatite Districts of Minas Gerais, Brazil." *Gems and Gemology*, vol. 24, no. 19 (Spring 1988): 74.

Rafferty, John P., ed. *Minerals*. New York: Britannica Educational Publishing, 2012.

Rapp, George R. *Archaeomineralogy*. New York: Springer-Verlag, 2002.

Raybould, Robin. *An Introduction to the Symbolic Literature of the Renaissance*. Victoria, Canada: Trafford Publishing, 2005.

Rice, Patty C. *Amber: Golden Gem of the Ages*. Bloomington, IN: AuthorHouse, 2006.

Richardson, Lawrence, Jr. *A New Topographical Dictionary of Ancient Rome*. Baltimore: Johns Hopkins University Press, 1992.

Rickard, David. *Pyrite: A Natural History of Fool's Gold*. New York: Oxford University Press, 2015.

Robinson, George W. *Minerals: An Illustrated Exploration of the Dynamic World of Minerals and Their Properties*. New York: Simon and Schuster, 1994.

Ropp, Richard C. *Encyclopedia of the Alkaline Earth Compounds*. Oxford, England: Elsevier, 2013.

Ross, Andrew. *Amber*. Cambridge, MA: Harvard University Press, 1999.

Roth, Philippe. *Minerals First Discovered in Switzerland and Named After Swiss Individuals*. Charlottesville, VA: Excalibur Mineral Corporation, 2007.

Rothenberg, Marc, ed. *The History of Science in the United States: An Encyclopedia*. New York: Garland Publishing, 2001.

Rudler, Frederick William. *A Handbook to a Collection of the Minerals of the British Islands*. London: Wyman & Sons, 1905.

Scarre, Chris, ed. *Monuments and Landscape in Atlantic Europe: Perception and Society During the Neolithic and Early Bronze Age*. New York: Routledge, 2005.

Schumann, Walter. *Gemstones of the World*, 5th ed. New York: Sterling Publishing, 2006.

_____ . *Handbook of Rocks Minerals & Gemstones*. Translated by R. Bradshaw and K. A. G. Mills. New York: Houghton Mifflin Company, 1993.

Scott, David A. *Copper and Bronze in Art: Corrosion, Colorants, Conservation*. Los Angeles: Getty Publications, 2002.

Semple, Sarah, and Howard Williams, eds. *Anglo-Saxon Studies in Archaeology and History 14: Early Medieval Mortuary Practices*. Oxford, England: Oxford University School of Archaeology, 2007.

Senning, Alexander. *Elsevier's Dictionary of Chemoetymology: The Whys and Whences of Chemical Nomenclature and Terminology*. Oxford, England: Elsevier, 2007.

Shipley, Joseph T. *Dictionary of Word Origins*. New York: Dorset House, 1993.

Shortland, Andrew J., Ian C. Freestone, and Thilo Rehren, eds. *From Mine to Microscope: Advances in the Study of Ancient Technology*. Havertown, PA: Oxbow Books, 2009.

Simmons, Robert. *Stones of the New Consciousness: Healing, Awakening, and Co-creating with Crystals, Minerals & Gems*. East Montpelier, VT: Heaven and Earth Publications, 2009.

Simmons, Robert, and Naisha Ahsian. *The Book of Stones: Who They Are and What They Teach*. East Montpelier, VT: Heaven & Earth Publishing, 2007.

Sinkankas, John. *Gemstones of North America*, vol. 2. New York: John Wiley & Sons, 1976.

Sinkankas, John, and Terry Ottaway, eds. "The Legendary Green Beryl," *Emeralds of the World*, extraLapis English, no. 2. Arvada, CO: Lapis International, 2002.

Smith, Henry G. *Gems and Precious Stones: With Descriptions of Their Distinctive Properties*. Sydney, Australia: Charles Potter, 1896.

Smith, Richard L. *Premodern Trade in World History*. New York: Routledge, 2009.

Sofianides, Anna S., and George E. Harlow. *Gems & Crystals from the American Museum of Natural History*. New York: Simon and Schuster, 1990.

Sonnendecker, Glenn. *Kremers and Urdang's History of Pharmacy*, 4th ed. Philadelphia: J. B. Lippincott, 1986.

Sorrell, Charles A. *Rocks and Minerals: A Guide to Field Identification*. New York: St. Martin's Press, 2001.

Spier, Jeffrey. *Ancient Gems and Finger Rings*. Malibu, CA: The J. Paul Getty Museum, 1992.

Staff Writer. *Fodor's South Africa,* 6th ed. New York: Fodor's Travel Publications, 2015.

Staff Writer. *Sri Lanka Mineral & Mining Sector Investment and Business Guide,* vol. 1. Washington, DC: International Business Publications USA, 2013.

Stewart, William. *Dictionary of Images and Symbols in Counseling*. London: Jessica Kingsley Publishers, 1998.

Streeter, Edwin W. *Precious Stones and Gems: Their History, Sources and Characteristics,* 5th ed. London: George Bell & Sons, 1892.

Sung, Ying-hsing. *Chinese Technology in the Seventeenth Century*. Translated by E-tu Zen Sun and Shiou-chuan Sun. Mineola, NY: Dover Publications, 1997.

Szőnyi, György E. *John Dee's Occultism: Magical Exaltation through Powerful Signs*. Albany, NY: State University of New York Press, 2004.

Thomas, Arthur. *Gemstones: Properties, Identification and Use*. London: New Holland Publishers (UK), 2008.

Thompson, Daniel V. *The Materials and Techniques of Medieval Painting*. New York: Dover Publications, 1956.

Thompson, Thomas. "Tanzania to Tiffany's," *Life Magazine,* vol. 66, no. 18 (May 9, 1969): 71.

_____ . *A System of Chemistry,* vol. 3. Boston: Adamant Media Corporation, 2005.

Tuider, Katherine, and Eval Caplan. *Other Places Travel Guide: Dominican Republic*. New York: Other Places Publishing, 2012.

Van den Berk, M. F. M. *The Magic Flute: Die Zauberflöte, An Alchemical Allegory*. Boston: Brill, 2004.

Vance, Erik. "The Lost Empire of the Maya," *National Geographic,* vol. 230, no. 3. Washington, DC: The National Geographic Society, September 2016.

Vaughan, David. *Minerals: A Very Short Introduction*. New York: Oxford University Press, 2014.

Warmington, E. H. *The Commerce between the Roman Empire and India*. Cambridge, England: Cambridge University Press, 2014.

Warren, John K. *Evaporites: A Geological Compendium,* 2nd ed. New York: Springer, 2016.

Weatherford, Jack. *The History of Money: From Sandstone to Cyberspace*. New York: Three Rivers Press, 1997.

Webb, H., and M. A. Grigg. *Modern Science,* vol. 3. New York: Cambridge University Press, 1964.

Webster, Robert. *Gems: Their Sources, Descriptions and Identification,* 3rd ed. Boston: Newnes, 1975.

Weinstein, Michael. *Precious and Semi-Precious Stones.* Redditch, England: Read Books, 2013.

Westropp, Hodder Michael. *A Manual of Precious Stones and Antique Gems.* London: Sampson Low, Marston, Low & Searle, 1874.

White, John Sampson. *Minerals and Gems.* Washington, DC: Smithsonian Institution Press, 1991.

White, Winston, C. *Labrador: Getting Along in the Big Land!* St. John's, Canada: Flanker Press, 2003.

Whitlock, Herbert. *The Story of the Gems.* New York: Dover Publications, 1997.

Wilburn, Andrew T. *Materia Magica: The Archaeology of Magic in Roman Egypt, Cyprus, and Spain.* Ann Arbor, MI: University of Michigan Press, 2012.

Willis, Tony. *The Runic Workbook: Understanding and Using the Power of Runes.* New York: Sterling Publishing, 1986.

Wilson, Eric G. *The Spiritual History of Ice: Romanticism, Science, and the Imagination.* New York: Palgrave MacMillan, 2003.

Wilson, Nigel, ed. *Encyclopedia of Ancient Greece.* New York: Routledge, 2006.

Woodman, Peter. *Ireland's First Settlers: Time and the Mesolithic.* Havertown, PA: Oxbow Books, 2015.

Xia, Nai. *Ancient Egyptian Beads.* New York: Springer, 2014.

Zebroski, Bob. *A Brief History of Pharmacy: Humanity's Search for Wellness.* New York: Routledge, 2016.

INDEX

To Write to the Author

If you wish to contact the author or would like more information about this book, please write to the author in care of Llewellyn Worldwide Ltd. and we will forward your request. Both the author and publisher appreciate hearing from you and learning of your enjoyment of this book and how it has helped you. Llewellyn Worldwide Ltd. cannot guarantee that every letter written to the author can be answered, but all will be forwarded. Please write to:

Sandra Kynes
℅ Llewellyn Worldwide
2143 Wooddale Drive
Woodbury, MN 55125-2989
Please enclose a self-addressed stamped envelope for reply,
or $1.00 to cover costs. If outside the U.S.A., enclose
an international postal reply coupon.
Many of Llewellyn's authors have websites
with additional information and resources.
For more information, please visit our website at
http://www.llewellyn.com

365 DAYS
OF
CRYSTAL
MAGIC

Simple Practices with Gemstones and Minerals

SANDRA KYNES

365 Days of Crystal Magic
Simple Practices with Gemstones and Minerals
SANDRA KYNES

Journey through the wheel of the year with daily crystal magic. This fun, approachable book features quick and easy ways to use crystals every day, even incorporating them into your sabbat, full moon, historical, and special occasion celebrations. Perfect for any age or interest level, *365 Days of Crystal Magic* provides valuable information on various topics, including prepping and cleaning crystals, understanding birthstones, and working magic according to the astrological bodies and the zodiac signs. For every calendar date, you'll discover ways to use crystals to deepen awareness, lift your mood, improve your divination, reduce stress, reach your goals, find love and community, strengthen your willpower, and much more.

978-0-7387-5417-8, 432 pp., 5 x 7   **$17.99**

Coming in January 2018

To order, call 1-877-NEW-WRLD or visit llewellyn.com
Prices subject to change without notice

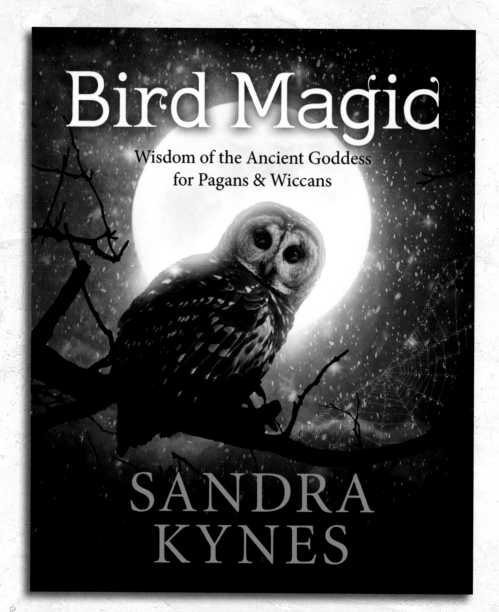

Bird Magic

Wisdom of the Ancient Goddess
for Pagans & Wiccans

SANDRA
KYNES

Bird Magic

Wisdom of the Ancient Goddess for Pagans & Wiccans
SANDRA KYNES

A thorough treatment of birds specifically for Pagans, Witches, and other magically-minded folks. Through background information and ritual, you will learn how to incorporate the Bird Goddess's meaning and symbols into your practices to enrich your spiritual path. A number of activities provide you with various ways to connect with birds on a personal level to enhance your everyday life.

You will learn how birds provide a simple yet powerful way to stay connected with the natural world. With an encyclopedic, listing of sixty birds, each profile highlights the bird's wisdom and what it has to teach and share. The book provides illustrations and practical info for identifying birds and where to look for them. In addition, *Bird Magic* will help you:

- Awaken intuition and psychic abilities

- Enhance your sabbat and esbat rituals

- Understand why the Bird Goddess was the major deity for millennia

- Recognize her influence on modern Pagan practice

978-0-7387-4864-1, 312 pp, 7 ½ x 9 ¼   **$19.99**

To order, call 1-877-NEW-WRLD or visit llewellyn.com
Prices subject to change without notice

Sandra Kynes

STAR MAGIC

MAGIC

The Wisdom of the Constellations for
Pagans & Wiccans

Star Magic
The Wisdom of the Constellations for Pagans & Wiccans
Sandra Kynes

Tap into the energy of the stars for divination, ritual, magic, and psychic work. Join author Sandra Kynes on an exploration of the night sky, looking beyond the moon to using the energy of the constellations in magic in ways meaningful to twenty-first–century Pagans and Wiccans. Explore the history associated with each constellation and notable stars, as well as ways to engage them, with help from seventy illustrations and a variety of star maps.

Organized around the wheel of the year, *Star Magic* lets you easily navigate chapters corresponding to both your current season and hemisphere. Discover the constellations of each season, from Virgo in spring to Aquarius in autumn, and dozens more. Use chakras, dream work, and astral travel to align with the stars and harness their power. With this comprehensive book's simple and straightforward methods, you'll reach a new level of magic and wonderment that is out of this world.

978-0-7387-4169-7, 336 pp., 7 ½ x 9 ⅛   **$19.99**

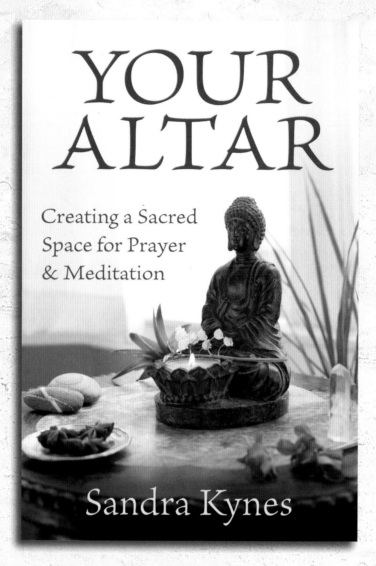

YOUR ALTAR

Creating a Sacred
Space for Prayer
& Meditation

Sandra Kynes

Your Altar
Creating a Sacred Space for Prayer & Meditation
SANDRA KYNES

In this fast-paced world of over-stimulation and distraction, keeping a private space for meditative retreat and spirituality is essential. Creating an altar using the power of numbers allows you to achieve spiritual stillness in a personal and meaningful way.

The numbers one through nine each carry a profound symbolic history and significance. Harness this energy and apply it to your life by selecting the number that best resonates with your intention and using it as a guide to your altar design.

With meditation techniques and many examples of prayers, practices, and rituals from all major faiths, popular author and Celtic scholar Sandra Kynes offers a new approach to altar-building. Using representations of elements from myth and nature as focal points, you can create an altar that best suits your spiritual needs.

Straightforward and practical, with easy-to-follow instructions and clear illustrations, this unique book allows you to experience the restorative benefits of altars—and ultimately reconnect with that sacred space within yourself.

978-0-7387-1105-8, 240 pp., 6 x 9   **$15.95**

To order, call 1-877-NEW-WRLD or visit llewellyn.com
Prices subject to change without notice